Who Wrote the Book of Love?

THE STORIES BEHIND THE HITS

— from Chuck Berry to Chumbawamba

Richard Crouse

Doubleday Canada Limited

Canadian Cataloguing in Publication Data

Crouse, Richard, 1963–
    Who wrote the book of love?: the stories behind the hits
    — from Chuck Berry to Chumbawamba

Includes bibliographical references and index.
ISBN 0-385-25732-5

1. Popular music — History and criticism. I. Title.

ML3470.C952 1998   781.64'09   C98-930073-0

Cover design by Heather Hodgins
Cover image courtesy Digital Stock
Author photograph by Greg Tjepkema
Text design by Heidy Lawrance Associates
Printed and bound in Canada

Published in Canada by
Doubleday Canada Limited
105 Bond Street
Toronto, Ontario
M5B 1Y3

WEB   10   9   8   7   6   5   4   3   2   1

"Credo Elvem ipsum etiam vivere."

—*Anonymous*

"The monkey speaks his mind. Yeah."

—*Dave Bartholomew*

Contents

Introduction 1

FIFTIES

1 "The Fat Man": *Fats Domino* 7

2 "Rocket 88": *Jackie Brenston and His Delta Cats* . . 10

3 "Hound Dog": *Big Mama Thornton* 13

4 "I Put a Spell on You": *Screamin' Jay Hawkins* . . . 17

5 "Bo Diddley": *Bo Diddley* 20

6 "(We're Gonna) Rock Around the Clock":
Bill Haley and His Comets 23

7 "Maybellene": *Chuck Berry* 27

8 "Tutti Frutti": *Little Richard* 30

9 "Heartbreak Hotel": *Elvis Presley* 34

10 "Blue Suede Shoes": *Carl Perkins* 38

11 "Great Balls of Fire": *Jerry Lee Lewis* 42

12 "Tequila": *The Champs* 48

13 "Book of Love": *The Monotones* 51

14 "The Purple People Eater": *Sheb Wooley* 54

15 "To Know Him Is to Love Him":
The Teddy Bears 57

SIXTIES

1 "The Lion Sleeps Tonight": *The Tokens* 63

2 "Can't Buy Me Love/"Twist and Shout"/"She Loves You"/"I Want to Hold Your Hand"/ "Please Please Me": *The Beatles' Top Five* 66

3 "Rag Doll": *The Four Seasons* 70

4 "Leader of the Pack": *The Shangri-Las* 72

5 "Oh, Pretty Woman": *Roy Orbison* 75

6 "Wooly Bully": *Sam the Sham and the Pharaohs* . . 78

7 "Hang On Sloopy": *The McCoys* 81

8 "When a Man Loves a Woman": *Percy Sledge* 85

9 "Did You Ever Have to Make Up Your Mind?"/ "Summer in the City": *Lovin' Spoonful* 88

10 "Hold On, I'm Comin'": *Sam & Dave* 93

11 "They're Coming to Take Me Away, Ha-Haaa!": *Napoleon XIV* 96

12 "Fire": *Jimi Hendrix* 101

13 "Green Tambourine": *The Lemon Pipers* 105

14 "(Sittin' On) The Dock of the Bay": *Otis Redding* . . 108

15 "Mony Mony": *Tommy James and The Shondells* . . . 111

16 "Na Na Hey Hey Kiss Him Good-bye": *Steam* . . 114

SEVENTIES

1 "American Pie": *Don McLean* 119

2 "Mother and Child Reunion": *Paul Simon* 123

3 "Bad, Bad Leroy Brown": *Jim Croce* 125

4 "Smokin' in the Boys' Room": *Brownsville Station* . 129

5 "You Ain't Seen Nothin' Yet": *Bachman-Turner Overdrive* 132

6 "Fame": *David Bowie* 135

7 "How Long": *Ace* 139

8 "Philadelphia Freedom": *Elton John* 142

9 "Only Women Bleed": *Alice Cooper* 145

10 "Jive Talkin'": *The Bee Gees* 150

11 Variety Is the Spice of Life: A 1970's Top Five . . . 153

12 "More, More, More": *Andrea True Connection* . . . 158

13 "Who Are You": *The Who* 161

14 "My Sharona": *The Knack* 164

15 "I Don't Like Mondays": *Boomtown Rats* 167

EIGHTIES

1 "Crazy Little Thing Called Love": *Queen* 173

2 "Whip It"/"Satisfaction"/"Jocko Homo": *Devo* . . 176

3 "Take Off": *Bob and Doug McKenzie* 181

4 "Burning Down the House": *Talking Heads* 185

5 "Maniac": *Michael Sembello* 189

6 "Billie Jean": *Michael Jackson* 192

7 "She Blinded Me With Science": *Thomas Dolby* . . 195

8 "Sweet Dreams (Are Made of This)": *Eurythmics* . . 198

9 "Jump": *Van Halen* 201

10 "Blasphemous Rumours": *Depeche Mode* 204

11 "Wake Me Up Before You Go-Go: *Wham!* 207

12 "Panic": *Smiths* 210

13 "Public Enemy Number One": *Public Enemy* 213

14 "Love Rescue Me": *U2* 217

15 "One": *Metallica* 220

NINETIES

1 "Smells Like Teen Spirit": *Nirvana* 225

2 "Jeremy": *Pearl Jam* 228

3 "Rhythm of My Heart": *Rod Stewart* 231

4 "Tears in Heaven": *Eric Clapton* 235

5 "Under the Bridge": *Red Hot Chili Peppers* 240

6 "Cop Killer": *Body Count with Ice-T* 244

7 "Informer": *Snow* 248

8 "Creep": *Radiohead* 251

9 "Spoonman": *Soundgarden* 254

10 "What's the Frequency, Kenneth?": *R.E.M.* 257

11 "The Macarena": *Los Del Rio* 260

12 "Ironic": *Alanis Morissette* 264

13 "Anybody Seen My Baby?": *Rolling Stones* 268

14 "I'll Be Missing You": *Sean "Puff Daddy" Combs with Faith Evans* 272

15 "Tubthumping": *Chumbawamba* 275

Selected Bibliography 279

Index 282

Introduction

The research for this book has taken twenty-five years to complete. I didn't spend the whole time in a cramped room poring over music magazines and spinning vinyl — the process was a little more organic. From the time I purchased my first record (a 45 of David Bowie's "Space Oddity") when I was nine years old, I have always been bewitched with popular music and the people who created it. *Hit Parader, Creem* and *Rolling Stone* became my textbooks. I investigated and learned about my fave raves, stockpiling much of the information that appears in this book.

If I had to pinpoint the day the research began, it would be August 25, 1977. It was a big day, an exciting day, just a week before I was set to go back to school, entering the eighth grade. After much thought, my father decided I was old enough to do a solo shop for school supplies. With five $20 bills in my pocket, I was set loose at the shopping mall. All these years later, I can still remember walking past the clothing stores and the department stores with all their loose-leaf binders and Bic pens and making a beeline to the nearest bookstore. Walking through the travel section, the Canadiana shelves, past the stacks of children's books, I settled in at the music area. You can probably guess the rest of the story. When I left the bookstore, I had a stack of music books and a few crumpled bills. I started that school year with eight 75¢ notebooks, $2 worth of pens and HB pencils, one $14 T-shirt, $80 worth of books on Janis Joplin, Jimi Hendrix, Elton John, the Rolling Stones and David Bowie — and a new mistrust from my father. It was a long time until I was allowed to shop on my own again.

Now, a little more than twenty years later, those books still sit on my shelf, along with hundreds of others gathered over the years. They form the basis of *Who Wrote the Book of Love?*. I love those books and the stories they contain. I have been entertained by them and educated about the artists who made my favorite music. I am reminded of that youthful shopping trip every time I go to a bookstore. I still enjoy leafing through the new music biographies, and I still spend too much money on them. I should thank my parents for not making me take back all those books in 1977. If they had, I might have paid more attention to my schoolwork, and this book might not exist today.

I also wish to thank Don Sedgwick whose early enthusiasm for this book encouraged me to proceed. Kathryn Exner handled the rough manuscript with great care and intelligence, sculpting the words into presentable form. I look forward to working with her again. Doubleday's Gloria Goodman, Christine Innes, Heather Hodgins and Dara Rowland offered invaluable assistance when I needed to tap their expertise.

Many people helped in the photo research. Thanks to Greg Jones, Tommy Cavalier, John Beaton, Allison at Mutato Muzika, Kirstan Andrews at Peg Productions and Pegi Cecconi at Anthem Records.

The following I would also like to thank for their generous contributions to the book: Stuart "word count" McLean, Scott Dobson, Blair Packham, Marjorie Wingrove,

Karin Chykaliuk, John Sebastian, Mark Mothersbaugh, Bob Ezrin, Jerry Samuels, Hilly Kristal, Marc Jordan, Cub Koda and Kathleen Scheibling.

This listing of acknowledgments does not begin to intimate the support, the advice and the many hours that considerate people gave me for this book.

FIFTIES

The Fat Man

Fats Domino

Fats Domino was the biggest-selling R & B artist of the 1950s. On his very first visit to a recording studio, he cut a track that would become his signature. "The Fat Man" reached Number Two on the R & B charts in February 1950.

Lew Chudd, the owner of Imperial Records, was looking to expand his label's sound. Based in Los Angeles, Imperial had tapped into the strong Mexican music scene in that city at the time. In December 1949, he visited Louisiana, hoping to discover some talent in the New Orleans' clubs. Setting up a temporary office in the Crescent City, Chudd's first order of business was to hire local trumpeter Dave Bartholomew as his tour guide and artists-and-repertoire man.

During one of their first meetings, Chudd asked Bartholomew if there were any hot, young unsigned talents currently playing in the clubs. Bartholomew paused for a moment, considering a list of talented New Orleans-based players. "I've heard about a guy called Fats Domino down at the Hideaway Club," he said. "I hear he's pretty good."

The next night, the pair headed down to Desire Street to hear Domino play piano with Billy Diamond's combo. As they walked into the club, Domino was doing a solo set,

Tommy Edwards's 1958 chart topper "It's All in the Game" is the only single to feature music written by a vice president of the United States. In 1912, Charles Gates Dawes (later VP under Calvin Coolidge) penned "Melody in a Major," a piece for flute. Forty years later, songwriter Carl Sigman added lyrics, and it climbed to the top of the hit parade.

singing "Junker's Blues," a New Orleans standard extolling the pleasures of reefer and cocaine use. It was a classic Domino performance — cool and jovial, one part rock and two parts roll. Chudd was impressed with Domino's laid-back style and instructed Bartholomew to set up a meeting. At this meeting, Domino walked away with a tentative recording deal and a date to lay down eight tracks at a local studio.

In mid-December 1949, Domino made his way to the J & M Studio at the corner of North Rampart and Dumaine streets in New Orleans. Located at the back of a record store, it was a bare-bones setup — a tiny room with only three microphones and three electrical outlets. The musicians were forced to crowd around Domino, the saxophonists sharing the piano mike while the bassist and guitarist shared a second. Domino sang directly into the third as the drummer tried to pound the traps loud enough to be picked up by any of the mikes at all.

First up was "The Junker." Chudd liked the melody but resisted releasing a tune about drug use. It was 1949, and while the term "junkie" wasn't yet in wide use, the tune's lyrics left nothing to the imagination. Chudd asked Domino to keep the tune but lose the lyrics. Not wanting to blow his shot at a recording deal (he was only making $3 a week at the Hideaway), Domino obliged, erasing all references to heroin and cocaine and replacing them with details of himself instead. The original "they call me a junkie, because I'm loaded all the time" transformed into the self-effacing "they call me the fat man, because I weigh two hundred pounds." The two verses of nonsense lyrics were peppered with

Domino's falsetto impression of a muted trumpet — a vocal trick he used in the clubs — and topped off with a round of barrelhouse piano in the style of his idol Fats Waller.

The band quickly moved on, laying down seven more tracks on that same December afternoon. Several of those cuts were released as singles, but "The Fat Man" was the lone hit from the December 1949 sessions. The revamped tune hit Number Two on the R & B charts in early 1950. But it would be two years before Domino really hit his stride, starting with "Goin' Home," a Number One in 1952. After that, he seemed unstoppable, writing and recording constantly, earning the 1955 and 1956 *Billboard* awards as America's Favorite R & B Artist and appearing in several films including the teen classic *The Girl Can't Help It*. The hits stopped in 1963, but by then, he had racked up an impressive fifty-eight R & B chart entries and thirty-seven Top Forty pop tunes including "Ain't That a Shame," "Blueberry Hill" and "I'm Walkin'."

In 1986, Domino was elected to the Rock-and-Roll Hall of Fame, and the following year, he was granted the Grammy Lifetime Achievement Award.

Rocket 88

Jackie Brenston and His Delta Cats

Recorded on March 5, 1951, "Rocket 88" was the first hit produced at the famed Sun Studios in Memphis. It was also the first Number One R & B hit released by Chess Records on their fledgling label. If that wasn't enough, many music scholars call it the first rock-and-roll record.

By his own admission, Jackie Brenston wasn't much of a saxophone player when he met Ike Turner in the late 1940s. The pair got together in Clarksdale, Mississippi when Turner was gathering musicians for his new band. Turner was a perfectionist, and he didn't unveil the Kings of Rhythm until extensive rehearsals had whipped them into a top-notch club band. During one of their fiery shows in Chambers, Mississippi, B.B. King happened to catch their set. He recommended they head off to Memphis to check out Sun Studios where he had recently recorded some sides.

The band arrived in Memphis after a trip fraught with mishaps. Turner claimed they were arrested three times on the drive from Mississippi, adding that the bass guitar blew off the top of the car, and that they were ticketed for speeding. They arrived in Memphis late at night on March 4, 1951 and had to scramble to find a place to stay.

The next day, they gathered all their instruments and made their way to 706 Union Avenue, Sun Studio's storefront office. The misfortunes continued. As they were unloading their gear, guitarist Willie Kizart dropped his amplifier, damaging the cone. The hole in the cone distorted any sound pumped through it, giving the band's guitar a fuzzy edge. Sun owner-producer Sam Phillips liked the sound, although it was toned down a bit by stuffing paper in the hole. When Kizart strummed his guitar, it sounded more like a saxophone than a six-string. Always after a new sound, Phillips miked the broken amp, turning it up in the mix, hoping it would accentuate Kizart's boogie-woogie guitar riff. Purely by accident, they may have created one of the staples of future rock and rollers — the fuzz guitar.

Once the tape was rolling, the band ran down two numbers, with Turner taking lead vocals and Brenston on alto sax. After a short break, the band reconvened, with Brenston on lead vocals for two songs: "Come Back Where You Belong" and "Rocket 88," a tune the band had written just the night before as they drove into Memphis. As they were stopped at the roadside with mechanical trouble, a Good Samaritan, driving a 1950 Hydra Matic Drive V-8 Oldsmobile 88 (nicknamed the Rocket 88), came to their rescue. It was a low-end luxury car, and its advertisements boasted a "rocket engine" and "sleek Futurmatic hood." Inspired by the late-model car, the musicians passed the time working up the tune on the remainder of the drive. Brenston, who grabbed the writer's credit on "Rocket 88," was clearly influenced by Jimmy Liggins's 1947 "Cadillac Boogie," liberally borrowing the melody and beat, but adding a blues sensibility not found in the original.

Phillips paid each of the musicians $20 for the session and promised to keep in touch. In 1951, Sun Studios was still a recording service, not a record label. Phillips would record bands and then sell or lease the tapes to record companies for distribution. His main customer, Modern Records in Los Angeles, had slighted him on past business deals, so he decided to send the Kings of Rhythm tunes to Chess Records in Chicago.

The Chicagonians released the two Brenston tracks in April 1951, earning Ike Turner's ire. Not only had they kept his songs in the vault, but his name wasn't anywhere on the label. Chess renamed the band Jackie Brenston and His Delta Cats. Insult was added to injury as "Rocket 88" zoomed up the charts, while Turner's two songs were released to less-than-enthusiastic response. This caused a rift between the two that broke up the original Kings of Rhythm. Brenston split to tour the country, cashing in on the immediate success of "Rocket 88." The singer spent the next two years driving from gig to gig in his own Olds Rocket 88, a gift from General Motors to show their appreciation for all the free advertising the song had given them.

Several more Brenston releases followed, but nothing matched the heat of that first single. By 1960, an alcoholic Brenston reteamed with Ike Turner, only this time he was a paid employee, playing sax for the Ike and Tina Turner Revue. Jackie Brenston died, drunk and homeless, in 1979.

Hound Dog

Big Mama Thornton

When band leader Johnny Otis contracted Jerry Leiber and Mike Stoller to write a song for Willie Mae Thornton, they were frightened. Thornton, known as "Big Mama," was a foul-mouthed, three-hundred-pound R & B singer who looked like she could eat the songwriters for lunch. They forged a tune to fit her personality — brusque and badass. "Hound Dog" topped the R & B charts for seven weeks in 1953.

In Los Angeles in 1950, Mike Stoller had just received a phone call from a friend of a friend. "I hear you play piano," Jerry Leiber said. "I'd like to get together and collaborate on some songs." Stoller was skeptical. He was a jazz baby and not interested in writing songs, which he took to mean Top Forty fluff. Leiber was insistent. He had a notebook full of lyrics and needed a piano player to help flesh out his ideas into songs. Twenty minutes later, Leiber was knocking at the door to where Stoller lived with his parents.

Once Stoller stopped staring at Leiber's eyes — one blue, one brown — the two bonded quickly. Referring to the battered notebook, Leiber sang his lyrics, dancing around the room, while Stoller banged out blues chords on the family's

THERE'S A RIOT GOIN' ON:
Leiber and Stoller's Top
Fifteen

1. "Hound Dog": Willie
   Mae "Big Mama"
   Thornton -- March
   1953
2. "Riot in Cell Block
   Number Nine": The
   Robins -- June 1954
3. "Black Denim Trousers
   and Motorcycle Boots":
   The Cheers -- August
   1955
4. "Love Me": Elvis
   Presley -- November
   1956
5. "Charlie Brown": The
   Coasters -- January
   1959
6. "Kansas City": Wilbert
   Harrison -- March
   1959
7. "Love Potion Number
   Nine": The Clovers
   -- August 1959
8. "Jailhouse Rock":
   Elvis Presley --
   September 1959
9. "Saved": LaVern Baker
   -- March 1961

upright piano. On the wall hung an auto-graphed picture of George Gershwin, a mentor perhaps, whose presence lent support to the teenagers. One of their early songs came easily. "It was like spon-taneous combustion," says Leiber on the creation of "K.C. Lovin'," a minor hit for Little Willie Littlefield in 1952. (Wilbert Harrison took the song, renamed "Kansas City," to Number One in 1959.)

The success of that song brought them attention in music circles. Band leader Johnny Otis invited the nineteen-year-olds to one of Big Mama's rehearsals — a meet-and-greet with the singer that would hopefully produce a new tune for her upcoming record. They watched her run through a few tunes when an idea hit them like a flash. By the time they reached the parking lot and Stoller's 1937 Plymouth, they already had the genesis of the tune. Banging out the beat on the car's hood, Leiber imagined Big Mama admonishing an unfaithful lover. "You ain't nothing but a...." He tried to come up with a low-down, dirty snub — one that would roll off Big Mama's tongue. Then it came to him. "...noth-ing but a hound dog." He scribbled lyrics furiously in the car on their way back to Stoller's apartment. Once at the piano, it took less than ten minutes to write the tune. That same afternoon, they returned to the rehearsal with the finished song.

Leiber and Stoller were hyped teaching the band their parts while Big Mama learned her lines. They were sure this could be a hit. But during the first run through, something was wrong. It sounded like a ballad, not the low-down dirty blues they had envisioned. What should they do? Neither one wanted to tell Big Mama how to sing the blues, but somehow they needed her to get dirty and growl out the lyrics. "We can't teach her," they thought, "but we can show her what we had in mind." The band howled as the two white boys played the song, with Leiber growling through the lyrics trying to impersonate a spurned woman.

10. "Stand By Me": Ben E. King -- April 1961
11. "I Keep Forgettin'": Chuck Jackson -- July 1962
12. "I'm a Woman": Peggy Lee -- December 1962
13. "Ruby Baby": Dion -- December 1962
14. "On Broadway": The Drifters -- March 1963
15. "I (Who Have Nothing)": Tom Jones -- July 1970

A few days later at the "Hound Dog" recording session, with Leiber and Stoller producing for the first time, the singer changed her tune. Big Mama snarled the lyrics, singing the hell out of every line. The band ran through the tune twice, and Thornton delivered incredible readings both times. The second one made the cut. "It was killer," said Stoller. By the time Leiber and Stoller turned twenty, in the spring of 1953, "Hound Dog" had reached the top of the R & B charts. Later that year, *Cash Box* named it Best Rhythm and Blues Record of 1953.

Three years later, a young singer named Elvis Presley would make "Hound Dog" world famous, selling seven million records in the process. Presley first heard the song in Las Vegas in 1956. It was his first time in Vegas, and he was keen to check out some of the local hot spots. Meandering into a casino lounge, he watched a band called Freddie Bell and the Bellboys perform a comic turn on "Hound Dog." They had been playing the watered-down version of Big

Mama's hit for several years, even recording it for Teen Records in 1955. Elvis, amused by their humorous interpretation of the tune, decided to cover it on his next record.

The success of Elvis's "Hound Dog" led to a profitable collaboration between Leiber and Stoller and the King of rock and roll. The pair scored several of Elvis's films including *Love Me Tender*, *Loving You* and *Jailhouse Rock*. With Elvis behind the microphone, Leiber and Stoller charted with "Love Me Tender," "(Let Me Be) Your Teddy Bear," "Loving You," "Jailhouse Rock" and "Treat Me Nice." With their reputation as speedy workers (they pumped out the score for *Jailhouse Rock* in one night) and a golden touch in the studio, by 1957, they were the hottest songwriters in the business.

I Put a Spell on You

Screamin' Jay Hawkins

A brokenhearted Screamin' Jay Hawkins penned "I Put a Spell on You" in hopes of wooing back an ex-girlfriend. The ploy didn't work, but his song of love's torment has been recorded many times since by acts as diverse as Nina Simone, the Alan Price Set and, most notably, Creedence Clearwater Revival.

In the summer of 1954, Screamin' Jay Hawkins, the former middleweight boxing champion of Alaska (1949), had retired from fighting for the less-grueling life of show business. At twenty-five, he was an accomplished sideman, playing piano with such luminaries as James Moody and Count Basie. However, his solo career was slow to take off. With a handful of failed singles under his belt, Hawkins was reduced to performing in honky-tonks and small clubs.

His love life wasn't going so well, either. One night, while playing to a sparse crowd at a club called Herman's in Atlantic City, his girlfriend paraded up, mumbled something in his ear and threw his house keys at him. Blowing him a kiss, she made a hasty exit out of the club. Cut the applause and dim the lights; Screamin' Jay had just been dumped. Later that night, Hawkins returned home to find a message written in lipstick on his bathroom mirror. "Good-bye my love," it read.

Hawkins was inconsolable. He had lost the best thing that had ever happened to him. Years later, he told one reporter that after reading the mirror's message, he collapsed on the bed, letting out the "most painful scream" of his life. Pulling himself together, he decided to entice her to come back in the best way he knew. He wrote "I Put a Spell on You" — a simple R & B tune of unrequited love. "I don't care if you don't love me," he wrote, "I'm yours."

Securing some studio time with the tiny Grand Records in Philiadelphia, he recorded the tender love ballad, crooning it in his operatic bass voice. The single sunk without a trace and apparently had no effect on his ex-girlfriend since she was nowhere to be found.

But all was not lost. Jay included the tune in his club act. Live, the song really came to life. Gone was the mournful crooning of the Grand Records' version. Hawkins pulled out all the stops for the audience, singing like a man who had lost everything, his soul stripped bare.

The live version impressed Columbia Records' label chief Arnold Matson. It had soul. But more importantly, it had a good beat, and you could dance to it. Matson suggested to Hawkins that he rerecord the song for Columbia's R & B offshoot Okeh. Hawkins leaped at the chance. Maybe this time, he would win back his woman.

In the studio, things didn't go so well. Take after take seemed to fall flat. The magic of Hawkins's live performance was missing. "What's wrong?" Matson asked. "Well, I usually like to drink a little before I go onstage," Hawkins replied. Matson stopped the session, went to the corner store and bought a case of Italian Swiss Coloney muscatel for Hawkins and the band.

Many bottles later, the session resumed. Hawkins was well oiled and let it rip. Screaming and hollering, Hawkins laid down one of the most outrageous vocal performances ever. It was the audible sound of a breaking heart. Rock historian

Dave Marsh described "I Put a Spell on You" as "an R & B classic that explicitly defines itself in terms more African than American, dabbling in voodoo imagery straight from ancient lands." In layman's terms, this was one wild record.

So wild, in fact, that it was banned immediately on most record stations. Hawkins's moans and groans were dubbed "suggestive and cannibalistic," unfit for public airwaves. To combat the bad press, Okeh issued a cleaned-up version, offering to compensate any DJ fired for playing the offending tune. All this was a surprise to Jay who didn't hear the finished product until after it was pressed and in the stores. He claims to have gotten so hammered at the recording session that he could barely remember the session, let alone moaning in phony sexual ecstasy at the end of the song.

Just like in a fairy tale, there is a happy ending to Jay's story. He got his girlfriend back. Ironically, it wasn't the A-side of the single that cast a spell on her; she liked the B-side, "Little Demon."

In the early days of his career, Paul Anka's mother was his biggest benefactor. On many occasions, Mrs. Anka loaned her son the family car to drive to talent shows and always acted as a sounding board for his new tunes, suggesting changes to improve them. In return, when he started making big money, Anka bought her a new car and house. The young heartthrob adored his mother. He was on tour in Pittsburgh when he was informed of her death from a liver ailment. Only seventeen years old, he felt alone in the world despite his great success. That night in Pittsburgh, he wrote "Lonely Boy," pouring out his grief in song. The tune reached Number One in July 1959.

Bo Diddley

Bo Diddley

He didn't know diddly. The guitarist didn't realize it at the time, but with the 1955 release of his eponymous first single, Bo Diddley was about to change the sound of rock and roll. His trademarked *bomp, bomp, bomp-bomp, bomp* beat — actually an African rhythm called "patted juba" — influenced hundreds of artists from Buddy Holly to the Sex Pistols. The tune "Bo Diddley" was Number One on the R & B charts in April 1955.

Otha Ellas Bates was born in 1928 in McComb, Mississippi. At age six, he was legally adopted by his mother's cousin Gussie McDaniel and ended up living in Chicago. With Gussie's encouragement, Otha studied violin while playing trombone in the church band. By his tenth birthday, Otha had taught himself guitar, hooking up an old acoustic to a radio for amplification. Soon he was busking on street corners with two friends, calling themselves the Hipsters.

His ambition to be a professional musician was put on hold while he attended Foster Vocational School, learning to build guitars and violins. On his off hours, Otha took up boxing as a defense against the city slickers who taunted him for being a country boy. Once, after a fight, a woman

congratulated him, saying, "Man, you're a Bo Diddly!" Much
to Otha's chagrin, the nickname stuck. However, a stage name
was born. "I could never figure out what the hell that meant,"
he said several decades later.

Returning to his first love, Diddley picked up the guitar
as a diversion to working in dead-end unskilled-labor jobs.
Forming a band called the Langley Avenue Jive Cats (after
his home address of 4746 Langley), he took up a nighttime
residency at the 708 Club on Chicago's south side. His chops
honed from constantly performing, Diddley auditioned for
Vee Jay Records in 1955. "What is this shit?" asked label owner
Ewart Abner before escorting Diddley out of the building.
More successful was his tryout for Leonard Chess at 2120
South Michigan Avenue, the home of the legendary Chess
Records. Founded in 1950, Chess Records was at the forefront of the Chicago blues sound by 1955, producing records
by Willie Dixon, Muddy Waters and Howlin' Wolf.

Chess was impressed with Diddley's "muted sound," his
unique method of rhythm-guitar playing that he transposed
from his training as a violinist. Diddley was invited back for
a three-hour session to record four songs. His regular band
were nonunion, and for the studio date, they were replaced
with seasoned pros including Otis Spann on piano.

"Bo Diddley," the third song recorded that day, wasn't
a completely new tune. Diddley had borrowed the distinctive beat from a record featuring the Hambone Kids with the
Red Saunders Orchestra. "Hambone" featured the young-
sters slapping out a rhythm on their chests, mimicking the
West African chant known as hambone. Musicologists would
call it the "patted juba," but it is probably more familiar as
the "shave and haircut, two bits" call-and-response beat
popular at the time. Diddley and his new band exaggerated
"Hambone's" beat, with the drummer, maracas and harmon-
ica player all keeping time with Bo's homemade guitar. The
effect was staggering. Almost totally without melody, "Bo

Songwriter Jean Dinning Surrey read an article by a disc jockey complaining that teenagers were getting a bad rap from the older generation. They weren't "little devils," he wrote. They were good kids, more like "teen angels." Recognizing a good song title when she saw one, she borrowed the phrase, writing a 1959 hit for her younger brother Mark Dinning.

Diddley" is all about the beat; it was a precursor to funk, although Bo called it a "jungle-type rhythm feel."

Of course, Diddley, in an audacious move, also rewrote "Hambone's" lyrics, placing himself directly in the center of the song. It was the first time in the rock era that an artist's name had been used as the title of a record. This style of song writing — known as "toasting" — would become popular in later years, particularly in black music. But Bo was there first, blazing a trail for those who would follow.

"Bo Diddley" was coupled as a B-side with "I'm a Man," another tune recorded that day, and released on Chess's subsidiary label Checker in March of 1955. Both songs reached Number One on the R & B charts although "I'm a Man" fell off the charts seven weeks before its mate.

The release of the double-sided single was the first time Bo had used his stage name professionally. A printing error on the label added an "e" in Diddley, which became his public name. But even now, forty years after the release of the record, the guitarist privately still spells his name Diddly.

(We're Gonna) Rock Around the Clock

Bill Haley and His Comets

Bill Haley is the first artist to score a Number One hit with a song that could be considered rock and roll. "(We're Gonna) Rock Around the Clock" tanked on its original release, only to have a second shot at chart action when it was used as the theme for 1955's juvenile delinquent film *The Blackboard Jungle*. The tune topped the charts for eight weeks in the summer of 1955.

"(We're Gonna) Rock Around the Clock" would have remained a footnote in the history of rock and roll had it not been for the persistence of one man — Jimmy Myers, known professionally as Jimmy DeKnight. It was his single-minded determination and belief in the song that saved it from the delete bins.

Myers and Max C. Freeman penned the tune in 1953, immediately offering it to Bill Haley who had scored a pop hit that year with "Crazy, Man Crazy." Haley liked "(We're Gonna) Rock Around the Clock," adding it to his live set that summer. Buoyed by good crowd response, the singer wanted to record the tune as his next single for Essex Records. He was thrice thwarted. Each time Haley tried to record the tune, Essex Records president David Miller vetoed it, reportedly because he disliked Myers and didn't want to help advance his career. Sensing that Haley would never be able to commit the song to vinyl, Myers offered it to Sonny Dae and His Knights. They scored a regional hit with it but were kept from the national charts by a lack of proper distribution. Refusing to let "(We're Gonna) Rock Around the Clock" fade away, Myers recorded his own big-band version under the name Jimmy DeKnight and His Knights of Rhythm. His fox trot-influenced version also failed to chart.

Luckily for Myers, Essex Records dropped Bill Haley at the end of 1953. With David Miller out of the picture, Haley was free to record "(We're Gonna) Rock Around the Clock." In the early months of 1954, Bill Haley and His Comets signed to Decca Records and were scheduled to record a single in April at New York's Pythian Temple studio. Two songs were chosen: "Thirteen Women," a Cold War fantasy about life after the bomb, as the only man in town, surrounded by a bevy of obliging women; and the long-delayed "(We're Gonna) Rock Around the Clock." Haley and his band were over an hour late for the session, drastically cutting into their studio time. With only two hours left to set up their gear and record the songs, Haley was rushed and eager to get the session under way. They spent most of the allotted time cutting the mid-tempo "Thirteen Women," a cover of an R & B song by Dickie Thompson. The original had been banned earlier that year because of its blues lyrics. Decca was counting on Haley's clean image to sell the song and prevent a backlash from radio programmers.

As the clock ticked down to the end of the session, they had only half an hour left to do "(We're Gonna) Rock Around the Clock." Guitarist Danny Cedrone didn't even bother to come up with a new guitar solo for the recording. Rushed, he recycled the solo from an earlier Haley tune, "Rock This Joint." The band ran through the song twice, but each take was lackluster. Haley's vocals were inaudible on the first take;

on the second, the producer bumped up the vocal, drowning out the band. With no time left for a third try, producer Milt Gabler turned to some studio wizardry to save the tune. He took the first two unsuccessful takes, synchronized them, blending them into one master tape that was radio ready.

Decca shipped copies of the single, with "Thirteen Women" as the A-side, to stores in May 1954. The song about nuclear holocaust didn't play well on radio, with most DJs ignoring the record completely. However, some radio stations flipped the 45, giving the B-side a shot. "(We're Gonna) Rock Around the Clock" managed to hit the charts the week of May 29, but the next week, it was gone, sinking like a stone.

Myers was upset. He knew the song could be a hit if only it was promoted properly. Snapping up hundreds of unsold copies, he loaded up his trunk and set out on a one-man publicity blitz. For the next seven weeks, he toured the country, stopping off at every mom-and-pop radio station he came across, using all his powers of persuasion to convince disc jockeys to play the record. Once back home after his two-thousand-mile trip, he mailed off the remaining two hundred copies to producers in Hollywood, hoping to place the song on a movie sound track.

Several months later, the call came. Director Richard Brook was looking for a tune to kick off his latest film. Returning home from the studio one night, he heard his daughter playing a record. It was the 45 he had received in the mail from Myers and had given to her as a present. "(We're Gonna) Rock Around the Clock" was the perfect song to underscore the rough-and-tumble theme of his movie *The Blackboard Jungle*. Based on the best-selling novel by Evan Hunter, the film was the first Hollywood product to deal with mid-fifties juvenile delinquency. Contacting Myers, he secured the film rights to the song.

The tune and film made headlines. As a result of riots in the theaters, Clare Booth Luce campaigned against *The*

Blackboard Jungle, succeeding in getting it pulled from the Venice Film Festival. *The New York Times* called it a "full-throated, all-out testimony to the lurid headlines that appear from time to time, reporting acts of terrorism and violence by uncontrolled urban youths." Several movie critics praised the film, including the influential Brosley Crowther who rated it the second best film of 1955. The inclusion of "(We're Gonna) Rock Around the Clock" established not only the trend of placing rock-and-roll songs in major motion pictures, but it also indelibly linked rock and roll with juvenile delinquency.

The furor surrounding *The Blackboard Jungle* convinced Decca to rerelease "(We're Gonna) Rock Around the Clock," this time as an A-side. Treating the reissue as a new record, Decca threw their full weight behind the promotion of the disc, pushing it all the way to Number One and displacing Prez Prado's "Cherry Pink and Apple Blossom White." On the charts, the rock era had arrived.

Maybellene

Chuck Berry

The year 1955 was auspicious in popular culture. On television, *The Adventures of Davey Crockett* was a top-rated show, sparking a craze for coonskin caps. The inaugural edition of *The Guinness Book of World Records* was published. At the bijou, *The Blackboard Jungle* helped kick off the rock-and-roll craze. And then, along came Chuck Berry. The thirty-year-old father of two scored his first hit with the sublime "Maybellene" in August.

Chuck Berry came to rock and roll late in life. After a few years spent on the assembly line at General Motors, he earned his cosmetology diploma, embarking on a career as a hairdresser. As a sideline, he moonlighted in clubs, fronting the Chuck Berry Trio with Johnnie Johnson on piano and Ebby Harding on drums. The band's musical vocabulary was broad — a melting pot of styles that gave birth to rock and roll. Berry was studied in jazz and blues, but he insisted on adding country and Tin Pan Alley standards — "Get Your Kicks on Route 66" and songs of that ilk — to their set to attract white audiences. Soon they were a hot item in the clubs.

One night in the spring of 1955, the twenty-nine-year-old Berry took a rare night off and went to see blues legend

Muddy Waters. Summoning up all his courage, he asked Waters if he could sit in on a song. The blues guitarist was blown away by Berry's inventive guitar playing, agreeing to put in a word for the unknown musician with Leonard and Phil Chess. A meeting was set up, and Berry dropped off two demo tapes that he and Johnson had recorded in Berry's living room, using a $79 tape recorder. The first was an original — "Wee Wee Hours" — a blues tune that was a particular favorite of the pair. The second track was the one that caught Leonard Chess's ear. "Ida May" was based on a country square-dance tune called "Ida Red," popular when Berry was an adolescent. Berry updated the tune, restructuring the chorus and, of course, writing new lyrics, turning the "Ida Red" into a teen dream of girls and cars.

On the strength of "Ida May," Chess invited Berry back to lay down some tracks. He asked Berry to come up with an alternate name for "Ida May," thinking the original too rural sounding for his uptown market. Johnnie Johnson remembered that there was a mascara box lying on the floor of the studio — made by Maybelline — that inspired the new name, although the spelling was changed to make it less brand specific. It has also been reported that

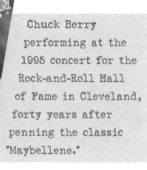

Chuck Berry performing at the 1995 concert for the Rock-and-Roll Hall of Fame in Cleveland, forty years after penning the classic "Maybellene."

Maybellene was the name of a cow from one of Berry's favorite childhood books.

Once "Maybellene" was in the can, Chess wanted to ensure that the tune would earn some airplay. To this end, he gave famed disc jockey Alan Freed and record distributer Russ Fratto cowriting credits on the tune. This was a practice some might have called "payola," but Chess preferred to think of it as greasing the wheels. Since the cowriters Freed and Fratto were making money every time a record was sold, it was in their best interest to give a little extra attention to the single. The dubious ploy worked. With the pump provided by Freed's top-rated radio show, "Maybellene" rocketed to the top spot on the R & B charts, staying at Number One for eleven weeks. On the pop charts, the hard-driving single paused at Number Five, the first of fourteen Top Forty singles Chuck Berry would record over the next eighteen years.

In 1986, Berry won back the full copyright to "Maybellene."

Chuck Berry's "Sweet Little Sixteen" was inspired by a fan at a Denver Auditorium rock concert. She wore a yellow flowered dress and enthusiastically gathered autographs from all the performers on the bill. Berry, amused by the gusto with which she pursued the artists, was struck by the purity and innocence of her zeal. He never did learn her name but credits her for inspiring his biggest pop hit of the 1950s.

Tutti Frutti

Little Richard

The earliest words to "Tutti Frutti" were so risqué that Little Richard was embarrassed to sing them for a female visitor at a recording session. "Tutti Frutti, good booty," the song went. "If it don't fit, don't force it. You can grease it, make it easy...Awopbopaloobopalobamboom."

September 13, 1955 was Little Richard's first recording session for Specialty Records. He had been summoned to New Orleans to lay down some tracks after bombarding Specialty owner Art Rupe with phone calls and letters for the better part of a year. Replacing Richard's tight nightclub band with Fats Domino's slick sidemen (including piano players Huey "Piano" Smith and James Booker), producer Robert "Bumps" Blackwell hoped to record eight songs in six hours.

The results were disappointing. Blackwell didn't even turn on the tape machine for the band's run through of "He's My Star." The gospel-tinged "Wonderin'" and "Baby" were better but didn't have the sound he was looking for. "I'm Just a Lonely Guy" by New Orleans songwriter Dorothy LaBostrie had good lyrics but an unremarkable tune. The trouble, however, ran deeper than weak material. Blackwell felt Richard was too inhibited, his vocal delivery too mannered. Richard's live act was over the top, and Blackwell wondered where that vigor was now that they were in the studio. Even worse, the producer didn't hear any songs with hit quality. Art Rupe would not be pleased.

Fretfully, he called a break. Specialty was spending a great deal of money on these sessions, and they weren't panning out. Needing time to rethink his approach, Blackwell took Richard to a nearby bar, the Dew Drop Inn. Once inside, Richard stood, stooped over the piano, furiously pounding out a rocking version of "Tutti Frutti." It was an old favorite he used to fire up the audience in his club act. Written years earlier while he was washing dishes at a Macon, Georgia bus station, Richard sang the song to himself while washing all the pots and pans. "Awopbopaloobopalobamboom" was a secret code. As much as he hated that job, he needed the money. So instead of swearing at his boss when he got frustrated, he would walk through the kitchen muttering this nonsense word. Over time, the song developed, but the lyrics were so dirty, it hadn't dawned on Richard to record it. It was, after all, a funny song about sodomy.

"That's it! That's a hit," shouted Blackwell as Richard finished up the song.

Desperate to salvage the costly sessions, Blackwell was set on committing "Tutti Frutti" to tape. The only obstacle was those obscene lyrics. After the recess, he spoke with Dorothy LaBostrie who had been hanging around the studio to hear Little Richard's take on "I'm Just a Lonely Guy."

LaBostrie was a neophyte tunesmith who had submitted dozens of songs to Blackwell. "The trouble was they all sounded like Dinah Washington's 'Blowtop Blues,'" he told Charles White, author of *The Life and Times of Little Richard*. She might not have had much melodic sense, but she could write lyrics. "So I said to her, 'Look. You come and write some lyrics to this [because] I can't use the lyrics Richard's got,'" recalled Blackwell. "He had some terrible words in there."

You didn't have to be a genius to figure out the double entendre of Hank Ballard and the Midnighter's 1954 hit "Work with Me, Annie." In ghetto slang, "work" meant sex. Young men would often boast, "I got some work last night." Ballard further pushed the tune's lascivious message with suggestive squeals and yelps. He said he wrote the song in tribute to childhood sweetheart Annie Butler. During one club performance several decades after the song had hit the top of the R & B charts, Butler was in the audience. Ballard introduced her and said "she had to sign more autographs than I did."

Richard was too shy to sing the song one-on-one to a woman. LaBostrie, for her part, having been told how dirty the song was, wasn't sure she wanted to hear it. "Time was running out," Blackwell told White, "and I knew it could be a hit. I talked, using every argument I could think of. I asked *him* if he had a grudge against making money. I told *her* that she was over twenty-one, had a houseful of kids and no husband and needed the money. And finally I convinced them."

Still feeling bashful, Little Richard faced the wall as he ran through the song for LaBostrie. She listened while he sang an uncensored "Tutti Frutti" — "good bootys" and all — three times. Richard was called back to the studio to work on two more songs. LaBostrie sat in the hall, ousting the scatological references, writing new, radio-friendly lyrics.

Fifteen minutes before the session was scheduled to end, LaBostrie was finished. Passing the new lyric sheet to Richard, Blackwell suggested recording the song.

"I got no voice left," protested Richard, who had been singing for six hours.

"You've got to sing it," said Blackwell. With no time to write an arrangement, Richard took Huey "Piano" Smith's place at the keyboard to lead the band. The hired hands were warmed up and followed Richard's fierce piano. For the first time during the sessions, Richard let loose. Paying homage to the gospel music he grew up with, he punctuated the song with "woos" reminiscent of the church singers of his youth. Three screaming takes and fifteen minutes later, "Tutti Frutti" was in the can. "Bumps" Blackwell knew he had the hit he had been fishing for.

But Rupe wasn't so sure. He saw "Tutti Frutti" as a novelty tune — one that might make back the money spent on the New Orleans' sessions. He tweaked the original recording with the addition of some echo and raised the pitch by speeding up the tape. Rewarding himself, he claimed a cowriter's credit under the pseudonym Lubin, a common practice by early rock-and-roll entrepreneurs to put a few extra dollars in their coffers.

"Tutti Frutti" became one of the seminal rock-and-roll records, an early experiment in fusing churchy R & B with rock and roll. It reached Number Seventeen on the *Billboard* charts in January 1956. The next month, Pat Boone's anemic cover version overshadowed Richard's original, climbing to Number Twelve. Boone, best known for wearing white buck shoes, took advantage of white-rock radio's reluctance to play black artists, covering a number of hits by Little Richard and Fats Domino such as "Long Tall Sally" and "Ain't That a Shame."

Heartbreak Hotel

Elvis Presley

Mae Axton, an amateur songwriter, was running Colonel Tom Parker's public relations office in Florida when she first met Elvis Presley. "You need a million seller," she told Presley when he signed to RCA Victor Records, "and I'm going to write it for you." Holding true to her word, she helped pen "Heartbreak Hotel," Presley's first Number One hit.

Tommy Durden, a Gainesville, Florida musician and an acquaintance of Axton's, was reading the *Miami Herald* when a headline caught his eye. Next to a photo of a suicide victim was the header "Do You Know This Man?" The corpse was a John Doe, having been found with no identification, only a note saying, "I walk a lonely street." Durden couldn't shake the image of the dead man and imagined how low down and blue he must have felt to take his own life.

Later that day, Durden visited Axton and told her about the story in the paper, suggesting they write a blues song about an unfortunate man who "walks a lonely street." She liked the idea, thinking it would be a good tune for Presley. But she wanted to expand on the note to include a stanza describing how the man's family would feel when they found out about his death. Together, they came up with the idea of placing a "Heartbreak Hotel" at the end of "lonely street" to represent the anguish of this man's family. Durden hammered out chords on Axton's piano as she improvised the lyrics. Legend has it that the pair finished the song in just twenty-two minutes.

Once the tune was written, Axton called Glen Reeves, a local singer, to come over and make a demo of the song. Reeves sang the song into Axton's tape recorder, trying to mimic Presley's voice. In lieu of payment, Axton offered Reeves a songwriting credit on "Heartbreak Hotel." He turned her down. "That's the silliest song I ever heard," he reportedly said.

With the demo completed, Axton's next call was to Presley. She asked that he meet her in Nashville so she could play him his first million seller. They hooked up in the country music capital where Elvis was scheduled to record his first album, and she played him the tape. He asked her to play

The last photo
ever taken of
Elvis Presley
and the
Jordanaires.
The Jordanaires
sang on almost
every Elvis
record from
1955 to 1970,
including
"Heartbreak Hotel."
Left to right: Neal Matthews,
Gordon Stoker, Elvis, Hoyt Hawkins
and Roy Walker.

photo courtesy of Gordon Stoker

it again, and again, until they had listened to it ten times. By the end of the meeting, Presley had agreed to release "Heartbreak Hotel" as a single from his upcoming LP for RCA.

Recording for the album, with producer Steve Sholes at the helm, commenced on January 10, 1956, just a few days after Presley's twenty-first birthday. Sholes assembled a band of Nashville heavyweight session players, including Chet Atkins on guitar and Floyd Cramer on piano, to try to re-create the Sun Records' sound that had been so effective on Presley's first singles. For his part, Elvis was still wet behind the ears in terms of working in a recording studio. Sholes had to surround him with three microphones to catch his voice at all angles because he moved around so much, often straying out of range.

The band warmed up by playing three or four songs, one right after the other. Elvis was so worked up by the time they settled in to record "Heartbreak Hotel" that he split the seat of his pants and kicked off his white bucks, releasing a waft of foot odor that hung in the studio air for the rest of the session. Elvis's vocal on the tune so closely followed Reeves's original demo that Durden commented later, "Elvis was even breathing in the same places as Glen Reeves did on the dub."

"Heartbreak Hotel" was released as a single on January 27, 1956, less than three weeks after the recording session. The next day, Presley made his first appearance on the Dorsey Brothers' television variety program *Stage Show*. He was such a hit, he was invited back five more times, singing "Heartbreak Hotel" on his third, fifth and sixth appearances. By the end of April, the single had reached Number One, knocking Les Baxter's syrupy instrumental "Poor People of Paris" out of the top spot.

The record sold an unprecedented quantity. It was to become 1956's biggest single, sitting at Number One for eight weeks and making a barrelful of cash in the process. The song's publishers Hill and Range refused to cash the first royalty check from RCA — in the amount of $250,000 — thinking the accountants at the record company must have added some extra zeros by mistake.

"Heartbreak Hotel" was the first of 107 singles Elvis Presley placed on the *Billboard* Top Forty in the next twenty-five years.

Blue Suede Shoes

Carl Perkins

A dancer at a honky-tonk gave Carl Perkins the idea for one of the most well-known phrases in rock-and-roll history. In 1956, "Blue Suede Shoes" was Sun Records' first million seller.

On December 4, 1955, Carl Perkins was playing a honky-tonk in his hometown of Jackson, Tennessee. His set was comprised of hillbilly songs with a twist; he filled in the space around the vocals with lead-guitar runs, a trick he learned from listening to old blues records. As an aspiring song-writer — having issued several self-penned singles by this time — he was always on the lookout for a snappy phrase to build a song around. This gig provided one that would echo through the next four decades.

A young couple were jitterbugging near the bandstand. "They were really good," he remembered. "You know, when you are playing, you often pick out a certain pair that are really rockin'." He kept his eye on the lively couple who continued to dance until the end of the set. At the end of the last tune, Perkins heard the boy admonish his date. "Don't you step on my suedes!" he said loudly, sounding annoyed. "I'm sorry," she replied, with a hurt look on her face. Suede shoes were getting popular around Jackson and Memphis at the time, but Perkins couldn't believe the way this boy had spoken. "I thought, 'You fool, that's a stupid shoe. That's a pretty girl, man.'"

Returning home after the show, he couldn't get the line out of his head, "Don't step on my suedes." As he was drifting off to sleep, he thought of an old rhyme: "One for the money, two for the show, three to get ready and four to go." That's it, he thought, leaping out of bed, grabbing his guitar and heading for the basement. "One for the money," he sang, strumming his guitar twice.

The clamor woke his wife Valda who came to the top of the stairs. "Carl, it's three o'clock in the morning! You're gonna wake up the children," she said. "Whose song is that?" "It's ours," said Perkins, already convinced he was writing a hit. "Write the song, and we'll rock them back to sleep," she replied, leaving him alone to work.

In his haste he didn't take any paper downstairs. He emptied three potatoes from a brown paper bag and quickly wrote the song on the potato sack, including the now-famous line, "Don't you step on my blue suede shoes." Never having owned a pair of the shoes, he misspelled suede as "swaed."

Later that month, Perkins showed the song to Sun Records' chief Sam Phillips who was willing to give him studio time. They ran through the tune three times. On the first try, Perkins sang "...three to get ready, now go boy go!" Phillips suggested he change it to "go cat go!,"

Songwriters Arthur Singer, John Medora and David White put their heads together to create a song that would cash in on a new dance craze. They came up with a tune called "Do the Bop," presenting it to Dick Clark for his consideration. Clark liked the melody but felt the tune needed new lyrics. He told the writers that the bop was a passing fad and wouldn't be popular when the song came out. He suggested "At the Hop" as a new title. They cut the revised song with Danny and the Juniors, scoring a Number One hit in January 1958.

giving the record a hipper sound. Four sides were recorded that day, two rockabilly and two country. Sun Records had a policy of coupling a rockabilly tune with a country song in an attempt to catch both markets. This time, though, Sam Phillips decided to break from his usual marketing strategy, going full ahead rockabilly. "Blue Suede Shoes," coupled with "Honey, Don't," was released on New Year's Day 1956.

Local reaction in Memphis was immediate. The song became a heavy seller, reaching Number One on the Memphis charts and sitting there for the next three months. By the following March, Blue Suede Mania had broken out of the South. *Billboard* Magazine rated the tune seventy-six out of one hundred, saying, "Perkins contributes a lively reading on a gay rhythm ditty with a strong R & B backing. Fine for the jukes." By this point, the song was selling twenty thousand copies a day.

In what is probably the clearest indication of its success, "Blue Suede Shoes" was covered by a dozen artists, including Pee Wee King, Boyd Bennett, Bob Roubian, Sid King, Lawrence Welk, Roy Hall, Sam "The Man" Taylor, Jim Lowe and, most notably, Elvis Presley. On March 10, 1956, Perkins became the first country

Ron Frehm/Canapress Photo Service

A dancer in a honky-tonk gave rockabilly legend Carl Perkins (pictured here in a January 1992 photo), the idea for one of the most well-known phrases in rock-and-roll history.

artist to breach the national R & B charts, beating Presley to them by three weeks.

Later, on the twenty-first of that month, Perkins and his band, including his brother Jay, left by car for New York. They were scheduled to make their first national television appearance on the *Perry Como Show* to receive a gold record on air for "Blue Suede Shoes."

Near Dover, Delaware, disaster struck. Driver Dick Stuart fell asleep at the wheel, slamming into a poultry truck. Perkins suffered a broken shoulder, lacerations and a cracked skull. The accident prevented Perkins from properly promoting "Blue Suede Shoes," and due to a loss in momentum, his next four singles fared poorly. "Boppin' the Blues," his follow-up release, only reached Number Seventy on the charts. Similarly, "Your True Love" failed to break into the Top Forty.

But even without Perkins to promote the tune, "Blue Suede Shoes" managed to top the country, pop and R & B charts, a feat never before accomplished. Many music historians consider it to be the first true rock-and-roll hit because it crossed over to all three major markets.

Until the time of his death in January 1997, the original potato sack with the words to "Blue Suede Shoes" hung in Perkins's house next to a gold record for his biggest hit. "After all those days in the cotton fields, the dreams came true on a gold record on a piece of wood," he said in an interview in 1985. "It's in my den where I can look at it every day. I wear it out lookin' at it."

Great Balls of Fire

Jerry Lee Lewis

Two souls, alas, are housed within my breast. — Faust

"Jerry is tormented by his religious influences," said *Great Balls of Fire* movie producer Adam Fields. "He sees himself forever torn between doing God's work and singing the devil's music." This dichotomy has plagued Lewis throughout his checkered career but never so strongly as when he recorded "Great Balls of Fire."

Otis Blackwell, the New York songwriter best known for penning "Don't Be Cruel" and "All Shook Up" for Elvis Presley, first heard Jerry Lee Lewis in a listening booth at a record store. As "Whole Lotta Shakin'" poured out of the booth's headphones, he became electrified. Already having scored several hits with Elvis, he sensed the same potential in Jerry Lee. In the coming weeks, as "Whole Lotta Shakin'" rose on the charts, Blackwell tried to come up with a song to present to Lewis. He uncovered a tune called "Great Balls of Fire" by a fellow New Yorker with the unlikely name of Jack Hammer. Changing some of the lyrics and pumping up the rhythm, Blackwell slapped a cowriter's credit on the song and submitted a demo disc to Jerry Lee at Sun Studios in Memphis.

Jerry Lee was knocked out by the demo. Sun staffers recall he walked around the office mouthing the words as if writing a musical arrangement in his head. Keen to get the tune on tape as quickly as possible, Sam Phillips, owner of Sun Studios, set aside studio time in October 1957. The night of the recording session, Jerry Lee had an unsettling revelation. Studying the lyric sheet, he realized "Great Balls of Fire" had a deeper meaning. It was actually about fire and brimstone — Judgment Day. Jerry Lee had been raised to be a God-fearing man. He may have lapsed at points in his life, but years later, he could still feel the power of his Pentecostal minister's words reverberating in his head. As much as he loved the song, he wasn't going to end up in hell for recording it — not without a fight, anyway.

While Sam Phillips tried to get the session under way, Jerry Lee went into a tirade. A glass or two of bourbon only

Jerry Lee Lewis, aka The Killer. After a 1958 performance, one fan had nothing but raves for the blue-eyed, fair-haired singer from Ferriday, Louisiana. "He's tall, he wears thick-soled white shoes and he hits the piano keys so hard that you can't understand why the piano doesn't collapse! All the time he's yelling 'go, go, go' and whips up the fans to such a pitch that it takes a bunch of police to stop them from tearing the place apart."

photo courtesy of Kerrie Lewis

fueled his mounting paranoia. "Great Balls of Fire" was the devil's song, he maintained. To sing it was sinful. Someone secretly switched on the tape machine, recording Jerry Lee's drunken sermon for all posterity. Years later, it appeared on a bootleg of Sun Studio outtakes called *Good Rocking Tonight.* Here's an edited version:

"H...E...L...L...!" Jerry Lee yelled.

"I don't believe this," Sam Phillips said, sensing what was to come.

"Great God almighty! Great balls of fire!" someone mockingly shouted in the background.

"It says make merry with the joy of God only," Jerry Lee ranted amid the comments from the band. "But when it comes to worldly music, rock and roll...anything like that...you have done brought yourself into the world, and you are in the world, and you are still a sinner. You are a sinner unless you be saved and borned again and be made as a little child and walk before God and be holy — and brother, I mean you got to be so pure. No sin shall enter there — no sin! For it says no sin. It don't just say a little bit; it says no sin shall enter there. Brother, not one little bit. You got to walk and talk with God to go to heaven. You have to be so good."

"Hallelujah," someone testified in the background.

"All right," said Phillips, warming up to a religious debate. "Now look, Jerry, religious conviction doesn't mean anything resembling extremism. All right. Do you mean to tell me that you are going to take the Bible, that you are going to take God's word and that you are going revolutionize the whole universe? Now listen, Jesus Christ was sent here by God almighty...."

"Right!" Jerry Lee agreed.

"Did He convince?" Phillips continued. "Did He save all of the people in the world?"

"No, but He tried to."

"He sure did. Now wait a minute. Jesus Christ came into

this world. He tolerated man. He didn't preach from one pulpit. He went around and did good."

"That's right. He preached everywhere," Jerry countered, talking over Phillips. "He preached on land. He preached on water. Man, He done everything. He healed."

"Now, now, here's the difference...."

"Are you following those that heal? Like Jesus did? Well, it's happening every day. The blind eyes opened. The lame were made to walk. The crippled were made to walk," Jerry Lee said, ignoring Phillips's attempts to interject.

"Jesus Christ, in my opinion, is just as real today as He was when He came into this world," Phillips sermonized.

"Right. Right. You are so right, you don't know what you are saying."

At this point the band was fed up with the polemic. "Aw, let's cut it," said one player disgustedly. "It'll never sell, man," said another. "It's not commercial."

"Wait, wait, wait. Just a minute," said Phillips, ignoring the band. "I'm telling you out of my heart, and I have studied the Bible a little bit...."

"Well, I have too," said Jerry Lee, recalling his days at the Southwest Bible College in Waxahachie, Texas. "I studied it through and through, and through and through, and I know what I am talking about."

"Jerry, Jerry," said Phillips, adopting the tone of an older, wiser man. "If you think that you can't...can't do good if you are a rock-and-roll exponent...."

"You can do good, Mr. Phillips. Don't get me wrong."

"Now wait. Wait. Listen. When I say do good...."

"You can have a good heart. You can help people."

"You can save souls," Phillips added.

"No. No. No. No!" Jerry Lee responded loudly, appalled at the idea.

"Yes."

"How can the devil save souls? What are you talking

about?" said Jerry Lee, clearly confused. "Man, I got the devil in me. If I didn't have, I [wouldn't] be a Christian."

"Well, you may have him...."

"Jesus!" Jerry Lee yelled in his best preacher voice, pounding his chest. "Heal this man. He casts the devil out. The devil says, 'Where can I go?' He says, 'Can I go into this swine?' He says, 'Yeah, go into him.' Didn't he go into him?"

"Jerry, the point I'm trying to make is, if you believe in what you are singing, you got no alternative whatsoever.... "

"Mr. Phillips. I don't care. It ain't what you believe. It is what is written in the Bible."

"Well, wait a minute."

"It is what is there, Mr. Phillips."

"No, no."

"It's just what's there."

"No, by gosh, if it's not what you believe, then how do you interpret the Bible?" said Phillips, exasperated, trying to end the argument. "How do you interpret the Bible if it is not what you believe?"

"Well, it's not what you believe. You can't just...." said Jerry Lee, confused.

"Let's cut it man!" said a frustrated and bored band member.

The band finally won out, and they laid down a furious track that writer Greil Marcus says "outsins the version Sam Phillips released to the public." The tired band did the song several more times, and sometime between midnight and dawn, recorded the version that pumped out of radios later that year. At the end of the session, someone joked to Jerry Lee that the royalties should be split with the Holy Ghost. He didn't laugh.

Held out of the top spot by Danny and the Juniors' "At the Hop," "Great Balls of Fire" sat at Number Two for four weeks. It was the biggest hit Sun Records ever had, proving to Jerry Lee that there was money to be made singing the devil's tune. He joked that there were almost as many zeros on his royalty checks "as there had been Fs on my third-grade report card."

More than twenty years after that night of drunken sermonizing, Jerry Lee was convinced he would burn for singing rock and roll. Being good isn't always easy, and most often, Jerry Lee seemed to have one eye looking to heaven while the other was looking for trouble.

In a 1979 interview, music critic Robert Palmer asked Jerry Lee, "What is it about rock and roll that damns you to hell if you play it?" Jerry Lee replied, "I can't picture Jesus Christ doing a whole lotta shakin'."

Tequila

The Champs

A solo artist named Dave Burgess thought he had a hit with an instrumental track called "Train to Nowhere." Previously, he had recorded four singles for Gene Autry's Challenge record label, all of which failed to chart. This time he felt in his gut he could hit the big time. "Train to Nowhere" didn't grab anyone's attention, but the 45's B-side, a hastily recorded instrumental called "Tequila," went to Number One in March 1958.

When lead guitarist Dave Burgess, pianist Danny Flores, drummer Gene Auden, guitarist Buddy Bruce and bass guitarist Cliff Hils recorded "Tequila," they were session musicians hired to play backup on a Jerry Wallace album. Wallace knocked off the session early, leaving the musicians with a few spare minutes to goof around in the studio. With Wallace picking up the tab for the studio time, Burgess grabbed the opportunity to record a B-side for his "Train to Nowhere" single.

Flores proposed they cut a tune he had written while visiting family in Tijuana. While on vacation in Mexico, he drank a lot of that famous local liquor, and a bartender suggested he write a song about his favorite drink. He took the advice and wrote the melody, often using it as a break song during his club dates. In the studio, he taught it to the other guys, writing a quick musical arrangement on the spot. After the first run through, Burgess thought something was missing. He asked Flores to shout "tequila" in his big baritone during the song. Using the last few remaining moments of studio time, the session players recorded the tune, committing it to tape just as the next band was arriving to set up in the studio. Time was so tight that they didn't even bother to listen to a playback of the tune before grabbing the reel-to-reel tape and going their separate ways.

Several days later, they met again to decide on a band name under which to release the single. They came up with the Champs in tribute to Gene Autry's horse Champion. Flores also decided on a name change for the writer's credit on "Tequila." Using a combination of his middle name and his father's given name, he came up with the stage name Chuck Rio.

The title "Train to Nowhere" proved prophetic. Released on December 26, 1957, the record sank without a trace until a disc jockey flipped the single and played the B-side. By March 1958, the quickly recorded throwaway "Tequila" was burning up the *Billboard* charts. Meanwhile, ABC Paramount recording artist Eddie Platt released a cover version of the tune that ultimately made it to Number Twenty, but it was eclipsed by the Champs' spirited rendering.

In mid-March, "Tequila" hit Number One, a spot it would hold for five weeks, establishing several firsts in rock-and-roll history. The Champs became the first instrumental group to top the charts with their first release. "Tequila" was the first tune of the rock era to jump from outside the Top Ten to the Number One spot. It also won the first-ever Grammy Award for Best R & B Performance.

The success of the tune took the band by surprise. Conceived only as a studio project, several of the guys were

Ricky Nelson's 1958 hit "Poor Little Fool" was penned by Sharon Sheeley, girlfriend of rock pioneer Eddie Cochrane.

unprepared for "Tequila"'s sweeping popularity. Buddy Bruce and Cliff Hils had families and were not able to tour with the band to promote the record, so they were replaced. After a nationwide series of shows, Flores, aka Rio, left for a solo career, with Alden following soon behind. Jim Seals and Dash Crofts, who would later find fame as Seals and Crofts ("Summer Breeze" and "Diamond Girl"), were brought on board to fill the gap. The band's last incarnation saw Burgess as the only original member, backed up by Glen Campbell on rhythm guitar.

Despite the ever-rotating lineup, the Champs placed two more singles — "El Rancho Rock" and "Too Much Tequila" — in the Top Forty before disbanding in 1965.

Book of Love

The Monotones

A radio jingle inspired Charles Patrick to write a novelty tune for the amusement of his friends, a New Jersey doo-wop group called the Monotones. "Book of Love" peaked at Number Five on *Billboard* magazine's Hot One Hundred in April 1958.

Warren Davis, George Malone, Charles Patrick, Frank Smith and brothers John and Warren Ryanes sang together in a church choir in Newark, New Jersey. Inspired by the success of Dionne Warwick, one of the choir's alumni, they formed a group to sing secular music. Fast friends, they dubbed themselves the Monotones because "the word means 'one tone,' and we were so close, like one," said one member.

The discipline of church singing served them well. Soon after forming the band, their four-part doo-wop harmonies won them a berth on the *Ted Mack Amateur Hour*, competing against other musical acts. Victorious the first week, they lost the second time around, but they had tasted the fame that television could provide. The next logical step was to record a single. Patrick went to a sheet-music store to look for songs for his band to record. An old Four Lads' tune called "Book of Love" caught his eye just as the shop's radio

Three Songs of Amour: Ritchie Valens's 1958 hit "Donna" was written for Donna Ludwig, a middle-class girl whose family disliked Valens because he was Chicano; "Oh Carol" was Neil Sedaka's 1958 ode of love to his high-school crush Carol King; "Claudette," the 1958 Everly Brothers' hit, was penned by Roy Orbinson in tribute to his first wife. The former Miss Frady was tragically killed in a motorcycle accident.

was playing a commercial for a popular brand of toothpaste.

"You'll wonder where the yellow went," the radio trumpeted, "when you brush your teeth with Pepsodent."

Patrick was amused by the jingle, humming it while paying for the sheet music and making his way home. He met with his friends where they worked on new material. Singing together, they came up with a new song based on Patrick's visit to the sheet-music store. Borrowing the Four Lads' title and combining it with the hook of the toothpaste commercial, they produced their version of "Book of Love." The band thought the up-tempo ditty was cute, but they were concentrating on ballads, which they thought were their strong suit. They agreed to play the song live but didn't consider committing it to tape.

They didn't consider recording it, that is, until another local band, the Kodacs, decided to release "Book of Love" as a single. The Monotones didn't want anyone else scoring a hit with their song, so they made a demo and shopped it to record labels. R & B giant Atlantic Records liked the song but wanted another band to sing it. "No way," they said, walking away from a lucrative recording deal, in search of another contract. Eventually, they came in contact with Ben Casalin, an executive with the smaller firm Hull Records, who agreed to release "Book of Love" with the Monotones.

They cut the tune at Bell Sound Studios in New York City. The instrumentation was kept to a minimum to emphasize the boys' voices. During the "keeper take" of the song, someone threw a baseball through a window in the studio, causing a loud crash in the recording booth. During playback, the engineer realized the uninvited noise was perfectly in time with the vocal and kept it in as the drum part. "Book of Love" hit the stores a few weeks later in December 1957.

The tiny label was unprepared to deal with the response to the song. Unable to keep up with the demand in the New York area alone, Casalin cut a deal with Argo Records to handle national distribution. Argo smelled a hit and promoted the hell out of the record, sending the Monotones out on an extended tour with teen idol Bobby Darin. The ploy worked, driving the song to the Top Five in April 1958.

However, the band was slow to record a follow-up single, waiting until May to enter the studio again. By then, momentum was lost, and their subsequent singles failed to chart. The Monotones were one-hit wonders, but they continued to perform at rock, roll and remember shows into the nineties.

The Purple People Eater

Sheb Wooley

Sheb Wooley was a successful actor and country musician before a friend told him a childish joke that inspired an unlikely hit. "The Purple People Eater" was Number One for six weeks in the summer of 1958.

The phrase "Been there, done that" could have been coined to describe Sheb Wooley's career. Born in 1921 near Erick, Oklahoma, Wooley, who is part Cherokee, made his first mark as a rodeo star while still in his teens. Trading in the saddle for a guitar, he next gave country music a try. World War II interrupted Wooley's burgeoning musical career, stopping it cold. After the war, he briefly worked as a welder in an oil field in California. Tired of the long hours, he decided to give music another shot. Relocating to Nashville, he performed on radio and cut a few sides for the local Bullet label. His big break came in 1946 when he signed on as front man for a national radio show sponsored by Calumet Baking Powder. The success of this show opened doors that Wooley would walk through for the rest of his career.

Hoping to further diversify his résumé, he headed west in 1950, seeking work as an actor and songwriter in Hollywood. He stayed busy in tinsel town, signing a record deal with

MGM Records and scoring with a tune called "Peepin' Through the Keyhole Watchin' Jole Blon" which became a hit in Texas. Soon others were recording his songs, and film and television work started coming his way. In his big-screen debut, he played opposite Errol Flynn in *Rocky Mountain* and in 1952, put in a memorable performance as the killer scheming to gun down Gary Cooper in *High Noon*. Other films followed: *Little Big Horn*, *Distant Drums*, *Giant* and *Rio Bravo*. With his film career gathering steam, Wooley signed on as Pete Nolan on television's *Rawhide* in 1958, costarring with Clint Eastwood.

During a break in shooting on the *Rawhide* pilot, Wooley had supper with an old friend, songwriter Don Robertson. Over dinner, Robertson told some jokes his young son had heard at school. One riddle was so stupid, so juvenile, that the pair couldn't help but laugh at it. "What has one eye, one horn, flies and eats people? A one-eyed, one-horned, flying people eater."

Once they stopped giggling, Wooley proposed that they turn the joke into a song. "Go ahead, that's more in your field," said Robertson, aware that Wooley had already written several novelty songs. Wooley wrote the song as a lark, filing it away in his guitar case. Several days later, he had a meeting with the honchos at MGM to audition new tunes. After playing a few new ballads, none of which excited the producers, they asked if he had anything else. Perhaps something more up-tempo. "I do, but it's nothing you'll want to hear," Wooley said, noticing the last piece of sheet music in his case. "It's the bottom of the barrel." He played "The

A John Wayne movie inspired one of Buddy Holly's best-known tunes. In *The Searchers*, Wayne plays an antiestablishment cowboy with an attitude. Wayne intones the film's most famous line that became a popular catchphrase of the time. "That'll be the day," the macho cowboy said, ending a disagreement with a foe. Holly liked the sound of the line, incorporating it into his first Number One hit.

Purple People Eater," expecting to get laughed out of the room. The bigwigs laughed alright, but they loved the song and wanted him to record it.

At the session, producer Neely Plumb used some studio trickery made popular by David Seville on his hit single "Witch Doctor" (and later on the Chipmunks' records). Recording the voice of the Purple People Eater and the saxophone part at a reduced speed, he played them back at high speed to create the People Eater's squeaky cry.

The resulting two minutes and eleven seconds of musical mayhem didn't thrill the MGM sales department. "We're Metro Goldwyn Mayer!" one salesman griped. "We don't want to be associated with this." Cooler heads prevailed, and the tune was released in May 1958. Just three weeks later, it was Number One. "The Purple People Eater" became a national sensation, with spin-off merchandising galore. For a few heady months, teenyboppers snapped up Purple People Eater T-shirts, horns, hats, ice cream and, of course, almost three million copies of the single. Hoping to cash in on the craze, other record companies released "answer" records, the most popular being Joe South's "The Purple People Eater Meets the Witch Doctor" which reached the Top Fifty in 1958.

"The Purple People Eater" was Wooley's only Top Forty chart entry, under his real name, that is. His alter ego, a goodtime drunk named Ben Colder, released song parodies such as "Hello Walls Number Two," "Harper Valley PTA (Later That Same Day)" and "Lucille Number Two." None of these songs equaled the success of "The Purple People Eater," but Wooley was never at a loss for work. He appeared in over forty major motion pictures, played on *Rawhide* for four and a half years and wrote the theme song for *Hee Haw*.

To Know Him Is to Love Him

The Teddy Bears

The light and airy production of the Teddy Bears' first single masks its sorrowful beginnings. A teenaged Phil Spector wrote "To Know Him Is to Love Him" in memory of his late father Benjamin. The song hit Number One just before Christmas 1958.

Benjamin Spector came to the United States in 1913. He was ten years old and just one of thousands of Russian Jews who immigrated to the US in the early 1900s. At Ellis Island, his Russian last name Spektor was anglicized by the immigration officer who spelled it with a "c" instead of a "k." Settling in the Soundview section of the Bronx, young Ben soaked up all things American. At age thirty-one, he married Bertha Spektor, another Russian who made her way to the US via France. They were meant to be together. After all, they already shared the same last name!

They married in 1934 and started a family right away with the birth of Shirley. Six years later, they had another child, Harvey Phillip, born on December 26, 1940. Ben worked hard to support his tightly knit family. Their home life was idyllic. At family dinners, young Harvey would entertain, singing songs of his own composition. Father and son were very close.

THE WALL OF SOUND: PHIL
SPECTOR'S TOP FIFTEEN

1. "To Know Him Is to
   Love Him": The Teddy
   Bears -- July 1958
2. "Corrine, Corrina":
   Ray Peterson --
   October 1960
3. "Spanish Harlem": Ben
   E. King -- November
   1960
4. "Pretty Little Angel
   Eyes": Curtis Lee --
   June 1961
5. "He Hit Me (It Felt
   Like a Kiss)": The
   Crystals -- June 1962
6. "He's a Rebel": The
   Crystals -- July 1962
7. "Da Doo Ron Ron": The
   Crystals -- March
   1963
8. "Chapel of Love":
   Darlene Love -- April
   1963
9. "Not Too Young to Get
   Married": Bob B. Soxx
   & The Blue Jeans --
   April 1963
10. "Be My Baby": The
    Ronettes -- July 1963

Just months before Harvey turned nine, his father changed. He spent more time alone and was silent at the dinner table. He told friends he felt he didn't make enough money to keep his family as comfortable as they deserved. He felt as though he had failed them. On April 20, 1949, he left for work at the steel plant as usual, kissing Bertha good-bye before he left. He drove a few blocks to Myrtle Avenue. Once there, he attached a hose to the exhaust pipe of the car and poked the other end through the window, rolling it up tightly. He sat in the car and turned on the engine. His lifeless body was discovered half hour later. The official cause of death was listed as "carbon monoxide poisoning — asphyxia; suicidal."

He was buried in Beth David Cemetery in New York on April 22. In accordance to Jewish law, a headstone was erected one year later. Festooned with a Star of David, there was a personal and touching epitaph from Bertha etched on the lower portion of the large stone.

Flash forward to 1958. Harvey Phillip Spector and family had moved to Los Angeles. At Fairfax High, Harvey took to introducing himself as Phil, a name he considered hipper than his given name. He studied guitar, learning the musical intricacies of Bach and Beethoven by day, and by night, strumming along to the tunes on the black R & B radio stations. He could identify with the raw emotion of those records, having lost his father — his best friend — at a young age. His late-night practices with the radio taught him the rudiments of R & B and rock and roll, while the daily lessons gave him the confidence to write down his musical ideas.

One night as he drifted off to sleep, he had a terrible dream. He saw himself as a young child standing in front of his father's grave at the Beth David Cemetery back East. Next to him was the ghostly apparition of Ben Spector, goading him, taunting him. Jolted awake, he sat upright, shaken and troubled. Instinctively, he reached for the guitar. Since his father's death, music had been a great pacifier. He strummed some chords to calm his tormented mind, letting his thoughts wander.

11. "Baby, I Love You": The Ronettes -- November 1963
12. "Walking in the Rain": The Ronettes -- September 1964
13. "You've Lost That Lovin' Feelin'": The Righteous Brothers -- November 1964
14. "River Deep, Mountain High": Ike & Tina Turner -- March 1966
15. "Save the Last Dance for Me": Ike & Tina Turner -- April 1966

Phil couldn't shake the dream. As the chords drifted from the guitar, he thought of his father and his final resting place. Tears stained his face as he remembered his mother's final tribute to Ben — "To Know Him Was to Love Him" — words engraved on the tombstone. To help him through his grief, he began to write a song — more of a dirge, really — to express the profound loss he still felt at his father's passing. By daybreak, the black mood had passed. It was seven o'clock, and Phil's therapy was complete. The dark, moody chords had slowly transformed into a light, lilting song Phil called "To Know Him Is to Love Him." Excited, he called his friend Marshall Lieb, playing him the tune over the phone.

"That's great, Phil," yawned Lieb before going back to bed. Phil wouldn't be put off, and later that day, he and Lieb

Phil Spector's "Wall of Sound" was born in an LA facility called Gold Star Sound Studios. Using dozens of musicians -- dubbed "Spector's Army" -- the producer crafted a monolithic clamor, one that threatened to blow radio speakers. The cacophonous sound produced by four guitars, three basses, three pianos, two drums, innumerable percussion instruments and layers of background vocals bounced around the studio's low ceilings and two echo chambers creating a din that one writer called "not of this earth." Spector expertly reigned in the clamor, mixing it down, creating something akin to aural poetry. This "Wall of Sound" was an integral part of some of the most exciting pop singles of the 1960s.

were hard at work putting together an arrangement for the new tune. Around this time, Phil was dating a girl named Donna whose best friend Annette Kleinbard had a lovely singing voice. Soon, she became the vocalist with the band Phil had formed with Lieb — the Teddy Bears. As Spector and Lieb worked out the arrangement, they shaped it to fit her voice. After intensive rehearsals in Lieb's garage, the trio secured a record deal with Dore, a small Southern California label. Bertha voiced her concern over her only son's choice of career. It wasn't stable. However, Bertha's concerns were unfounded. "To Know Him Is to Love Him" was released in August 1958 and finally settled in at Number One in December.

It would be the Teddy Bears' only hit, but the members would have an impact on the charts that would span decades. Phil Spector distinguished himself as a songwriter/producer, creating the famed "Wall of Sound" production technique, becoming one of rock's great eccentrics along the way. Kleinbard, under the name Carol Connors, became a noted songwriter, penning "Gonna Fly Now" (Theme from *Rocky*), "With You I'm Born Again" and "Hey Little Cobra" which she claims is the only hot-rod song written by a woman.

SIXTIES

The Lion
Sleeps Tonight

The Tokens

The debt popular music owes to African music is inestimable. Many of rock-and-roll's traits can be traced back to the music of that continent — the beats, the call-and-response formation, the use of husky voices rather than the trained clear vocals of European music. The Tokens brought their brand of African music to the hit parade. "The Lion Sleeps Tonight" hit Number One in December 1961.

In the 1930s, a song by Soloman Linda called "Mbube" was a hit in Swaziland. In the Zulu language, "Mbube" is pronounced "wimoweh." Twenty years later, Miriam Makeba recorded a folk version of the tune, sung in its original dialect. Later, the American folk act the Weavers anglicized "Mbube," renaming it "Wimoweh," and included it on their Carnegie Hall live album.

In 1955, Neil Sedaka brought together the best singers in his Brooklyn high school to form a doo-wop group called the Linc-Tones. After Sedaka left for a solo career, the remaining members split, leaving Hank Medress without a band. He quickly regrouped, forming Darrell & the Oxfords in 1958. More personnel changes followed, leading to the Tokens' lineup of Medress, Jay Siegal and Phil and Mitch

Margo in 1960. Signing a one-off deal with Warwick Records, the quartet scored a doo-wop hit with "Tonight I Fell in Love," a Number Fifteen hit in 1961.

Later that year, they were offered a chance to audition for RCA Records' hit makers Hugo (Peretti) and Luigi (Creatore). By then, however, their musical focus had changed. Siegal had discovered *The Weavers at Carnegie Hall*, and now that doo-wop music was quickly falling out of favor, he had convinced his bandmates to give folk music a shot. Trying to emulate the smooth folk sound of the Kingston Trio and the Highwaymen, they chose "Mbube" for their audition.

Hugo and Luigi enjoyed the lively African melody but felt it needed more lyrics. The Tokens' version had almost no words, just the rhythmic "wimoweh" chanted over and over to a light guitar backing. Putting their heads together, they came up with the African-themed "The Lion Sleeps Tonight." They didn't realize it at the time, but the new lyric sheet was very faithful to the original intent of the Soloman Linda tune. Over the years and after many translations of the song, it came to be known as "Wimoweh," basically a phonetic transcription of "Mbube." The word "wimoweh" means nothing in Zulu, but its root "mbube" can be translated as "lion." The Italian/ American producers had unwittingly created an authentic-sounding African folk song.

The band, who by now considered themselves folk purists, didn't want to record the tune but relented when RCA made them an offer they couldn't refuse. The session was called for early May 1961 at RCA Studios on East 24th Street in Manhattan. This facility was RCA's recording headquarters until the end of the sixties. Elvis recorded "Hound Dog," "Don't Be Cruel" and "Blue Suede Shoes" here; now it was the Tokens' turn in front of the microphone. They cut two songs that day — a Portuguese folk tune called "Tina" and the rewritten "The Lion Sleeps Tonight."

Hugo and Luigi brought in opera singer Anita Darien to

supply the high soprano part, while drummer Panama Francis was told to pile newspapers on top of his drum kit to muffle the sound. The single was released in October. In the meantime, Siegal got married and started a day job to help pay the bills. When the record started to sell, his manager called advising him to quit working. "'The Lion Sleeps Tonight' is going to be a smash," he said.

With the help of DJ Dick Smith at WORC in Worcester, Massachusetts, who pumped the song mercilessly on his show, "The Lion Sleeps Tonight" broke nationally, becoming a Number One hit in December 1961. The success of that song was never equaled by the Tokens who only managed to place two more singles in the Top Forty. Their greatest triumph came as producers of other people's records. While "The Lion Sleeps Tonight" was racing up the charts, the band signed a production deal with RCA that would eventually yield the Chiffons' "He's So Fine," "Tie a Yellow Ribbon" for Tony Orlando and Dawn and a remake of their biggest hit by Robert John which hit Number Three in 1972.

Those Are People Who Died: Dion's 1968 Top Five folk-rock hit "Abraham, Martin and John" was written by Dick Holler as a eulogy to a quartet of American heroes -- Abraham Lincoln, Martin Luther King and the Kennedy brothers John and Robert. The younger Kennedy was also memorialized by Crosby, Stills and Nash in the album cut "Long Time Gone."

Can't Buy Me Love/Twist and Shout/ She Loves You/ I Want to Hold Your Hand/ Please Please Me

The Beatles' Top Five

For one week in 1964, the Beatles accomplished something unheard of in the history of pop music. Riding the wave of Beatlemania that was sweeping North America, the Fab Four were breaking sales records, monopolizing the charts in a way that no band before or since has been able to do. In the week of April 4, 1964, they were the "toppermost of the poppermost," with a staggering ten singles in the Hot One Hundred — and all the positions on the Top Five.

CAN'T BUY ME LOVE: Number One

This song was composed in January 1964 in Paris during an eighteen-night stand at the Olympia Theater. The band was put up at the ritzy George V Hotel, just off the Champs Elysees. They were virtual prisoners in their rooms, having attained such a degree of popularity that venturing out in public presented a risk to their security. To pass the hours, Paul had a grand piano moved into his suite so he and John could work on songs. At the hotel, they collaborated on "One and One Is Two" for Billy J. Kramer while Paul wrote "Can't Buy Me Love."

They entered Paris's Pathe Marconi Studio on George Harrison's twenty-first birthday to record the song. Producer George Martin rearranged the tune, suggesting they kick it off with the chorus. The simple twist in song structure gave the song an exciting start that grabbed listeners from the opening notes. "Can't Buy Me Love," originally released as a single, was later included on the sound track for *A Hard Day's Night.*

In 1966, McCartney laid to rest the rumors that "Can't Buy Me Love" was inspired by the prostitutes the band met in Hamburg in their early career.

"Absolutely not," was his answer, "that's going a bit too far."

TWIST AND SHOUT: Number Two

"Twist and Shout" was the final number recorded for the *Please Please Me* long player. After an intense day of recording, George Martin needed one more song to round out the album. Lennon had almost lost his voice from singing non-stop but agreed to do one more tune. The boys chose the Isley Brothers' "Twist and Shout" (written by Bert Russell and Phil Medley), a song they had covered in their early club gigs. John's throat was sore and raw, so he was only able to run through the song once. He delivered a fine raspy vocal but could be heard hacking and coughing at the end of the tune. A live version of "Twist and Shout" recorded at the Star Club in Hamburg, Germany in 1962 was released in 1977.

SHE LOVES YOU: Number Three

McCartney wanted to try something a little different with this song. Holed up at the Turk's Hotel in Newcastle while on tour in June 1963, John and Paul sat on their beds strumming

Three Tunes About One Woman: George Harrison's first A-side single release, 1969's "Something," was a tender love song in tribute to his wife Patti Boyd. Eric Clapton hit the charts twice with songs about Boyd. "Layla," the 1972 Top Ten hit for Clapton's group Derek and the Dominoes, was written as a locution of love for Boyd who was still married to the Beatle. Several years later, after Boyd had left Harrison for Clapton, he penned "Wonderful Tonight." On the surface, it was a gentle gem of a song, but bubbling underneath was Clapton's true meaning. He wrote the song to voice his aggravation in waiting for Boyd to finish getting dressed to go out. Apparently, it took her some time to put on her face, and she wouldn't

guitars. Previous tunes had been written as statements of love — "Love Me Do," "Please Please Me," "From Me to You." This time, he wanted to add a third party. Together, they wrote a tune about a broken relationship, offering advice to a friend on how to mend it. The "woo woo" section was borrowed from the Isley Brothers' hit "Twist and Shout," a refrain that Lennon says "we stuck into everything — "From Me to You," "She Loves You" — they all had that 'woo woo.'" Paul's father recommended changing the now-famous "yeah, yeah, yeah" to the more proper "yes, yes, yes" to maintain some sense of British dignity. The boys luckily rejected this idea.

I WANT TO HOLD YOUR HAND: Number Four

The Beatles' first US Number One hit was written in the basement of McCartney's girlfriend's home. He and John would spend hours at Jane Asher's house working out tunes on the family's piano. One afternoon, while they were hanging out, they worked out the structure and lyrics of "I Want to Hold Your Hand," with Paul on piano and John on pedal organ. For the chorus, John borrowed a technique from an LP loaned to him by a friend — a record of French experimental music with a musical phrase repeated over and over as though the needle was stuck in the groove. John appropriated this effect on the "I can't hide, I can't hide, I can't hide" part of the tune. At the time of its release, "I Want to Hold Your Hand" was the biggest-selling British single of all time, with advance orders of 940,000 copies. Worldwide sales now have exceeded fifteen million.

leave the house without positive feedback from her husband. Tired of waiting, the frustrated guitarist would always reply, "Darling, you look wonderful tonight."

PLEASE PLEASE ME: Number Five

John Lennon claimed complete credit for this song. Sitting in his bedroom at 251 Menlove Avenue in Liverpool, he intended to write a song in the style of Roy Orbison. He started off with an idea lifted from a 1932 Bing Crosby song called "Please." He was intrigued by the double use of the words "please" and "pleas" in this Leo Robin/Ralph Ranger tune. Then, after listening to a 45 of Orbison's "Only the Lonely," he penned "Please Please Me," trying to emulate Orbison's style. When the song was presented to producer George Martin, he thought it sounded so much like Orbison that he changed the arrangement to avoid any comparison to the American rock legend. "Please Please Me" was the Beatles' first Number One hit in Britain.

On the stereo remix of "Please Please Me," careful listeners will note a mistake as John and Paul sing different words.

Rag Doll

The Four Seasons

A young girl who made her living washing car windows at a stoplight in Hell's Kitchen inspired Bob Gaudio to write "Rag Doll," the Four Seasons' last big hit of the sixties.

In 1964, Gaudio, a former member of the Royal Teens (who joined the Four Seasons after scoring a Number Three hit in 1958 with the Teens' "Short Shorts"), was on his way home to New Jersey after a recording session with the Four Seasons in New York City. Driving through the Lincoln Tunnel, he exited on Westside Highway near 10th Avenue in an area known as Hell's Kitchen. While stopped at a traffic light, a kid approached his car, washcloth in hand. In that neighborhood, youths streamed into the streets, cleaning windshields, hoping for a quarter tip for their trouble. He couldn't tell whether the kid was a boy or a girl until he saw her unwashed face, with a little cap perched on her head. He took in her whole appearance — ragged clothes, holes in her stockings — and immediately felt sorry for her. Digging in his pockets for something to give, he was embarrassed to discover he didn't have any change. The smallest he had was a $5 bill, an astronomical amount to a street kid in 1964.

He hesitated to give her the bill, but a second look at her

dirty, sad face convinced him to turn over the cash. She took the money without saying thank-you. Instead, tears welled up in her eyes. Pulling away, he caught one last look at her in his rearview mirror, standing in the road, staring in amazement at the $5 bill.

Over the next two weeks, he worked on "Rag Doll," turning the story of the street waif into a ballad about class struggle. Written from the singer's point of view, Gaudio wrote about a man in love with a young woman who is scorned by his family and society. But the creative process wasn't a smooth one. Suffering from writer's block, Gaudio found himself unable to finish the song and considered shelving it. Enlisting the help of producer Bob Crewe, they fleshed out the story, wrote musical arrangements and presented it to the Four Seasons.

The recording session for "Rag Doll" almost didn't happen. Unable to use their usual studio or engineer, the band had second thoughts about doing the song. However, they decided to go ahead with the session. Instead, they used a New York demo studio, and worked with an engineering crew they had never met before.

Despite their qualms, the session was fruitful, producing a song Dave Marsh called a "gorgeous blast of Italian R & B." Complete with Frankie Valli's gliding falsetto and Bob Crewe's grandiose Phil-Spectorized production, the tune — all crashing drums and thick-layered harmonies — soon roared out of radios and rose to the top of the charts. However, the sublime American pop of "Rag Doll" was knocked out of the Number One position by "A Hard Day's Night," beckoning the beginning of the British Invasion. The Four Seasons continued to place songs in the Top Twenty, but they were never again able to hit the top spot in the 1960s.

Leader of the Pack

The Shangri-Las

Two sets of sisters, Mary and Betty Weiss and Marge and Mary Ann Ganser, were billed as "The Queens of the Musical Melodrama." Working under the name the Shangri-Las, they released a string of mid-sixties' hits that featured sound effects in their songs of teen angst and rebel boyfriends. "Leader of the Pack" was their crowning achievement, reaching Number One on the *Billboard* charts in October 1964.

August 1964 was a thrilling time for the two sets of sisters from Queens, New York. "Remember (Walking in the Sand)," a teen soap-opera song complete with the plaintive cries of seagulls in the background, was quickly climbing the charts. The fresh-faced teens were becoming overnight stars. "One day they're eating pasta," said producer George "Shadow" Morton in Alan Betrock's book *Girl Groups: The Story of a Sound*, "the next day they're eating chateaubriand, and they don't even know how to pronounce it."

In the early summer of 1964, Morton had bluffed his way into the studio after a meeting with crack songwriter/producer Jeff Barry. The brash Morton talked Barry into giving him some studio time to record a "hit song." The only problem was, he had never written a song. He couldn't even play an instrument, pretty much a prereq- uisite for a songwriter/producer. He could, however, hear the song in his head, and he was convinced he could come up with a hit. Booking studio time and rounding

> Baby boomer President Bill Clinton named his daughter Chelsea after a Joni Mitchell song, "Chelsea Morning."

up musicians (including a fifteen-year- old Billy Joel on piano and, if you believe the rumors, a teenage Iggy Pop on drums), Morton headed to record a demo. On the drive there, he pulled the car to the side of the road and in twenty minutes, wrote "Remember (Walking in the Sand)." Once at the studio, he described the sounds in his head to the musicians. "You play boom boom boom," he instructed the piano player, and so on. At the end of the session, he had produced a seven-minute version of the tune. It was too long for the radio, but he had proved he could do the job. After editing and rerecording a tighter version of the song, it was released and took off like wildfire. Now they needed a follow-up.

Even Morton hadn't expected success so quickly, and he didn't have another tune ready. When Barry asked what he planned to do for the next single, he said the first thing that popped into his head. "It's called 'Leader of the Pack.'" The record company hated the idea. They said that a song about a girl falling for a biker who is killed in a motorcycle crash had no commercial appeal. Morton insisted it could be a hit, and with "Remember (Walking in the Sand)" riding high on the charts, the company couldn't refuse him. He was offered time at Ultra-Sonic Studios.

The day of the session, with twenty-two musicians being paid scale to wait around for Morton to show up, he had yet to write the song. The studio manager called in a panic. "Where are you?" he demanded. "I'll be right there," replied Morton. He poured a bath, and accompanied by two bottles of champagne and two cigars, Morton wrote "Leader of the Pack" on a shirt cardboard insert with his kid's crayons.

Finally, in the studio, Morton applied his unusual method of arranging the song. Showing the cardboard lyric sheet to the singers, he instructed one set of sisters to sing the blue lines and the others to vocalize the red lines. The young singers, barely sixteen years old, were so green that they were intimidated by the studio and Morton's peculiar directions. Jeff Barry had to sit across from Mary Weiss and mouth the words along with her to keep her in sync with the music. Once familiar with the song, she became so caught up in the drama of the lyrics that she began to cry. A careful listen to the record reveals her audible sobs.

A suggestion from Jeff Barry and Ellie Greenwich added extra drama to the song. They asked Joey Veneri, a studio engineer, to bring his motorcycle to the echo chamber and recorded its revving for the opening of the song. The recommendation earned them a writing credit on the tune (and, no doubt, hundreds of thousands of dollars in royalties). As sound effects were not the norm on Top Forty records, the realistic motorcycle din, the addition of the noise of screeching tires and the collision of the vehicles set this record apart from anything else heard on the radio in 1964.

The tragic tale of girl meets boy and girl loses boy to a terrible traffic accident was an instant hit with record buyers. But the mainstream press wasn't as enthusiastic. Editorials dubbed the tune "teenage trash," and "Leader of the Pack" was banned at some radio stations. Despite the controversy (or perhaps because of it), the "death disc shocker" nonetheless reached the peak of the *Billboard* charts only six weeks after its release.

Oh, Pretty Woman

Roy Orbison

Roy Orbison's first wife Claudette inspired two songs during their nine-year marriage. The first, "Claudette," recorded by the Everly Brothers, barely made the Top Thirty, but the second one was enormous, selling over seven million copies and becoming a rock-and-roll classic in the process. "Oh, Pretty Woman" was Number One for three weeks in November 1964.

"Oh, Pretty Woman" was written one afternoon at the Orbison home in Nashville. Writing partner Bill Dees and Roy were in the living room, trying to come up with a song. The Big "O" was a regular visitor to the charts, placing fourteen songs in the Top Thirty between 1960 and the spring of 1964. His glass-shattering falsetto propelled a series of tragic teen operas like "Only the Lonely (Know How I Feel)," "Crying," "In Dreams" and "Blue Bayou" into the public consciousness. After the Top Ten success of 1964's "It's Over," the duo had to come up with another chart topper.

As Orbison and Dees strummed their guitars, Claudette interrupted, announcing that she was going downtown to do some shopping. "Do you have any money?" Roy asked. "A pretty woman never needs any money," Dees said, laughing at his own joke. The three of them thought the remark was funny, but when the laughter had died down, Dees said, "Hey, that would make a great song title." "No," said Roy, "but 'Pretty Woman' would."

By the time Claudette left to do her errand, the men were already working on the song. Roy picked at the guitar as Dees banged out a rhythm on the coffee table. Forty-five minutes later, Claudette returned, and Orbison and Dees had written "Oh, Pretty Woman," a tune that would become the biggest hit of Orbison's career.

Orbison liked to keep his recording sessions loose. He rarely wrote out arrangements for the band, preferring to leave room for improvisation. This method paid off for him during the recording of "Oh, Pretty Woman," resulting in the tune's most distinctive vocal tics. Roy was known around the studio for saying "Mercy" as the reply to a rude joke or comment. As they were committing the song to tape, they

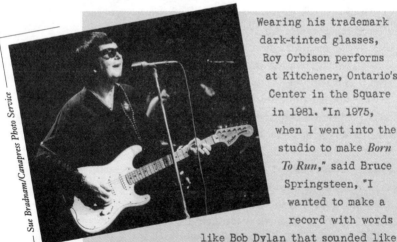

Sue Bradnam/Canapress Photo Service

Wearing his trademark dark-tinted glasses, Roy Orbison performs at Kitchener, Ontario's Center in the Square in 1981. "In 1975, when I went into the studio to make *Born To Run*," said Bruce Springsteen, "I wanted to make a record with words like Bob Dylan that sounded like Phil Spector. But most of all, I wanted to sing like Roy Orbison. Now, everybody knows that nobody sings like Roy Orbison."

came to a note that wasn't in Orbison's range. Instead of straining for the note, he substituted "Mercy." Everyone in the studio smiled, thinking it sounded hip, so it was left in. In a playful mood, he added the growls before the tune's famous guitar riff in an effort to make the band laugh. Later, he remarked that the "Mercy" line had an interesting effect on foreign audiences. "In France," he said, "'Mercy' sounds like I'm saying 'thank-you.'"

Released on Monument Records in the fall of 1964, "Oh, Pretty Woman" was an instant hit. "Great dance beat coupled with a fine arrangement," said *Billboard* magazine. Legendary guitarist/producer Chet Atkins raved it was the best commercial record he had ever heard, but, more importantly, record buyers snapped up seven million copies of the tune, pushing it to Number One.

It was to be Orbison's last Top Five record. Shortly after the release of the single, Roy left Monument, the home of his past success, for MGM Records, hoping for a greater opportunity to appear in films, like his contemporaries Elvis and Jerry Lee Lewis. One movie followed — *The Fastest Guitar Alive* — proving that Roy was no actor. The hits dried up. Roy's next Top Ten hit was the posthumously released "You Got It" in 1989.

Like so many aspects of Orbison's life, "Oh, Pretty Woman" was tinged with tragedy. On June 7, 1966, his muse Claudette was killed in a motorcycle accident. Two years later, a fire destroyed his home in Tennessee, claiming the lives of firstborn son (by Claudette) Roy Jr. and his half brother Tony (from Orbison's second marriage).

On a happier note, Van Halen took a rocky version of "Oh, Pretty Woman" to the Top Fifteen in 1982.

Wooly Bully

Sam the Sham and the Pharaohs

For Domingo Samudio, coming up with a Top Five hit was as easy as "uno, dos, one, two, tres, cuatro." Sam the Sham and the Pharaohs broke out of obscurity in Texas to place "Wooly Bully" at the top of the charts in 1965.

Domingo Samudio (his friends called him Sam) always wanted to be in show business. At his Dallas high school, he formed a rock-and-roll band with Trini Lopez who later scored a Top Five hit with "If I Had a Hammer" in 1963. After graduation, and following a four-year stint in the Navy, Sam studied classical music, moonlighting as a rock and roller in the evenings. The rigid regimen of college wasn't for him, and, after two years, he quit to become a carny. But the draw of music was stronger than the lure of carnival life, and soon he was back in the clubs, playing keyboard for a variety of bands.

In 1963, he decided to start his own group. He needed a catchy name. One night, a musician gave Sam a new nickname. Watching Sam gyrate around the stage when he sang, the guy called him a sham artist — R & B slang for someone who dances, shaking his hips as he performs. Sam the Sham — he liked the sound of it. It was a good start, but he still needed a name for the backup musicians. A trip to the local bijou solved that problem. Taking in *The Ten Commandments*, the band members thought the king of Egypt looked rather hip. That next day, they became the Pharaohs, investing a few dollars in brightly colored material to make flamboyant Arab-inspired stage clothes.

> Procal Harum's "A Salty Dog" was inspired by a wood carving in a Cleveland bar that read "Good God, Skipper, We done run aground!" and not by some ancient tale of mariner mishap.

Sam the Sham and the Pharaohs' good-time shows quickly gained a following in the Texas clubs, and a handful of independent single releases fared well locally. In 1964, MGM Records came calling, offering to bring Sam the Sham and the Pharaohs' rollicking sound to a larger audience. Sam had the perfect song for the first single. It was a dance song, featuring a heavy beat provided by drummer Jerry Patterson. With words based on "The Hully Gully," a popular dance that had been the subject of several hits ("Baby Hully Gully" by the Olympics, "Hully Gully Again" by Little Caesar and the Romans and "Hully Gully Baby" by the Dovells), Sam was sure he had a song that couldn't miss.

In the studio, just minutes before they were set to record, an MGM executive notified the band that MGM wasn't interested in releasing another "Hully Gully" record. They would have to come up with something else. Sam counted in the band, making up new lyrics on the spot. Wooly Bully was the name of his cat and fit the meter of "Hully Gully," so he started from there. He improvised a whole new set of lyrics as the band recorded three takes of the song. The now-famous Tex-Mex "Uno, dos, one, two, tres, cuatro" countdown to the song was also done on the spur of the moment. Sam wanted it taken off the record, but the rest of the band loved it. So the bilingual opening stayed.

The danceable novelty struck a chord with record buyers who lapped up a million copies of the single in 1965.

Radio programmers were a little more cautious. Convinced that Sam's nonsense lyrics were obscene, the tune was banned by many stations. This only piqued the public's curiosity, and it propelled "Wooly Bully" to Number Two in May 1965. Later that year, it was nominated for Best Contemporary Performance by a Group at the Grammys, losing to the Statler Brothers' "Flowers on the Wall." *Billboard* magazine named it Record of the Year for 1965.

Sam the Sham and the Pharaohs placed several more songs in the Top Forty before splitting up in 1968. Sam continued a career in music — after a brief stint as a street preacher in Memphis — writing songs for others and scoring films.

Hang On Sloopy

The McCoys

In the music business, timing is everything. Nobody learned this lesson better than Rick and the Raiders who, under the name the McCoys, registered a Number One hit with 1965's "Hang On Sloopy."

This is a story of two bands. In Dayton, Ohio, a combo of teenage musicians called Rick (Zehringer) and the Raiders were enjoying local success playing sock hops, school dances and local clubs. The 1965's single "You Know That I Love You" sold well in Dayton but failed to make any impact on the national charts.

Meanwhile, another group, the Strangeloves, had a single — "I Want Candy" — in heavy radio rotation. As the name intimates, the Strangeloves were a bizarre group. Their public persona was that of three brothers — Miles, Giles and Niles from Armstrong, Australia — who wore garish suits and aboriginal headgear. The catch was that they weren't siblings, and they weren't Australian. In reality, they were American writer/producers Bob Feldman, Jerry Goldstein and Richard Gottehrer. The writers for hire operated out of New York's renowned Brill Building, producing a Number One hit in 1963 with "My Boyfriend's Back" by the Angels.

Like many American rock and rollers, the writers were bumped off the charts in the early sixties by the wave of British talent led by the Beatles. They concocted their Australian band as the exotic "Down Under" answer to the British Invasion.

Their first 45, "I Want Candy," fusing a Bo Diddley beat with the band's mimicry of African Masai tribal percussion patterns, became fashionable enough for them to embark on a tour. The stint on the road proved to be wildly successful. The pseudo-Aussies were greeted in most cities by throngs of fans waving "Welcome to the US" signs. The Australian Invasion was a hit, but they needed a follow-up single. Dusting off a song that had been written in 1954 by their boss, Bang Records' label head Bert Berns (with Wes Farrell), "My Girl Sloopy" became their next planned single. The Strangeloves added the song to their live set.

Back in Dayton, Rick and the Raiders were honing their craft, building up a repertoire of pop and soul covers that guaranteed them work every weekend. A chance meeting with the Strangeloves at a mid-summer concert for station WING in Ohio was about to change their lives. Retained as a backup band for the Strangeloves, Rick and the Raiders belted out a raucous set that impressed the canny New Yorkers despite drummer Randy Zehringer having to stand to play so his foot could reach the kick drum pedal.

The timing couldn't have been better for the young band. The counterfeit Aussies had just received word that after hearing the response "My Girl Sloopy" garnered at the Strangeloves' shows, British Invasion act the Dave Clark Five planned to rush release a cover of the tune. This would effectively squash any chance of the Strangeloves' version seeing any chart action. It was a real catch-22. They couldn't release "Sloopy" without cutting into the sales for "I Want Candy" which was still climbing the charts. The timing couldn't have been worse.

Then Feldman, Goldstein and Gottehrer had a brain-storm: Hire the Raiders to rerecord a vocal track on the existing Strangeloves' track, thereby scooping the DC5. The Raiders were an obvious choice. They were a good band, but more importantly, they had teen appeal with Beatle-style mop-top haircuts. In a scene that could have been ripped out of a Mickey Rooney/Judy Garland flick, after the show, as the roar of the crowd still rang in their ears, Rick and the Raiders were offered a recording deal with Bang Records. Because they were minors, the producers had to convince Mr. and Mrs. Zehringer to let the youths go to New York. The parents agreed, booked time off from work and left the next day for the Big Apple.

Many changes were to come. The producers felt that the band's name was too similar to another up-and-coming group — Paul Revere and the Raiders — and asked the boys to come up with a new moniker. A family photo album showed the young Raiders in a previous incarnation as the McCoys in tribute to a Ventures' song the boys favored. The Raiders once again became the McCoys. The producers were so pleased with the name that they briefly discussed pairing the lads up with an all-female act called the Hatfields to get some free publicity.

Also, they felt that Rick Zehringer wasn't a catchy enough name for the lead singer of their next chart buster. But the sixteen-year-old wasn't keen to change his name. He wanted his parents to be proud of their family name's good fortune, but he softened after seeing a small derringer gun on Bang Records' logo. Rick Derringer was similar enough to his real name to satisfy his parents and hip enough to appease the producers. Finally, the title of the song was changed from "My Girl Sloopy" to the groovier-sounding "Hang On Sloopy."

On arrival in Manhattan, the newly christened Derringer was given a copy of the instrumental track and guidelines on how to sing it. Several days of rehearsal, with brother

Randy singing harmonies, followed. At the recording session, the brothers added a vocal track, with Rick throwing off a now-classic garage-rock guitar solo after the second chorus. When the track was complete, the brothers could see the producers through the control-room window jumping up and down, yelling, "It's gonna be a Number One!"

Less than two months later, "Hang On Sloopy" was at the top of the charts, and the McCoys became teen idols. It just goes to show, being in the right place at the right time makes some rock-and-roll dreams come true.

When a Man Loves a Woman

Percy Sledge

A hospital orderly with woman troubles improvised a heart-tugging soul ballad live on stage. "Wasn't no heavy thought to it," he said in Gerri Hershey's *Nowhere To Run*. "I was just so damned sad." "When a Man Loves a Woman" was Number One for two weeks in May 1966.

By day, Percy Sledge worked as an orderly at Colbert County Hospital. On Sundays, he sang in the choir at the Galilee Baptist Church in his hometown of Leighton, Alabama. Most nights, though, he could be found onstage at any one of the area's local clubs, singing lead in the Esquires Combo. They played Motown and Beatles' covers and were a popular draw with the dance set.

One night, other band members noticed Percy was off. He flubbed the lines to songs he had sung dozens of times. Finally, he stopped completely, unable to sing the band's usual repertoire. After a lengthy pause, with the eyes of the audience burning through him, he asked the band to play something. Anything. It didn't matter. Bass player Cameron Lewis and keyboardist Andrew Wright chose a key and played a slow blues. Sledge, upset about a love gone wrong, improvised

Al Kooper maintains that the 1968 hit "I Can't Quit Her" that he wrote for Blood, Sweat and Tears was the only song in rock-and-roll history to contain the word "proselytized."

lyrics that sprung deep from his broken heart. Tears stained his face as he bared his emotions for all to see. The crowd went crazy. They loved the tune.

Weeks later, he was able to control his emotions and work on refining the song. After a few hours of rehearsal, the band molded Sledge's improvised rap into a polished ballad. Sledge gave song-writing credit to Lewis and Wright, a move that earned them hundreds of thousands of dollars in the decades to come. With the song in good shape, Sledge approached Quin Ivy, a well-known Alabama producer, in hopes of committing the song to vinyl.

Ivy was swayed by both Sledge and "When a Man Loves a Woman," as the tune was now called. After an audition at Ivy's Tune Town, a record shop, a deal was struck to record the tune, using engineer Marlin Greene on guitar and Rick Hall's Muscle Shoals musicians from Fame studios as backup. They laid down the track at Ivy's South Camp Studios, with Sledge turning in an impassioned vocal that, as Dave Marsh wrote, makes it "...easy to forget that there's anybody on earth except him, his girl and you."

Fame studio honcho Rick Hall was so taken with the song that he submitted it to a friend at Atlantic Records, fishing for a national distribution deal. They picked up the demo, turning it into a Number One record, selling a million copies in 1966. The deal also reaped benefits for Hall. As a result of the runaway success of "When a Man Loves a Woman," his session men became in demand. Atlantic Records was so keen to cash in on the Fame Studio's Muscle Shoals sound that they sent their latest soul sensation to Alabama in hopes that some of the magic would rub off on him. His name was Wilson Pickett, and under Rick Hall's tutelage, he would turn out a stunning string of soul hits including "Land of 1,000 Dances," "Funky Broadway" and "Mustang Sally."

"When a Man Loves a Woman" was Sledge's only Top Ten hit, although he continued to produce fine soul records into the eighties.

Did You Ever Have to Make Up Your Mind?/ Summer in the City

Lovin' Spoonful

Like many musicians, John Sebastian was motivated to put together a rock-and-roll band after seeing the Beatles on the *Ed Sullivan Show* in February 1964.

The night of the broadcast, Cass Elliott invited Sebastian and Canadian-born Zal Yanovsky to her apartment. As they (and seventy-three million others) watched the show, John and Zal were excited by the potency of the Beatles' four-piece rock-and-roll setup. The two young men played guitars for hours afterward, cementing a personal and professional friendship that would blossom over the next four years.

In 1965, subsequent to a brief stint with Cass Elliott and Denny Doherty (later of the Mamas and the Papas), John and Zal enlisted bassist Steve Boone and drummer Joe Butler. Taking their name from a Mississippi John Hurt blues song which included the verse, "I love my baby by the lovin' spoonful," songwriter Sebastian merged a unique blend of jug-band, rock-and-roll, folk and blues influences into a winning formula of electric good-time music that *Rolling Stone* called "effervescent pop."

During their heyday — 1965–67 — the Lovin' Spoonful placed ten Sebastian-penned tunes in the *Billboard* Top

Twenty. "I only wrote songs out of desperation," says Sebastian. "I can't say that I came at it with high aspirations. I didn't consider myself a songwriter [when] I was writing several of those songs that were visible at the time [1965-66]. It was mainly that we were running out of material. I was just trying to supplement with *feels* we didn't have. We needed to play a lot of different things."

Here are the stories of two of the Lovin' Spoonful's biggest hits.

DID YOU EVER HAVE TO MAKE UP YOUR MIND?: Number Two, May 14/66

"Nothing was ever consummated," chuckles Sebastian, on the teenage crushes that inspired the Lovin' Spoonful's hit "Did You Ever Have to Make Up Your Mind?" "This was a time before that kind of thing started to happen. We were a little young."

One of Sebastian's most sparkling pop offerings was the Spoonful's fourth single in May 1966. Two sets of sisters — the Robinson girls and the Lorch twins — were Sebastian's co-muses.

Jump back to summer vacation 1960. During the school year, sixteen-year-old Sebastian discovered that playing Duane Eddy-style rock and roll — twanging guitar and squealing sax — was a good way to meet girls. "I was using this band experience as a way of having a life while I was going to prep school," he said. He signed on as a drama counselor at Apple Hill Camp with the idea of wowing women with his rock-and-roll attitude.

"I went up to this summer camp thinking, 'I'm going to pull my collar up and grease my hair back, and these girls are going to go crazy,'" he said. "Well, nothing could be farther from the truth. Nobody was even interested. What was happening was that all these girls from Massachusetts and New York were actually into folk music."

John Sebastian was a fine songwriter, but he should have hired a fact checker to go over the lyrics of "Nashville Cats," the 1966 Lovin' Spoonful hit. In the song, he sang about those "Yellow Sun Records from Nashville." Sun Records was, of course, located in Memphis. Right state, wrong city.

He rethought his strategy, threw away the Brylcream and eventually learned to play the Autoharp to impress the folk-loving vacationers. "I was crazy for two different sets of sisters over the course of five years that I was a summer camp counselor," he said. "These sisters worked as counselors as well and, in fact, had many things in common. Their parents were all educators, and they were very worldly New York kids. I was falling in love, usually with the first sister and then the second."

Six years after his first summer at Apple Hill Camp, Sebastian recalled his unrequited teenage love triangles in music, penning the song in the back of a cab on the way to a recording session. A near flawless guitar pop song, "Did You Ever Have to Make Up Your Mind?" secured Sebastian's reputation as a mainstream rock-and-roll songwriter of exceptional quality. The tune settled at the Number Two spot on the *Billboard* charts for two weeks in 1966, held out of the top position by the Rolling Stones' "Paint It Black."

"Sometimes things don't pay off right away," he said, reflecting on the song's success. "They pay off in the long run. Although nothing ever happened [with the sisters, the song] was one of the ways that those unconsummated love affairs paid off."

SUMMER IN THE CITY: Number One, July 23/66
Lovin' Spoonful legend has it that the lyrics to this 1966 Number One hit were written as a school project by John's brother Mark who received a failing mark for his efforts. Three decades after the release of "Summer in the City," John Sebastian wanted to set the record straight.

"I have gone back to my brother with that story because it has circulated," he told me in 1997. "He is a little [more vague] on it now than when the story was fresh out of school. Here's what I can assure you: The form you hear on the record was never before seen in print. What Mark had was a song about 'Summer in the City.' You know, 'It's gonna get hot...the shadows of the buildings will be the only shady spot,' something like that, and this cool chorus. I said, 'Boy this just kills me. Let me try and write a different verse.' When I asked him about it, Mark said, 'You know I don't remember now whether I just thought about doing it, or when it was a successful song, I submitted it just to make the [teacher] look like an idiot, letting him give me a low mark and then going back and saying, "Here's what you know. This thing is a Top Forty record.' So that is the way the song evolved."

The Spoonful collaborated on the tune, hammering it out over two nights in the studio. "It kind of evolved," says Sebastian. "We had the verse and the chorus, and there was this fragment that Steve Boone had been playing. Steven's fragment, which became the instrumental bridge [between the verse and the chorus], was something [he] had been playing on the piano for months. Then suddenly, once the verse and chorus came together, I don't remember if it was Steven, me or Zally who said, 'You know, this thing fits really well in the middle of the song.' But once we put it in there, I remember saying, 'You know, this kind of reminds me of Gershwin — the section of *An American in Paris* which is the traffic.'

"Once that sentence was out, we began to talk about the idea of putting car horns over this [musical] bridge. We invited this wonderful old Jewish radio soundman who showed up with records of lots of different traffic jams and individual car horns. We knew we wanted car horns, and I think I came up with the idea of finishing it off with a big blast from a pneumatic hammer. He had three or four pneumatic hammers, all different [ranges]. I remember the traffic jam [we chose to include] was a 48th Street traffic jam. As soon as we heard it, we said, 'This is *the* traffic jam' because 48th Street was *the* music street. That was where we went to get our guitars. So we used that traffic jam, and then I heard this Volkswagen car horn, and I said, 'Just to make it comical, let's have this little Volkswagen start it off.' So you hear beep, beep, beep then whoosh. You know, it sounded like a real New York traffic response to one poor lonely guy stuck in traffic who dares to touch his horn. Those were the components. They kind of fell together."

Steve Boone, John Sebastian and his brother Mark all share the songwriting credit. "[Mark] is a songwriter and continues to write songs, but somehow or another, we never actually collaborated on anything else." "Summer in the City" was the Lovin' Spoonful's fifth single and first Number One, sitting atop the charts for three weeks.

Hold On, I'm Comin'

Sam & Dave

A recording session, interrupted by a songwriter's bathroom break, produced one of the best soul records of the sixties. *Billboard* magazine called Sam & Dave's 1966 hit "Hold On, I'm Comin'" "a soulful wailin'-blues shouter with exceptional vocal performance." The single peaked at Number Twenty-One in June 1966.

The "Double Dynamite" duo of Sam & Dave met in Miami in 1958. The high-voiced Sam Moore abandoned a burgeoning career as a gospel singer for the lure of a grittier secular sound. The son of a Baptist minister, he paid his dues working in a series of gospel groups until he was hired by the Soul Stirrers, a front-running inspirational group that had been around since the 1930s. On the eve of his first tour with the church singers, Sam faced a dilemma. Jackie Wilson, his favorite *profane* (or so the Soul Stirrers would have thought) performer, was playing in town the night he was to depart to spread God's word. The R & B seduced Moore, and instead of leaving with the Soul Stirrers, he witnessed Wilson's exciting and ecstatic live show. Moore decided to fuse the gospel music with which he grew up with the dynamic R & B he loved. His life was changed.

Working up a club act, he hit the road. One night at the King of Hearts Club in Miami, he was spontaneously joined on stage by Dave Prater, the club's gritty-voiced cook. They hit it off, and an R & B legend was born.

Popular in nightclubs, the duo earned the nickname "The Sultans of Sweat" for their hard-driving, energetic shows. They didn't find acceptance on vinyl until they hooked up with the songwriting team of Isaac Hayes and David Porter. Hayes and Porter were the house hit makers at Stax Records in Memphis. Between them, they came up with a song called "You Don't Know Like I Know," a Top Ten hit on the R & B charts, but one that barely breached the *Billboard* Top One Hundred.

Their next effort established Sam & Dave on both the R & B and pop charts — but it wouldn't have happened if Dave Porter hadn't had to relieve himself during a session.

The four men were working on new material in Stax's main studio, trying to come up with a song that could top the success of "You Don't Know Like I Know." Porter suddenly disappeared without a word. The session chugged along for another few minutes before Hayes became impatient. With no idea where his partner had gone, he checked every room in the studio, starting with the control room. He had no luck until he started down the corridor to the washrooms. Pounding on the men's room door, Hayes yelled for Porter to hurry up.

"Hold on. I'm comin'," was Porter's reply. A light went on in Hayes's head. "Hold On, I'm Comin'" was a superb title for a song. It would be a life-affirming tune about a husband extending his support to his wife, offering to come to her when times were bad. The songwriters quickly wrote the tune and added Sam & Dave's blistering vocal.

However, radio misinterpreted the song's message. DJs picked up on the double entendre, and many stations banned the song for its supposed libidinous content. In an effort to save the tune, Stax reissued it with the title, "Hold On, I'm A-Comin'." But the damage was done. The soul classic stalled at Number Twenty-One on the pop charts. It would be one full year before Sam & Dave hit the Top Five with their next single, "Soul Man."

They're Coming to Take Me Away, Ha-Haaa!

Napoleon XIV

Dr. Demento called the song "the most sensational novelty record in American history," naming its creator the Rembrandt of the novelty art form. "We believed the record was either going to be a big dud," said Jerry Samuels, aka Napoleon XIV, "or a gigantic monster." Released in 1966, "They're Coming to Take Me Away, Ha-Haaa!" was the fastest-selling record in history to that date.

Jerry Samuels was twenty-eight years old when "They're Coming to Take Me Away, Ha-Haaa!" was released. "It was my second hit," he said. "I wrote a song in 1963 that was a hit in 1964 called 'The Shelter of Your Arms.'" Recorded by Sammy Davis Jr., it ranked Number Seventeen. "I had written for other people, including Johnny Ray. ["To Ev'ry Girl — To Ev'ry Boy (The Meaning of Love)"] came out when I was sixteen. I couldn't believe that my idol recorded my song."

In addition to his career as a recording engineer, Samuels played piano in nightclubs, cutting a record in 1956 ("Puppy Love") in the style of Johnny Ray. He continued to write for others, but by 1966, he had a solo career in mind. The song that catapulted him to fame wasn't like anything else he (or anybody else) had ever penned. It was a strange tune about a man who goes insane after his pet runs away.

"I was thinking about an old Scottish song called 'The Campbells Are Coming,'" he said. "I didn't even know the name of it back then, but the tune was running through my head. I thought to myself, 'What kind of lyric would go with that? "They're coming to take me away, ha ha."' See it? I decided to do it without any melody at all because it was a rhythmical recitation. As soon as I wrote the first verse, I knew I was writing what some people would call a sick joke. It took me about three months to decide where to go with the second verse. I still realized I had a sick joke, and it took another six months for me to decide to go and refer to a dog in the third verse. You realize that the person is talking about a dog having left him, not a human."

A cartoon rendering of Napoleon XIV taken from the cover of Rhino Records' compilation disc *The Second Coming.* "They're Coming to Take Me Away Ha-Haaa!" singer Jerry Samuels has never been photographed in costume, preferring the public to conjure up their own idea of what the character of Napoleon XIV looks like.

photo courtesy of Rhino Records

Lou Reed was cagey when talking about his inspiration for the Velvet Underground's "Femme Fatale." "We wrote "Femme Fatale" about somebody who was one," he said in the Victor Bockris, Gerard Malanga book *Up-Tight.* "She has since been committed to an institution for being one and will one day open up a school to train others." The tune was commonly thought to be about Nico, ex-Andy Warhol superstar and sometimes Velvet singer, who died in 1988 of a cerebral hemorrhage.

Using a great deal of ingenuity, "They're Coming to Take Me Away, Ha-Haaa!" was recorded on a tight budget at Associated Recording Studios in New York City. "The tape was $25 — that's a four-track tape, half inch. It cost $5 for the rental of the hand-cranked siren.

"We had trouble with the hand clappers. I invited a bunch of my friends. We couldn't get the studio until two o'clock in the morning. I said, 'Come on down,' and only two people besides me showed up. I said, 'Look, we're here to do hand clapping on this record, but we [only] have three pairs of hands. That's not enough, and I'd rather not overdub if I don't have to.' In an analogue format, overdubbing loses quality. I said, 'Here's what I want us to do. Instead of clapping our hands, I want us to sit around in a semicircle and slap our thighs. That will give us the sound of two claps, and that will mean six instead of three. However, you can't slap your clothes because clothes muffle the sound. You have to slap skin. You've got to take off your pants.' They wouldn't do it. So we had to overdub several times just to get enough hand-clapping sounds."

Recording the song presented some other, more complicated technical problems. Samuels had very specific ideas about how it was to sound. Against a rhythmic backing track, he wanted his voice to gradually rise in pitch to highlight the comic anguish of the song. Now all he had to do was create the technology to bring the sound in his head to tape. Working with engineer and lifelong business partner Nat Schnapf, the two concocted a device to change the pitch of his voice while leaving the rhythm track in sync.

Once done, "They're Coming to Take Me Away, Ha-Haaa!" had a sound unlike anything heard on the radio in 1966. "Many record companies didn't know how we did it. They actually called us and asked us how so they could cover the record. We said, 'We're not going to tell you how, and you can't cover the record because it's not a song. It doesn't fall under compulsory licensing as a song does. It's a lecture. We're not going to give you permission to cover it.' Our attorney was brilliant."

Another bit of advice from his attorney resulted in the pseudonym Napoleon XIV. Samuels didn't want to release the song under his own name lest he be labeled as a novelty artist. He asked drummer Howie Farmer if he had any suggestions for a stage name. Farmer jokingly proposed Napoleon. "Our attorney Alan Arrow, who was smart as a whip, said, 'Napoleon Something,'" recalled Samuels. "Why? Because you can't trademark Napoleon. But you can trademark Napoleon Something. I picked XIV because it looked good in Roman numerals. We were able to trade-mark it."

George Lee, an executive with Warner Brothers Records won a bidding war to release "They're Coming to Take Me Away, Ha-Haaa!" Schnapf and Samuels had learned from experience to take money on the back end — that is, accepting a lower advance for a bigger cut of the profits. The standard industry royalty rate in 1966 was 7 percent. The producers wanted more. "We were looking for a 10-percent deal," said Samuels, "because we knew it was doable. Alan Stanton offered us $25,000 up front and 7 percent. Warner Brothers offered us $500 up front and 10 percent. We took the 10 percent because we believed the record was either going to be a big dud or a gigantic monster. As a monster, that $25,000 meant nothing. We took the shot."

Warners released the single in the summer of 1966. Even the record itself was unusual. The B-side was completely reversed, with "They're Coming to Take Me Away Ha-Haaa!" played backward, and even the title was transposed. Sales of the wacky song skyrocketed, moving half a million copies in just one week before some radio stations refused to play the song because of its subject matter.

"I knew it was touchy, but I was never afraid of it," said Samuels. "I figured we'd probably get away with it for about a month, and then somebody would say, 'Hey, wait a minute, this guy is making fun of the sickies.' I never felt there was a problem with the thing. The reason I put [the dog] in is that I thought it might throw off the naysayers long enough to give us a little more time. Somebody would say, 'Oh wait, it's about a dog. That's alright.' If...you're talking about something that pokes fun at insanity, it doesn't make any difference who or what the object is — whether it is a human being or a dog or anything else. You either object to the premise, or you don't. I felt it would cause some people to say, 'Well, it's alright.' And it did. It worked."

A full-length Napoleon XIV LP, *They're Coming to Take Me Away, Ha-Haaa!*, was quickly recorded and released. However, by then, the mania had passed, and the record stiffed. Subsequent single releases, "They're Coming to Take Me Away Again, Ha-Haaa!," "I Live in a Split-Level Head" and "I'm in Love With My Little Red Tricycle" didn't chart either.

These days, Samuels runs a talent agency in Philadelphia that specializes in providing entertainment to senior-citizen facilities. "I gotta tell you something," he said on the phone from his office, "I love my job. It is a joy to do it."

Fire

Jimi Hendrix

"Fire," a cut from Jimi Hendrix's debut album *Are You Experienced?*, may be the guitar hero's definitive tune. Drenched with sexual braggadocio, Hendrix lasciviously advises a young woman to leave home so he can warm himself next to her fire. Hendrix wrote the song after a particularly cold, rainy English night.

Jimi Hendrix touched down in England on September 21, 1966. The American-born guitarist had been spotted by Animals' bassist Chas Chandler at a club gig at the Cafe Wha? in New York's Greenwich Village. Chandler, impressed by the left-handed guitarist, coaxed him to come to swinging London to find a more open-minded audience. Jimi, who had never been outside the United States, readily agreed.

Auditions were held to recruit a backup band. By October 12, drummer Noel Redding and bassist Mitch Mitchell were dubbed the Experience, playing showcase gigs in London's hippest clubs. Jimi's natural sense of showmanship quickly caught on with London's underground in crowd, making fans out of Eric Clapton, the Rolling Stones and Pete Townsend.

The press were a little slower to jump on the Hendrix bandwagon. His wild onstage antics — playing the guitar behind his back and with his teeth — inspired ridicule. "For one thing, Jimi is scarcely likely to qualify for a best-looking bloke competition," wrote Donald Bruce in *Pop Shop*. Another paper labeled him a "Wild Man From Borneo," making no mention of his virtuoso fretwork.

Following up on the buzz created in the clubs, the trio quickly entered Olympic Studios, recording the blues standard "Hey Joe." Released just before Christmas 1966, the band took the holidays off to work on new material for a proposed album. Itching to play for a crowd after several weeks of rehearsing, the band accepted an invitation from the Hillside Social Club in Noel Redding's hometown of Folkestone to perform on New Year's Eve.

At the stroke of twelve, the Experience took the stage and did their standard set — a mix of blues covers and contemporary material — that brought in the New Year with the band's patented aural onslaught. After the show, Redding suggested the band stay at his mother Margaret's house rather than risk the late-night drive back to London. It was a rainy, wintry evening, com-

Canapress Photo Service

"Hendrix was the only person I ever knew who could play on acid," marveled David Crosby. "Whenever I tried it, the strings always melted."

pounded by the brisk cold wind blowing off the English Channel.

Once at the small house, the band — particularly Hendrix who wasn't yet used to the damp English winters — were chilled to the bone. Spotting a blazing fire, Jimi uttered a line that would form the basis of "Fire." "Can I get you anything?" asked Mrs. Redding. "Let me stand next to your fire," replied Hendrix, hoping to warm himself against the dancing flames.

As Hendrix vied for position in front of the berth, he was stymied by a large sleeping German Shepherd. After a few attempts to share the warmth with the dog, Jimi uttered a line that would become a classic: "Oh, move over Rover and let Jimi take over."

"Fire," inspired by the New Year's Eve incident at the Redding house, became a favorite of Jimi's. After the release of *Are You Experienced?*, the hard-driving tune became a centerpiece of the band's live show. It was at Finsbury Park in March 1967 that the song entered rock-and-roll history. The Experience was on the same bill as teen idols the Walker Brothers. At the beginning of the tour, it was announced that they would split up after this series of shows. Hendrix wanted to divert some of the attention from the Walkers to the Experience, but he needed something new to punch up his act. Backstage, music writer Keith Altham proposed that as a climax to the show, Jimi set his guitar aflame during "Fire." Lighter fluid was secretly procured to keep Hendrix's new bit of pyrotechnics under wraps until show time. Not even Redding or Mitchell had any idea that Jimi planned to torch his Fender Stratocaster.

Jimi pulled out all the stops for the Finsbury Park show. All the tricks he learned from the American R & B bands he had played with whipped the crowd into a near frenzy. They stomped and cheered as he reclined on stage, coaxing sounds from the guitar with his teeth. The show's capper came when he lit the fluid-soaked guitar, gyrating around the flames like a shaman.

Hendrix later admitted that he had trouble getting the matches lit, but once he did, the guitar "went up like a mini meteorite striking earth." The response from the press was immediate. With the sound of the crowd still roaring in the background, a press conference was quickly assembled backstage. Press agent Les Perrin blamed the fire on a short circuit in the guitar, not mentioning the lighter fluid lest it seem like a calculated attempt to steal the Walker Brothers' thunder.

In the coming days and weeks, the Experience and Jimi's scandalous onstage mischief became front-page news. The same press that had jeered at Jimi now proclaimed him to be "The Black Elvis." The resulting publicity propelled the band's new single "Purple Haze" to the upper reaches of the charts. After the pyrotechnic event, musician Curtis Knight stated that Jimi cryptically said he "succeeded in awakening some inner range of cosmic consciousness within that fucking guitar."

Green Tambourine

The Lemon Pipers

A song that had been turned down by dozens of music publishers excited an executive at Buddah Records enough to order one of his bands to record it. They reluctantly agreed, scoring their only hit in the process. "Green Tambourine" took the Lemon Pipers to the top of the charts in 1968.

Shelley Pinz was a neophyte songwriter with a satchel full of lyrics but no musical arrangements. Paul Leka was a musician/producer who worked at Circle Five Productions. They were introduced by Stan Costa whose uncle was well-known record producer Don Costa. The pair hit it off, working hard to set music to Pinz's extensive collection of lyrics. One afternoon, she showed up at the office with a new lyric inspired by a newspaper article she had read. It was a story about an elderly busker from England who played music on the street. He was a one-man band, entertaining passersby, collecting money in a tambourine he kept at his feet. Pinz came up with the phrase "green tambourine" after imagining a tambourine filled with money.

Dropping their other projects, the pair worked exclusively on "Green Tambourine," sure they had a hit on their hands. The problem was, nobody else agreed. Leka shopped the tune

"MacArthur Park," song-writer Jimmy Webb's surreal seven-minute-and-twenty-one-second ode to lost love is actually based on a real place. Webb and girlfriend Susan used to meet for box lunches at MacArthur Park (at Alvarado and Wilshire), a thirty-two-acre patch of greenery in a now-shabby part of Los Angeles. When their relationship ended, he wrote a song about their picnics in the park. "That's where the image of the cake comes from," he told writer Joe Smith. "The image is, the rain comes, and the whole thing is going or melting, and then it is gone."

to every publisher in New York, only to be turned down every time. All seemed lost until Gary Cannon (who, under the name Gary Katz, would later produce Steely Dan), a young executive for Buddah Records, heard the tune. He flipped out and convinced Buddah president Neil Bogart that it could be a smash. Now they needed a band to record "Green Tambourine."

The Lemon Pipers were an Oxford, Ohio psychedelic band signed to Buddah. Bogart explained to Leka that he wanted to drop the band but had decided to give them one more chance if they would record "Green Tambourine." It was Leka's job to fly to Oxford, present the song and convince them to commit it to vinyl. He flew to Ohio and in the band's rehearsal space, played them the tune on an upright piano. They hated it. It was too pop sounding for the band who favored longer, drug-influenced psyche-delic works. Sensing he was losing his shot at getting this song recorded, Leka told the band that they would be dropped from the label if they didn't accept it. The Lemon Pipers agreed to get back to him.

Leka took the next plane back to NYC and waited by the phone. The next day, the band called, having had a change of heart. Better than that, they wanted Leka to produce the song. He booked time at the Cleveland Recording Studio in Oxford and cut the tune along with several other tracks including "Jelly Jungle (Of Orange Marmalade)" and "Rice Is Nice," both of which bubbled under the Top Forty. The recording — featuring the band playing foghorn, green tambourine, toys and other more conventional instruments — was rudimentary. Once back in New York, Leka doctored the track, replacing the drums and adding a string section.

The improved mix of "Green Tambourine" was rushed to radio stations in the New York area. Programmers were told they had an exclusive from a hot new band. The ploy worked, and the single broke big in the New York market. Weeks later, it entered the national charts. Seven weeks further, on February 3, 1968, it was Buddah Records' first Number One.

The Lemon Pipers followed "Green Tambourine" with several psychedelic offerings, none of which captured the record-buying public's imagination. Neil Bogart ultimately did drop the Lemon Pipers from the Buddah roster after a self-produced sophomore album failed to produce any chart action.

(Sittin' On) The Dock of the Bay

Otis Redding

During a well-earned vacation, Otis Redding wrote a song he knew would be a hit. Unfortunately, he didn't live long enough to see it become the biggest pop hit of his career. "(Sittin' On) The Dock of the Bay" was recorded just three days before he died in a plane crash on December 10, 1967.

Otis Redding was exhausted. He had just finished his record company's promotional European shows, The Stax/Volt Tour. As the headliner, he had to work extra hard to provide a cap to a show that included Booker T & the MGs, Arthur Conley, Carla Thomas, Eddie "Knock on Wood" Floyd and Sam & Dave — showstoppers all. The response in Europe surprised the Memphites. Police intervened in Liverpool, England, nearly stopping the show, when the audience almost collapsed the theater's balcony. Redding played some of his finest shows on this tour, the intensity of which is captured on the long-playing *Live in Europe*.

Once back in the United States, Redding had only one more concert commitment — a nonpaying gig at the Monterey Pop International Festival — before taking a rest. This one-off show would be the most important of Redding's career. Sharing the bill with acts like the Association, Jefferson

Airplane, Janis Joplin and Jimi Hendrix, this concert would bring his soul music to a whole new audience. Redding put in an electrifying show that brought together black and white music and saw him embraced by a primarily white crowd. Writer Kevin Phinney wrote, "...the bundled up energy of the sixties seemed to pour out through Otis and the band." History records the event as the first major pop-music revolution since the Beatles. Redding was primed for rock superstardom.

In the weeks following his watershed performance at Monterey, Redding rented a houseboat just across from San Francisco's Golden Gate Bridge in the small town of Sausalito. On the turntable was *Sgt. Pepper's Lonely Heart's Club Band*, a record Redding listened to over and over, soaking up each note. Encouraged by the refined songwriting of the Beatles, he wrote a song, but it was a different sort of tune. He labored over the lyrics which were inspired by his surroundings. "(Sittin' On) The Dock of the Bay" was a moody, introspective tune with a folky feel that he hoped would appeal to the flower-power kids he had wowed at the pop festival.

Back home in Memphis, there wasn't much enthusiasm for the tune. His wife Zelma particularly detested it. "I really couldn't get into it," she told writer Peter Guralnick. "I said, 'Oh, God, you're changing.'"

Stax Records owner Jim Stewart agreed with Zelma, telling Otis he didn't think "Dock of the Bay" was nearly as strong as "I've Been Loving You Too Long," Redding's 1967 hit. Redding's business partner Phil Walden felt the folky tune was too radical a change and tried to talk the soul singer out of recording it. In retrospect, he admitted that "Dock of the Bay" wasn't that different from Redding's back catalog, but at the time, it seemed a little too pop. Redding was adamant. "I think it's time for me to change in my music," he said. "People might be tired of me."

"(Sittin' On) The Dock of the Bay" was recorded on December 6 and 7, 1967. As usual, Redding entered the

> John Fogarty wrote
> "Proud Mary," Creedence
> Clearwater Revival's
> first gold disc, on the
> morning he was dis-
> charged from the Army.

studio with a rough version of the tune, relying on guitarist Steve Cropper to flesh out his musical idea. Cropper took Redding's intro and one verse, molding it into a finished song. The pair worked out an ad lib rap for Redding to sing over the fade-out. During recording, Redding, who often had trouble remembering the words to his songs, forgot what he was supposed to do. So he whistled instead, perfectly capping the tune. It was a perfect counterpoint to the laid-back surf sounds that swell as the song fades.

Redding never heard the finished recording of "(Sittin' On) The Dock of the Bay." Three days after recording it, he and all but two members of his band were killed when his twin-engine Beechcraft crashed into the icy waters of Lake Monona, just minutes away from their destination of Madison, Wisconsin. Otis Redding was twenty-six years old.

In the months following his death, Steve Cropper spent countless hours in the studio remixing the unfinished tapes Redding had left behind. The "(Sittin' On) The Dock of the Bay" track was completed and sent to Atlantic Records in New York. To Cropper's surprise, it was rejected. Label head Jerry Wexler felt the vocal was buried too deep in the mix, and the surf sound effect was too predominant. Cropper doctored the tape to Wexler's specifications, and the single was released in early March 1968. "(Sittin' On) The Dock of the Bay" reached Number One, sitting atop the charts for four weeks.

The tune is notable for two charts firsts. It was the first posthumous Number One single. In 1980, when the singer's sons Dexter and Otis III, performing as the Reddings, brought the tune back to the Hot One Hundred, it became the first time a Number One single had been covered by an artist's children. Their version hit Number Fifty-Five.

Mony Mony

Tommy James and The Shondells

Tommy James had a problem. He had written and recorded a catchy track but was having difficulty coming up with words to go along with it. After a fruitless night of brainstorming with writing partners Ritchie Cordell and Bo Gentry, a fortuitous glance at the skyline of New York City provided the inspiration they were after.

Tommy James had been making music his entire life. Born Thomas Gregory Jackson in Dayton, Ohio in 1947, he began playing ukulele when he was three years old because a regular-size guitar was too large for his small hands. At age nine, he switched to guitar, and by thirteen, he had formed Tommy & the Tornadoes, recording his first single, "Long Pony Tale." At nineteen, he hit the top of the charts with "Hanky Panky," a party-rock gem that had been recorded two years previously. The next five years saw James place fourteen songs in the Top Forty including "I Think We're Alone Now," "Crimson and Clover," "Crystal Blue Persuasion" and "Mony Mony."

The early months of 1968 saw James in search of a Top Ten hit. It seemed that his good-time sound had been replaced on the charts by the Motown sound out of Detroit or acid rock from California. The New York-based singer needed a bona fide killer tune to reestablish his career. He had an upbeat instrumental track he thought could be a hit — just no lyrics.

James, Cordell and Gentry gathered at James's Manhattan apartment to trade ideas. One thing they agreed on was that the hook of the song had to be an unusual-sounding girl's name — something along the lines of "Bony Maronie" or "Sloopy" — something nobody had heard before. Time passed. The pressure mounted. James had to record the lyrics the next day, but no title was forthcoming. Searches through dictionaries and thesauri yielded nothing.

In frustration, James walked out to his terrace to take in the cool night air. Looking across the skyline of New York, Tommy James found what he was looking for. In the distance he saw a sign for a major insurance company. The forty-story Mutual of New York building at 1740 Broadway displayed a flashing sign spelling MONY with a dollar sign in the O. That was just the title they had been looking for. "If I had been looking in the other direction," James told writer Parke Puterbaugh, "it would have been called 'Hotel Taft.'" The lyrics flowed quickly, with James commenting

Greg Jones

The logo that saved Tommy James's career: Manhattan's Mutual of New York. The original flashing neon sign is gone now, replaced by a glistening chrome emblem, but the significant dollar sign remains.

later, "The song [is] kind of etched in stone in New York."

Rounding up a posse of musicians, friends and people off the street to clap hands and lend a party atmosphere to the recording, James recorded the vocals the next day, confident of the song's success. "A lot of people thought I was nuts to put out a record like 'Mony Mony' in the middle of the Vietnam War," James said in the liner notes to the 1989 Rhino Records' retrospective *Tommy James & The Shondells Anthology*. "How dare somebody come out with a dance record at a time when things were that serious! My feeling was, hey man, there's enough garbage on the news every night. Who needs to be depressed anymore? If music can't make you feel good, then what's it for? We literally had a party going on in the studio. 'Mony Mony' was a party on top of a very simple track."

"Mony Mony" reached Number Three on the *Billboard* charts. It proved even more popular in Britain where its garage-band sound shot to the top of the charts. The tune got another kick at the can in 1987 when Billy Idol's live version reached Number One on the American charts.

Na Na Hey Hey Kiss Him Good-bye

Steam

Many bad records get played on the radio, but artists don't often set out to make an inferior record. Gary DeCarlo, Dale Frashuer and Paul Leka did, only to see it climb to Number One in 1969.

After a failed stab at pop stardom in the early 1960s, the Chateaus split up. Paul Leka became a songwriter for hire, most notably penning the Lemon Piper's 1967 hit "Green Tambourine." He then hooked up with Mercury Records, convincing the label to sign his old Chateaus bandmate Gary DeCarlo to record four solo singles.

With Leka producing, the pair laid down four tracks, all of which were deemed hitworthy. The friends were sent back to Mercury Sound Studios to record a throwaway song to be used as the B-side for the first single. At six o'clock pm, Dale Frashuer, the third member of the Chateaus, dropped by to say hello. They started mulling over old times when someone brought up the 1961 Chateaus' up-tempo ballad "Kiss Him Good-bye."

They decided to record the tune, but it needed some work. It was only two minutes long, and Leka reckoned it had to be at least four minutes to discourage DJs from playing it as an A-side. Reworking the tune, Leka sat at the piano, singing "na, na, na, na, na, na, na, na" when he couldn't think of new lyrics. Someone else chimed in with "hey hey hey." Thinking they were banging off a quick and nasty B-side, the trio of friends quickly threw together "Na Na Hey Hey Kiss Him Good-bye."

To keep costs down, no additional musicians were brought into the session. A drum track was spliced together from another song, and Leka played keyboard while DeCarlo banged out the rhythm on a block of wood. The vocal track including the working lyrics — "na, na"s and all — were left in because nobody could think of anything better. However, Leka fattened it by overdubbing it several times, calling on DeCarlo's cousin for assistance. He sang off key, but what the hell, it was never going to get played on the radio. Right?

Three Quick Hits from Burton Cummings: The mysterious "Albert Flasher" of the Guess Who song was a play on the "alert flasher" red light Cummings once saw flickering in a studio. The phrase "Break It to Them Gently" was borrowed from a detective movie. The zip code for Indianapolis, taken off the return address of a letter from a female fan, is the basis for the obscure "46201" reference in the ballad "Sour Suite."

Wrong. Mercury A&R head Bob Reno loved the song, insisting it be pressed as a 45 on their subsidiary Fontana label. Leka was appalled. In his words, "Na Na Hey Hey" was an "embarrassing record," an "insult." He didn't want his name connected to the record. Neither did DeCarlo or Frashuer. Leka thought back to the night of the recording. Leaving the studio at five o'clock a.m., someone pointed out a manhole cover billowing steam. The weary producer filed away "steam" as a possible group name for future use. Since no one wanted their name on this record, now seemed like a good time to use the epithet.

The recording of "Na Na Hey Hey Kiss Him Good-bye" credited to Steam was released on Fontana in late 1969. As it rose on the charts, all four of DeCarlo's singles, released under the stage name Garrett Scott, stiffed. Mercury Records shifted their focus from DeCarlo's failing career to the rising fortunes of Steam. Leka and Frashuer pulled together some other Chateaus' tunes and headed for the studio to put together an album for the nonexistent group.

DeCarlo, stung from the failure of his solo singles, refused to participate. Leka recruited a Bridgeport, Connecticut band to record and tour as Steam. They placed one song ("I've Gotta Make You Love Me") in the Top Fifty before vaporizing. "Na Na Hey Hey Kiss Him Good-bye" sold a million copies, hitting Number One in December 1969. DeCarlo, though bitter from the experience, wasn't an all-around loser. Songwriting royalty checks continue to come in from the dozens of cover versions — including an Italian translation "Na Na Hey Hey Ciao Ciao" — of the song he didn't want to be a hit.

SEVENTIES

American Pie

Don McLean

Don McLean's "American Pie" has some of the most confounding lyrics to ever hit the top spot on the *Billboard* charts. The eight-minute, twenty-seven-second tune is packed to overflowing with oblique references and metaphoric images that have inspired university theses and fervent barroom dialectic.

One thing is certain — "the day the music died" is a reference to February 3, 1959, the date of the plane crash that claimed the lives of Buddy Holly, Ritchie Valens and J.P. Richardson (The Big Bopper). Beyond that, the meaning is hazy. McLean offered no help, telling *Life* magazine's P.F. Kluge in 1972, "I can't necessarily interpret 'American Pie' any better than you can."

For a quarter of a century, McLean has steadfastly refused to break the tightly coded lyrics. But the tune could be an apocalyptic vision about the death of music's redemptive powers and the "we shall overcome" optimism of the flower-power generation. Or maybe it is about the death of rock and roll itself subsequent to Holly's passing. Or perhaps it is about rock and roll's refusal to die. The lyrics can have as much meaning as you are willing to grant them, or none at all, depending on where you sit in the great "American Pie" debate.

The roots of the song go back to 1959 when McLean was a thirteen-year-old paperboy. "February made me shiver/ With every paper I'd deliver" refers to the chilly winter morning in his hometown of New Rochelle, New York when he delivered the sad news that Buddy Holly had been killed. McLean later admitted that Holly was the first and last person he had idolized as a kid.

The chorus, with its refrain "Bye, bye Miss American Pie," is conjectured to refer to the death of the apple-pie-in-the-sky American dream, although one internet source wonders whether the "Miss" allusion has a beauty-pageant connection. It has also been submitted that the Beechcraft Bonanza, the red-and-white, four-seat light airplane that crashed on February 3, 1959, was called the American Pie.

"This'll be the day that I die" is a plain reference to Buddy Holly and his 1957 hit "That'll Be the Day," a song title that was inspired by a quote from the John Wayne film *The Searchers*.

From here on in, McLean muddies the waters, piling pop-culture references on top of one another fast and hard. A longtime fan of early rock-and-roll radio, McLean cribs lines from his favorite tunes to flesh out his epic poem. "Did you write the book of love?" cites the Monotones' 1958 hit "Book of Love." "If the bible tells you so" might quote 1955's "The Bible Tells Me So" by big-band singer Don Cornell.

"You both kicked off your shoes" refers to high-school "sock hops," so named because dancers had to remove their shoes to prevent damaging high-school gym floors with their street shoes. "I was a lonely teenage broncin' buck/ With a pink carnation and a pickup truck" sounds like a reference to Marty Robbins's 1957 hit "A White Sport Coat (And a Pink Carnation)."

No critical history of rock and roll would be complete

without a nod to Bob Dylan, and "American Pie" doesn't disappoint. "When the jester sang for the King and Queen" refers to a Martin Luther King rally, attended by John F. and Jackie Kennedy, at which Dylan performed. "In a coat he borrowed from James Dean" likely refers to the red windbreaker Dean wore in *Rebel Without A Cause*. Dylan wears a similar coat on the cover of *The Freewheelin' Bob Dylan*.

> Bruce Goes to the Library: Bruce Springsteen based "Darkness on the Edge of Town" on Tom Joad's last speech in John Steinbeck's *The Grapes of Wrath*. Ron Kovic's Vietnam tome *Born on the Fourth of July* (later a movie by Oliver Stone) inspired Springsteen to pen "Born in the USA."

The line about "Lennon reading a book on Marx" seems to allude to John Lennon and his growing political awareness in the late 1960s. "I met a girl who sings the blues" probably refers to Janis Joplin who died from a heroin overdose just as the 1970s began.

Verse four opens with "Helter Skelter in a summer swelter," an obvious reference to the Beatles' song Charles Manson mistakenly took to be a warning to Americans of a racial conflict that was "coming down fast." "The birds flew off with the fallout shelter/ Eight miles high and falling fast" could have something to do with the Byrds and their 1966 single "Eight Miles High."

In the homestretch, things get even more ambiguous. "And there we were all in one place" is probably referring to Woodstock. "And as the flames climbed high into the night/ To light the sacrificial rite" seems to allude to the Kent State tragedy where student demonstrators where shot after setting fire to military buildings. "And in the streets the children screamed" may be a comment on the flower-power protests and the death of 1960s idealism.

The song closes with what seems to be a religious analogy (McLean had studied in several Catholic schools): "The three men I admire the most/The Father, Son and Holy

Ghost." But it is more likely a reference to Holly, the Big Bopper and Ritchie Valens. Or, alternatively, as is sometimes suggested, it may allude to JFK, Bobby Kennedy and Martin Luther King. "They caught the last train for the coast" is undeniably a reference to death.

The symbolism doesn't end with the lyric sheet. "American Pie" uses studio technology to represent the evolution of rock and roll. The song starts in monaural and is gradually boosted into stereo, illustrating the change in recording techniques in the rock era. Full stereophonic sound is reserved for the last chorus.

Although the song was reviled by critics (the *Village Voice*'s Robert Christgau called it a novelty song, rating it D plus), it was an immediate hit in 1971, selling seventy-five thousand copies a week for several months before hitting the top of the charts in January 1972. The song was so celebrated that it even inspired another Number One hit. Singer Lori Lieberman saw McLean perform "American Pie" at the Troubadour in Los Angeles, and the next day, she told songwriters Norman Gimbel and Charles Fox about McLean's moving rendition of the song. They took her experience and turned it into "Killing Me Softly With His Song," a Number One hit for Roberta Flack in 1973.

In recent years, the enigma surrounding the lyrics to "American Pie" have become a source of amusement for McLean. In 1996, he teased that he was considering starting a 900 phone line to explain the song (and to help pad his bank account). Once, when asked to analyze the lyrics, he joked to a reporter that it meant that "I don't ever have to work again if I don't want to."

Mother and Child Reunion

Paul Simon

A chicken and egg dish from a Chinese restaurant in New York City was the unlikely source for Paul Simon's first solo hit record. The soft reggae rhythms of "Mother and Child Reunion" took Paul Simon to the Top Five for the first time without his sidekick Art Garfunkle.

Near the end of Simon & Garfunkle's run at pop stardom, Paul Simon found himself moving away from the pop/folk formula that had fueled their biggest hits. Simon had been listening to ska, the up-tempo dance music of Jamaican dance origin that emphasizes the offbeat rather than the Westernized onbeat. This reversed beat was extremely popular in Jamaica during the first half of the sixties, producing the first wave of homegrown Jamaican pop stars.

The final album of S & G's golden years, 1970's *Bridge Over Troubled Water*, was to have included a ska track, "Why Don't You Write Me." But it didn't turn out the way Simon had hoped, so it was scrapped. When he got the chance to record a solo album, he decided to take another run at the world-beat rhythm. He booked the Dynamic Sound Studio in Kingston, Jamaica — the same studio that can be seen in

Henry Gross claims to have written his 1976 hit "Shannon," the story of a dear-departed pet dog, in only ten minutes. He threw in the falsetto vocals as a tribute to Brian Wilson of the Beach Boys.

the Jimmy Cliff film *The Harder They Come*. Now all Simon needed was a song.

While having supper at New York's Say Eng Look Restaurant, Simon came across an elaborate chicken and egg dish called Mother and Child Reunion. Starting with the poultry dish's name, he crafted a tale about a "sad and mournful day" — the day he lost his "little darling" to a car accident. In actual fact, the little darling was a beloved pet dog that had recently been run over and killed. It was the first death he had experienced personally. He said that at the time, he couldn't remember a sadder day. The lyrics for his proposed ska tune came directly from that incident.

Arriving in Jamaica, he was told by his band of hired musicians that they didn't play ska anymore. Now they played reggae. "What does that sound like?" Simon asked. The band cranked up and introduced Simon to the repetitive bass riffs and offbeats of reggae music. He quickly wrote a reggae arrangement of his new song and rehearsed the band. "It was a good band," Simon told Giles Smith of *Q Magazine* in 1993, "a lot of ganja smoked." Later, many of his hired hands would go on to join reggae pioneers Toots & The Maytals.

Simon's first foray into musical globe-trotting was warmly received. Reviewing the eponymously titled album in the *Village Voice*, Robert Christgau gushed, "I've been saying nasty things about Simon since 1967, but this is the only thing in the universe to make me positively happy in the first two weeks of 1972." "Mother and Child Reunion" hit Number Four on the *Billboard* charts in February 1972.

The Say Eng Look Restaurant has since taken Mother and Child Reunion off the menu, but the chef will still whip up this exotic dish given twenty-four hours' notice.

Bad, Bad Leroy Brown

Jim Croce

Jim Croce was the living embodiment of the singer-songwriter. A writer of heartfelt tunes, he drew from his own life experiences to craft the melodic narratives that took him to the top of the charts. His first Number One, "Bad, Bad Leroy Brown," was based on a real person.

Jim Croce started his career in music as a disc jockey at the Villanova University campus radio station. In the mid-sixties, he got caught up in the performing side of music, playing guitar in rock bands in the Phillie area. Never really a rocker, he soon found himself in New York's Greenwich Village. Croce spent the Summer of Love playing guitar in folk clubs such as The Bitter End and Cafe Wha? He and wife Ingrid released one album of their songs, 1969's *Approaching Day*, to a tepid response. Discouraged by the failure of the record, they moved back to Pennsylvania where he took a job as a truck driver.

Continuing to write songs, Croce would soon meet the man who inspired his first big hit. Yearning for a stable career, Croce joined the Army, going to school to learn how to become a telephone lineman. While stationed in Fort Dix, New Jersey, he met Leroy Brown. Brown wasn't cut out for army life nd only lasted for about a week before going AWOL. Not the sharpest knife in the drawer, Brown returned at the end of the month to collect a paycheck. He was taken away in handcuffs and placed under military arrest. "Just to listen to him talk and see how 'bad' he was, I knew I was going to write a song about him one day," Croce told Bob Gilbert and Gary Theroux, authors of *The Top Ten*.

Croce's experience as a truck driver gave him a good knowledge of engines and the inner workings of vehicles. He put this to good use during his lean years, scavenging junkyards in search of spare parts for his "$29 cars." Each of these junkyards would have a guard dog with "an axle tied around their necks or an old lawn mower to hold 'em or at least slow them down." He incorporated that image into "Bad, Bad Leroy Brown."

Blending both these experiences, he created an indelible image of a badass that would eventually come to life on the radio. An accident with a sledgehammer had damaged one of his hands, forcing him to develop a unique way of playing guitar. Nonetheless, he always wrote on acoustic guitar. Once he had completed "Bad, Bad Leroy Brown" and five other tunes, he contacted his old university friend Terry Cashman, now a record producer in New York. Cashman and partner Tommy West thought the songs had potential and invited Croce to the Big Apple for a recording session at the Hit Factory.

There they recorded the demos that would land Croce a deal with ABC Records. "Bad, Bad Leroy Brown" wasn't considered polished enough to be included on the debut album *Don't Mess Around With Jim* although it yielded the hits "Operator (That's Not the Way It Feels)" and the title track. Eager to re-create the success of the first album, the same team was assembled to cut 1973's *Life and Times*. While gathering material for the new disc, Croce pulled out several songs left over from the initial sessions.

Cashman and West liked "Bad, Bad Leroy Brown," but they made some suggestions to improve the tune. On Croce's demo, the song was a straight acoustic number with a shuffle beat. The producers felt it would work better on piano, so they lifted the distinctive piano vamp from the 1958 Bobby Darin hit "Queen of the Hop" to open "Leroy Brown." Croce liked that idea, but he put his foot down when they asked him to change the lyrics. They thought the "meaner than a junkyard dog" line was hard and crass and didn't belong in the song. Croce disagreed, arguing that it was the tune's most memorable phrase. Fortunately, the line was saved.

ABC released *Life and Times* in February 1973 to favorable critical response. One writer called it "perfect commerciality," while another called it "a relief from post-hippie confessionalism." "One Less Set of Footsteps," the initial single release from the album, only reached Number Thirty-Seven in March 1973. Croce would have to wait until July of that year to score his first Number One with "Bad, Bad Leroy Brown."

Today, complex sound-effect loops are produced with the aid of samplers and computers. In 1973, when Pink Floyd was recording *Dark Side of the Moon*, it took some elbow grease to get the job done. Recording the opening rhythmic cash-register sequence for "Money" was a lengthy process involving several feet of reel-to-reel tape. Recording the sound of a bag of 50p coins being dropped to the floor on one set of tape loops, the cash register and paper tearing (from a sound-effects album) on others, David Gilmour cut and pasted the long loops of tape, skillfully manipulating them to play in 7/4 time.

With a Number One single and a best-selling long player on the charts, Croce suddenly had a high profile. Another cut from *Life and Times*, "Time in a Bottle," was used as the theme for *She Lives*, a television movie of the week starring Desi Arnaz Jr. and Susan Hubley. The exposure the film gave the song convinced ABC to release it as a single. It went to Number One in December, but Croce would not live to see its success.

On September 12, 1973, the night of the television movie's broadcast, Croce finished his third album *I Got A Name*. A week later, he flew to Northwestern Louisiana University in Natchitoches to give a concert. After the show, a chartered plane was waiting to take him and the band to their next gig seventy miles away. The light aircraft crashed on takeoff, killing Croce and five others including guitarist Maury Muehleisen. Jim Croce was just thirty years old. ABC mined his existing albums for posthumous singles, placing "I Got a Name," "Time in a Bottle," "I'll Have to Say I Love You in a Song" and "Workin' at the Car Wash Blues" in the Top Forty.

Smokin' in the Boys' Room

Brownsville Station

Anyone over the age of thirty will remember the summer of 1974 when Cub Koda's band, Brownsville Station, ruled the radio with "Smokin' in the Boys' Room." From its opening guitar riff and spoken word introduction — "How you doin' out there? Did you ever have one of those days where it just seems that everybody's on your case, from your teacher all the way down to your best girlfriend?" — the song positively drips with attitude. It's an anthem to teenage rebellion from a band who were punk long before punk meant bondage pants and spiky hair. Brownsville Station were brash, loud and proud.

"Smokin'" is two minutes and fifty seconds of rock-and-roll posturing. "It's a good simple rock-and-roll song," said Koda. "When you see what it was up against at the time on the charts, it really stuck out. It was different. It was straight-ahead rock and roll at a time when there wasn't a lot of that out. There was a lot of hippie stuff, and there was certainly all types of big-hair pop at the time."

The inspiration for the song dates back to Koda's pre-adolescent days in Michigan. Every Friday night, his parents would drop him off at the Clinton Theater "so they could go out drinking.

"When we were eight or nine years old," said Koda, "me and my buddies would swipe some of our old men's cigarettes and go downstairs into the boy's room. They had a little hole in the wall where they had this Chase and Sanborn coffee can to stick your butts in. We'd be down there puffin' away, actin' like tough guys, and you could hear the theater manager Frank "the Crank" Mendez coming up the stairs after our asses. He knew something was up. This guy sounded exactly like Edgar Kennedy, the guy who played the cop in the *Little Rascals*. He started every sentence with the word 'Say.' 'Say! What are you kids doing down there?' 'Nothing Mr. Mendez,' we'd say, stuffing the cigarette can into the hole. We'd get the faucet going and sprinkle water all over the place to cut down on the fumes."

"Smokin' in the Boys' Room" was written on the recommendation of record company executive Doug Morris. "He would throw out song titles at me and say, 'Go ahead, see if you can write a song about this,'" remembered Koda. "It would be some ridiculously outrageous title like 'They Call It Teenybop, But the Money's FM to Me.'" Morris proposed the title "Smokin' in the Boys' Room," and Koda,

photo courtesy of Trod Nossel Productions

Former Brownsville Station leader Cub Koda still records and performs two decades after his biggest hit "Smokin' in the Boys' Room" hit Number One.

with bassist Michael Lutz, banged out the tune in half an hour.

The song made it all the way to number three on the *Billboard* charts. "'Smokin'" was just another cut on the album," said Koda. "There were other things we wanted to release as 45s and did, preceding that, but ['Smokin' in the Boys' Room'] took off on its own."

You Ain't Seen Nothin' Yet

Bachman-Turner Overdrive

A song that inspired millions of rec-room air guitarists was recorded as a joke. "You Ain't Seen Nothin' Yet" was never meant to be released to the public, but it brought Bachman-Turner Overdrive to the top of the *Billboard* charts in November 1974.

Randy Bachman split with the popular Guess Who after the success of 1970's *American Woman* LP. Several failed projects later, including a solo album and two records with the countrified Brave Belt, the guitarist hit on a winning formula — brawny rock with pop and heavy-metal touches. Along with bassist C.F. "Fred" Turner and Bachman brothers Robby (drums) and Tim (rhythm guitar), Randy chose the name Bachman-Turner Overdrive, borrowing it from a trucking trade magazine. This was not surprising considering the four heavyweight guys looked more like truckers than rock stars.

After suffering twenty-five record company rejections, BTO found a home with Mercury Records in 1973. Churning out two records with assembly-line precision, the predictably titled *BTO* and *BTO II* motored up the Hot One Hundred as high as Number Twelve with "Takin' Care of Business" in

1974. Eager to follow up their 1974 chart success, the band
sped to a Seattle, Washington studio to record their third
album *Not Fragile*.

One night, after a session inspired by the work of Traffic
rhythm guitarist Dave Mason, Bachman improvised an instrumental track. Later, clowning around, he made up some jokey
lyrics to add to the mix. In rehearsal, he tried to make the
band laugh, singing the new song, vocally impersonating
James Cagney and other movie stars. While taping the tune,
Bachman changed his approach, recording the vocals in one
take, stuttering through them as a backhanded tribute to
BTO's manager and Randy's other brother Gary who had a
pronounced speech impediment. "You Ain't Seen Nothin'
Yet," as the song came to be known, was tucked away. Bachman
was planning to send it to Gary after the sessions were over.

Completing the album, they offered the finished eight
songs to Mercury's Charlie Fach. He griped that he didn't
hear the magic single that would duplicate the success of
"Takin' Care of Business." Bachman told Fach he *did* have
one other song, but it wasn't good enough to release. The
vocal, he explained, was by turns sharp and flat, the band could
be heard laughing at the end and worst of all, he stuttered
through the whole thing.

Fach gave it a listen and immediately smelled gold. To
him, "You Ain't Seen Nothin' Yet" was just the vehicle to take
BTO to the top of the charts. There was a brightness to the
track that was missing on the rest of the album. He insisted
it be added to the *Not Fragile* lineup. Bachman yielded, but
only if he could rerecord the vocal. The next day, he made
several attempts to clean up the vocal track, each one worse
than the last. "I tried to sing it," Bachman is quoted in Fred
Bronson's book *The Billboard Book of Number One Hits*, "but
I sounded like Frank Sinatra. It didn't fit."

Fach got his way, and the original version of the
song was included on the album. But Bachman, who, as

producer, had final say on single releases, refused to allow "You Ain't Seen Nothin' Yet" to be put out as a 45 despite the substantial radio play the song was earning as an album track. He was embarrassed by the song, thinking it was childish and dumb, and he would turn down the radio when it came on. Three long weeks passed before Bachman gave in and allowed "You Ain't Seen Nothin' Yet" to be pressed as a single. He still wasn't convinced the song would be a smash. But he realized it carried the tradition of "Louie Louie" — great dumb rock and roll — so why not give it a chance?

The song entered the *Billboard* charts at the end of September 1974, and just seven weeks later, it soared to Number One for a week, becoming BTO's biggest hit. "It's a gold single now," said Bachman in 1975. "I'm not so embarrassed anymore."

Fame

David Bowie

"About ten, fifteen minutes a song," said David Bowie in 1975. "[They didn't] take very long to write. It wasn't too hard, really." The chameleon-like singer is referring to the time it took to put together the soul-powered *Young Americans* LP which included his biggest hit — "Fame."

David Bowie finished production on his "plastic soul" album at Sigma Sound Studios in Philadelphia. His producer Tony Visconti returned to England to mix the tapes, then called *The Gouster* (Philly street slang for cool guy) at his home studio. Bowie set up camp in New York City, renting a large house on 20th Street. John Lennon was a frequent guest, and Bowie recalled that the two "spent endless hours talking about fame and what it was like not having your own life anymore."

During one of those visits, Bowie decided to record a Lennon/McCartney song and proposed that Lennon sit in on the session. Lennon was pleased to have a chance to work with Bowie and agreed to play guitar on "Across the Universe," a track that appeared on the Beatles' *Let It Be* LP.

Time was booked at the Electric Lady Studios at 52 West 8th Street. The sessions began amid the psychedelic murals and dramatic lighting of the studio (originally installed by the studio's founder Jimi Hendrix). Like most Bowie sessions, musicians didn't arrive until midnight and worked through the night.

Things got off to a slow start. As Bowie fiddled with the recording console in the control booth, Lennon and guitarist Carlos Alomar jammed a version of Shirley and Company's "Shame, Shame, Shame," a current Top Forty hit. "What are you playing?" Bowie asked over the studio intercom. "A disco tune called 'Shame, Shame, Shame,'" replied the former Beatle.

Bowie listened to the two men play, then he put pen to paper. Drawing on his conversations with Lennon, he wrote the words to "Fame" in under twenty minutes. "God!" said Bowie, "That session was fast. That was a whole evening's work."

Bowie grafted lyrics about the price of fame and the sting of being in the public eye to an unreleased R & B song called "Foot Stomping." Commenting on the record in the *Village Voice*, Robert Christgau noted that Bowie's rhyming "Fame" with pain "makes you believe it." Running part of the "Foot Stomping" tape backward and cutting and pasting the melody, Bowie spliced together the basic disco-tinged track for "Fame." Alomar and Lennon added finishing touches — guitar overdubs and a piano played backward.

Lennon was fascinated by Bowie's writing process, which differed from his own workman-like approach. "[He] writes in the studio," said Lennon. "He goes in with about four words and a few guys and starts laying down all this stuff and he has virtually nothing — he's making it up in the studio."

Bowie credited Lennon with providing the spark for "Fame." "With John Lennon, it was more the influence of having him in the studio that helped," said Bowie in November 1976. "There's always a lot of adrenaline flowing when John is around, but his chief addition to it all was the high-pitched singing of 'Fame.' The riff came from Carlos, and the melody and most of the lyrics came from me, but it wouldn't have happened if John hadn't been there. He was the energy, and that's why he's got a credit for writing it; he was the inspiration."

Meanwhile, Tony Visconti had finished mixing the rough Sigma Sound tapes, now called *Young Americans*. Visconti picked up the story. "About two weeks after I'd mixed the album," he told John Tobler and Stuart Grundy in *The Record Producers*, "David phoned to say that he and John Lennon had got together one night and recorded this tune called 'Fame.' 'I hope you don't mind, Tony, but it was so spontaneous and spur of the moment. And we did "Across The Universe"...we got on great.' He was very apologetic and nice about it, and he said he hoped I wouldn't mind if we took a few tracks off and included these, and I said that was all right."

Visconti didn't hear either of the new tracks until the record was released. "I wish I'd been in the studio with them," he continued. "But

C. Pizzello/Canapress Photo Service

David Bowie unveils his star on Hollywood's Walk of Fame. In 1975, he released Young Americans, a soul music tribute. "I tried to do a little stretch of how it feels musically in America," he said, "which is sort of relentless plastic soul."

David wasn't really elbowing me. It was really spontaneous — I was in England, and David was in New York with John — and that's exactly the way it happened."

"Fame" earned David Bowie his first American Number One single. Lennon took a metaphysical view of the song's good fortune. After the breakup of the Beatles, Paul, George and Ringo all topped the charts. But Lennon was unable to emulate their solo success. It took "Whatever Gets You Through the Night," a 1974 duet with Elton John, to get the Liverpudlian back at the Number One slot. "I felt like that was a karmic thing, you know," he told a reporter in 1975. "With me and Elton, I got my first Number One, so I passed it on to Bowie, and he got his first...I like that track."

How Long

Ace

In 1974, the pub-rock band Ace were poised on the verge of stardom. They were receiving favorable notices in the press and were about to record their debut album. Then disaster struck. A band member decided to leave just as things were starting to happen. Band leader Paul Carrack was hurt and angry and wrote a song about it. "How Long" hit the *Billboard* Top Five in 1975.

A keyboardist with the soul of a roving minstrel, Carrack has sung and played on many hits including chart entries by Roxy Music, Eric Clapton, Squeeze and Mike and the Mechanics. As a well-respected session player, he had enjoyed a prolific and lucrative career without ever becoming a household name. However, in the early seventies, he had his eye on rock-and-roll stardom.

By 1974, it looked like he was well on his way. The London newspapers were running hundreds of column inches on a new music trend. For several years immediately preceding punk rock, there was a proliferation of groups who played guitar-based American-tinged rock in pubs and hostelries. Dubbed pub rock by the press, the scene produced many players who would later find fame. Brinsley Schwartz, one of the

The original recording of Pink Floyd's "Time" included a cuckoo clock in the opening cacophony of clanging timepieces. David Gilmour felt the chiming birdcall destroyed the mood of the piece, so it was removed. The raw sound effects for the clock section were provided by engineer Alan Parsons (who hit the US Top Five in 1982 with the Alan Parson's Project single "Eye in the Sky"). Parsons recorded all the clocks separately on a Uher portable tape machine at an antique shop in St. John's Wood, close to Abbey Road Studios. They were originally intended to be released on a quadrophonic sound-effects album.

leading lights of pub rock, produced both Dave Edmunds and Nick Lowe. Another popular player on the scene was Paul Carrack, singer in the band Ace. With a smooth-as-silk vocal delivery, he lent credibility to Ace's attempts at re-creating American soul music.

As fast-rising pub rockers, Ace were offered the opening slot on a Hawkwind tour. At one show, they were scouted by record producer John Anthony who offered them a deal on the Anchor Records' label. On the eve of the first sessions for their debut *Five-A-Side*, Drummer John Woodward tendered his resignation to join the Sutherland Brothers & Quiver, a more successful group. Carrack was furious, fearing the departure would queer his deal with Anchor and his shot at stardom. Why hadn't Woodward said something earlier? "How long," he wanted to know, "had this been going on?"

Feeling cheated and spurned, he wrote a song, changing the context to a story about a girl who has discovered that her boyfriend had two-timed her. As a jab at his former bandmate, he dedicated the tune to Woodward. The playlist for the LP had already been decided on, but when Carrack presented "How Long" to the band, they voted to drop another track and release the new tune as a single. It was a fortuitous decision. "How Long" peaked at Number Three on the *Billboard* charts in 1975. It was Ace's only hit.

The band limped along for the next three years, unable to top the success of their first single. More albums followed, with Woodward returning to the drum kit on *Time for Another*, the third and final Ace album.

Philadelphia Freedom

Elton John

A gift of tennis gear inspired a song that topped the *Billboard* charts for two weeks in 1975. "Philadelphia Freedom" was Elton John's musical tribute to Wimbledon champ Billie Jean King.

In the spring of 1974, Elton John (real name, Reginald Kenneth Dwight) was appointed the director of the Watford Football Club, trumpeting his passion for sports to the world. This wasn't a new interest for John. As a child, he pinned up posters of soccer players on his walls and, with his father as chaperon, often attended games at his local playing field. The heavy burden of constant piano lessons thwarted any hope of John becoming a first-line pick at school soccer games. He was a better tennis player, but ultimately his love of Chopin and Brahms won out over a sporting life. By 1974, having secured worldwide fame, he rekindled his childhood interest in two typically English pastimes — tennis and soccer.

While John was devising methods to rescue the failing Watford team, the World Team Tennis League was being formed in the United States. The piano player became a fan of Billie Jean King's team — the Philadelphia Freedoms — and once, much to his delight, even played a match against the seasoned champion.

John frequently attended games, often allowing his English reserve to melt away as he hooted and hollered his support for the Freedoms. He was such an ardent fan that King commissioned tennis-clothing designer Ted Tingling to make up a customized Philadelphia Freedoms warm-up suit for John. He was so touched by the gesture that he vowed to write a song as a thank-you note.

After consulting with lyricist Bernie Taupin, the duo came up with a tribute to Philadelphia and the indefatigable spirit King showed in starting the World Tennis League. The musical arrangement pays tribute to Philadelphia record producers Gamble and Huff whose influence is indelibly stamped on the single's slick Tamla/Motown-cum-disco backbeat. Bed tracks for the song were recorded at Caribou, a studio on a ranch nine thousand feet up in the Colorado mountains.

King heard the song in Denver several months later while preparing for an important match when John brought a rough demo tape of the song to her dressing room. She was flattered and astounded that the biggest music star in the world had written a song for her. Snapping the tape into a cassette deck, John asked

Elton John performing onstage in November 1995. Twenty-two years before he recorded a musical eulogy for Diana Spencer, John topped the American charts with "Philadelphia Freedom," a tribute to Wimbledon tennis champ Billie Jean King.

Alan Singer/Camapress Photo Service

King to pay special attention to the thudding beat behind the chorus. "Hear the beat? That's you when you get mad on the court," he teased.

"Philadelphia Freedom" was Elton John's third Number One hit in the US in twelve months. But it didn't fare as well back home. Before the advent of MTV in Britain, the BBC1 television show *Top of the Pops* was the main means of exposure for new singles. John was caught in a dispute with the British Musicians' Union which demanded that any song performed on television have its orchestra track specially recorded by British musicians. John argued that the distinctive Philadelphia sound of the tune couldn't be reproduced by British players and as proof, offered a tape from the original American sessions. The Musicians' Union balked at John's proposal, and the singer was prevented from appearing on the hit-making show. As a result, the record stalled at Number Twelve on the British charts.

Since then, the original 45 of "Philadelphia Freedom" has become quite a collectable. As with John's other 1975 Number One "Lucy in the Sky With Diamonds," "Philadelphia Freedom" was released only as a single. Coupled with a rare concert B-side recording of "Whatever Gets You Through the Night" featuring John Lennon, the "Philadelphia Freedom" 45 is a much-sought-after piece of Elton John memorabilia.

Only Women Bleed

Alice Cooper

It's not all fun and games in the studio. It takes a lot of hard work to record an album, but sometimes fun and games is just the diversion a band needs. "We were in the middle of "Only Women Bleed," and we just couldn't get it," said Bob Ezrin, producer of Alice Cooper's megahits of the seventies.

In 1970, Vincent Furnier's dream of being as famous as the Beatles and the Rolling Stones seemed a long way off. "…Tuneless singing, tuneless playing, tuneless tunes…." was one critic's reaction to 1970's *Easy Action*, his band's second album. "A tragic waste of vinyl," said another. Their outrageous live show garnered lots of column inches, but with no hits and no sales, Alice Cooper (as both Furnier and his band were called) seemed to be withering on the vine.

During a stopover in Toronto to play at the Strawberry Fields Festival in April 1970, Cooper's manager Shep Gordon tried to get an audience with producer Jack Richardson. Best known for producing a string of Guess Who hit singles, Richardson ran Nimbus Nine Studios. As the singer recalled in his long-out-of-print biography *Me, Alice*, "It wasn't that Richardson was the only producer in the world, he was the *last* producer who hadn't turned us down." Richardson, used to working with more conventional bands, saw no future in producing an act that seemed to value theatricality over music. Instead, junior producer Bob Ezrin, described by Cooper as "a nineteen-year-old Jewish hippie," was sent to deal with the band.

A meeting was set up, but Ezrin was unprepared for what he would find. "He walked into our hotel room, and I saw panic on his face," recalled Cooper in his memoirs, "as if he had just opened a surprise package and found a box full of maggots." The teenage producer turned the band down, citing a lack of salable sound or talent.

However, he had a change of heart in October 1970 after seeing the band perform live in New York City. "I flipped," said Ezrin in an interview in 1994. "I thought I had seen the future. I was in a club — Max's Kansas City — full of people in spandex and spider eyes, and every song that Alice did, they knew the words to. And they knew all the actions. It was kind of like the *Rocky Horror Picture Show* where you get that cult following, and people show up in the same uniforms and costumes. It was audience-participation rock. Rock theater.

"When I came back to Toronto, I said, 'This isn't music. This is a cultural movement. We have to do this.' Jack said, 'If you think this is so fuckin' good, you do it.' Then the question became how? How was I supposed to do it? They didn't want me. They wanted Jack Richardson. It wasn't that we created a fiction, but what happened was that Jack only accepted the gig if I was going to be on the front line. He didn't really want to have much to do with these weirdos. I had to go off to Pontiac, Michigan by myself and do the preproduction. That's a story. A book in itself."

Ezrin devoted November and December 1970 to working with the band in Michigan, rehearsing ten or twelve hours a day. At first, the *Love It to Death* sessions seemed futile — akin to rearranging the deck chairs on the Titanic — as the band resented Ezrin's newfound creative control. His enthusiasm soon won out, and the band became tighter. Cooper wrote about the process. It was painfully slow as Ezrin pulled the melody out of the songs and formulated riffs, bridges and hooks. "He ironed the songs out note by note, giving them coloring, personality.

> Phil Rizzuto, the official radio announcer for the New York Yankees, provided the blow-by-blow account of Meatloaf's date with Ellen Foley on the 1978 teen classic "Paradise by the Dashboard Light."

"My musical background was far more classical than it was rock — classical and folk — so I brought a different point of view to the thing," says Ezrin. "Mainly because of my lack of comfort with the medium, I required a certain order that they were never able to achieve. We went from complete uncontrolled lunacy to a slightly more ordered, slightly more classical or folk-based musical style. I mean *slightly* more than what they had before, and that was all they needed to be righted by ten degrees."

Most successful from the *Love It to Death* sessions was a tune Ezrin called "I'm Edgy," misunderstanding the lyrics the first time Alice sang them. "I'm Eighteen" became Alice Cooper's first Top Forty single. The success of "I'm Eighteen" led to a record deal with Warner Brothers and one of the most prolific relationships between producer and artist of the seventies. In the next six years, Ezrin and Cooper would pump out a series of theatrical hard-rock records (*Killer, School's Out, Billion Dollar Babies*) that served as sound tracks for Cooper's macabre stage show. Necrophilia, sadomasochism, infanticide — no topic was off limits.

Their final collaboration, 1975's *Welcome to My Nightmare*, brought them full circle back to Nimbus Nine Studios. During one session, Alice was working on the ballad "Only Women Bleed." "He would write lyrics in the studio," said

Ezrin. "It wasn't that there were no lyrics. It's just that they weren't finished. We always had a verse and a chorus of everything. Always. We never went in without knowing what a song was called."

Once the song was finished, Ezrin put the band through the paces learning the tune. Several hours passed, but the band couldn't quite get the spirit of the song that Ezrin wanted. Nerves began to fray. Then Ezrin had an idea. "We had a small circus company in Toronto, a little private circus company [called] Puck's which became Puck's Farm. It was a real Toronto perennial, a hippie perennial. I hired the circus but didn't tell anybody. We were in the middle of a take. Suddenly the door bursts open, and in come midgets and acrobats and a juggler and a magician and people blowing whistles. The funny thing was, [the band] were in the middle of playing "Only Women Bleed" which is a pretty intense ballad, and the door bursts open and in comes the circus. The band took one look and broke into a little circus march without losing a beat. It was really great. They just fell into the spirit of it. The circus went to work.

"However, Alice was sitting there. He was completely poleaxed, sitting in

Canapress Photo Service

Alice Cooper poses onstage with a hatchet, flanked by the Billion Dollar Baby Band. In 1975, while on tour promoting "Only Women Bleed," Cooper tumbled off a stage in Vancouver, breaking six ribs.

his chair saying, 'What the hell is going on?' But they got into the spirit of it. We had a great twenty-minute diversion. It was fabulous — they dropped eggs all over the studio. Everybody laughed, and then they marched right back out again as though nothing had happened. Then I counted it in, and we played the take of 'Only Women Bleed' —the one that made it on the album. It all went without any talking. There was no verbal communication, it just sort of happened. It was a magical moment."

"Only Women Bleed" rose to Number Twelve on the charts in May 1975, but not without a dose of controversy. "It's funny because at first, people thought, of course, that it was about menstruation," Cooper later told Headly Gritter, author of *Rock 'N' Roll Asylum*. Many DJs referred to the song as "Only Women" for fear of offending their listeners. Cooper denied this accusation, calling "Only Women Bleed" a "sympathetic song." "It was kind of a Tennessee Williams kind of way of saying it, you know," Cooper said, explaining the song's feminist bent in Gritter's book. "I thought 'Only Women Bleed' would have been something Tennessee Williams would have said. And I like to honor certain writers, dedicating certain things to them. So I wrote that whole song with Tennessee Williams in mind."

Most critics missed the Williams's connection, but at least one scribe praised its hastily written feminist lyrics. "Alice's nose for what the kids want to hear is as discriminating as it is impervious to moral suasion," wrote Robert Christgau, "so perhaps this means that the more obvious feminist truisms have become conventional wisdom among at least half our adolescents. Encouraging."

Jive Talkin'

The Bee Gees

The early seventies were not kind to the Bee Gees. After a string of Beatlesque pop hits, the trio's career cooled. Reduced to playing cabaret shows, a low point came at the Yorkshire Variety Club performance in front of an audience more interested in drinking than listening to love songs. Atlantic Records' refusal to release their LP *A Kick in the Head Is Worth Eight in the Pants* seemed to be the band's *danse macabre*. It took producer Arif Mardin and a chance remark by Barry Gibb's wife to send them back to the top of the charts.

Mardin brought the Bee Gees (short form for Brothers Gibb) to Criteria Studios in Miami, Florida. Founded in the late 1950s by jazz fanatic Mack Emerman, it became the unofficial recording base of Atlantic Records in the sixties and seventies. With a client base that read like a who's who of popular music — everyone from Abba to Frank Zappa to Count Basie to Neil Young to the Allman Brothers to Placido Domingo have laid down tracks there — it seemed like a natural place to breathe some life into the Bee Gees' faltering career. Giving the band room to work, Mardin left them alone in Miami for a week. He advised them to keep their ears to the ground and listen to what was happening at the local discos. Most importantly, he urged them to write some new songs.

Inspired by the dance music they were hearing in the nightclubs of Miami, they would report to Criteria every day to work on new material. Late one afternoon, driving across the Sunny Isles Bridge on their way to the studio, they crossed some railroad tracks. Chunka-chunka-chunka. As the tires rode over the raised tracks, Barry's wife Linda commented on the noise. "Do you ever listen to the rhythm when we drive across the bridge at night. It's the same every evening. It's our drive talking," she said. Picking up on the rhythm, Barry started to improvise some lyrics. When Robin and Maurice joined in, "Drive Talking" was born.

Refining the song in the studio, "drive" became "jive" (American slang for "bullshit"), and Mardin added fire to the brother's arrangement. Finger-popping bass and swishing high-hat cymbals jostled with the Brothers' Gibb pop falsettos, sweetening the song's disco pulse. The resulting blue-eyed R & B marked a radical change in their sound, moving away from their repertoire of heart-tugging love songs to the slick, radio-friendly sound of 1970s urban dance music. The Bee Gees had reinvented themselves. Now they had to sell "Jive Talkin'."

Atlantic Records knew radio programmers wouldn't care a hoot about a new record from the Bee Gees. In an effort

Rod Stewart recognized that "Do You Think I'm Sexy?" "just pissed everybody off." Coming off a string of critically lauded rock albums, Stewart jumped on the disco bandwagon and rode it all the way to the top of the charts. It wasn't until the song was in the can that Stewart realized that he had unwittingly stolen part of the melody from a Brazilian hit called "Taj Mahal" by Jorge Ben. "I put me hands up and said, 'Sorry mate,'" Stewart told *Mojo* writer Mick Brown in 1995. "And he was okay. He earned a bit of money out of it. I gave my share of the royalties to UNICEF, I felt so guilty about nicking somebody else's song."

to whip up some enthusiasm for the single, Atlantic released the promotional 45 with a plain white label and no artist information. The ploy worked. Given the chance to hear the tune, without the Bee Gees' bias, radio loved the song.

"Jive Talkin'" became a Goliath hit. Released in May 1975, it attacked the charts with hammer and tongs, reaching Number One in August. It was their first Top Five hit since 1971's "How Can You Mend a Broken Heart." Making an impressive comeback, Barry, Robin and Maurice Gibb went on to top the charts seven more times in the 1970s.

Variety Is the Spice of Life: A 1970's Top Five

Convoy: C.W. McCall/*I Write the Songs:* Barry Manilow/*Theme from* Mahogany *(Do You Know Where You're Going to?):* Diana Ross/*Love Roller Coaster:* Ohio Players/*Saturday Night:* Bay City Rollers

In the beginning, there were pop, country and R & B charts. Rarely did they cross over, and all was good. Then came Elvis and rock and roll, and things became muddled. Pop songs hit the R & B charts. Rockabilly appeared on the country charts. Confusion reigned, and a change had to come. In the nineties, niche charts abound — adult-oriented rock, college, dance, new country, urban, alternative. But in the seventies, it was a different scene. Here is the story of one week — the week of January 10, 1976 — that could never be repeated today.

CONVOY: C.W. McCALL -- Number One

There is no C.W. McCall. It is a pseudonym for Omaha native and advertising-agency director Bill Fries. While working at the Bozell and Jacobs Agency, he created the character of C.W. McCall, borrowing the name from a one-armed trucker from Missouri. He was fascinated with truckers and installed a CB radio (a simple version of a police radio) in his jeep to

154   WHO WROTE THE BOOK OF LOVE?

CB LINGO
Bears in the air:
  helicopters
Smokeys: cops
Modulate: talk
Checking out the seat
  covers: on the lookout
  for women drivers with
  short skirts
Keeping my nose between
  the ditches and Smokey
  out of my britches:
  driving safely and
  obeying the speed
  limit

learn the big-rig lingo truckers used. Soon he had a handle, "Rubber Ducky," and an idea. He conceived an ad campaign for the Mertz Baking Company of Iowa featuring a trucker named C.W. McCall who delivered bread to the Old Home Filler-Up an' Keep on A-Truckin' Café. The spots were very popular, earning him a Cleo Award, the ad business's highest honor.

The ads were so popular that Fries was approached by Don Sears, president of Sound Recorders, who suggested spinning off a country single from the commercials. Under the assumed name C.W. McCall, the first single, "Old Home Filler-Up an' Keep on A-Truckin' Café" sold well, reaching Number Forty Five on the country charts. Several more truckin' tunes followed, but it was a traffic jam that inspired his biggest hit. One night, driving on the interstate in his jeep, he found himself last in line in a string of cars and trucks, all communicating with one another via CB. He imagined a convoy of truckers slowly gaining power until they had an army of one thousand trucks. Using CB lingo, he penned "Convoy" which topped both the country and Hot One Hundred charts in 1976.

I WRITE THE SONGS: BARRY MANILOW --
Number Two
Barry Manilow has written many popular songs, but ironically, he didn't pen his 1976 hit "I Write the Songs." That tune was composed by Bruce Johnson, a member of the Beach Boys. Written as a tribute to bandmate and songwriting genius Brian Wilson, "I Write the Songs" had been recorded twice

before Manilow got hold of it. The Captain and Tennille included it on their debut album but didn't release it as a single. Later, David Cassidy scored a Top Twenty hit in Britain with the tune. On a visit to London, label head Clive Davis heard Cassidy's version and decided it would be perfect for Manilow. The Brooklyn, New York-born singer recorded what Johnson declared "the definitive version" of the tune for his 1975 Tryin' to Get the Feeling LP. Manilow's "I Write the Songs" entered the charts at Number Forty-Eight, reaching the Top Five nine weeks later.

THEME FROM MAHOGANY (DO YOU KNOW WHERE YOU'RE GOING TO?): DIANA ROSS -- Number Three

Michael Masser had written several hit songs but had never scored a film. When he was approached by Berry Gordy Jr. to pen the sound track for Diana Ross's upcoming film about the fashion industry, he was nervous about accepting the job. The silver-tongued Berry talked him into taking on the task, and now he had to figure out how to do it. Masser read a book on film scoring but learned little about the actual mechanics of the job. He developed his own system. Renting a Beta video player, a rare thing in 1975, he played a tape of the completed movie with the sound off. He carefully watched the interaction between costars Ross and Billy Dee Williams, noting the depth of emotion in their expressions. After one run through, he rewound the tape and watched it again, this time recording an improvised piano score in sync to the action. "Theme from *Mahogany* (Do You Know Where You're Going To?)" was written using this unusual emotional approach rather than the cerebral technique used by most film songwriters. Nominated for an Academy Award for Best Song, Masser's tune lost out to Keith Carradine's "I'm Easy."

LOVE ROLLER COASTER: OHIO PLAYERS --
Number Four

The Ohio Players liked to keep things spontaneous. From 1968, when they recorded the first of their experimental funk albums, the band never wrote a note of music before they entered the studio. With no preconceived notions of what they were about to record, they preferred to jam and let the music grow organically. The sessions were private (only the band and an engineer were allowed near the studio), and they worked quickly. In an era where most major acts took weeks or months to produce an album, the Ohio Players could pound out a hard-driving funk album in as little as four hours (1971's *Pain*). *Fire* was produced in 1974 in three days, which, for them, was considered quite leisurely. Applying their usual jam technique to the recording of 1975's *Honey*, they rapidly laid down funky bed tracks, adding finishing touches, vocals and effects later. The first single from *Honey*, "Sweet Sticky Thing," broke into the Top Thirty. But it was the extremely danceable "Love Roller Coaster" that went to the top of the charts. Twenty years later, the Red Hot Chili Peppers resurrected the tune, with a remarkably respectful cover, for the sound track of *Beavis and Butthead Do America*.

SATURDAY NIGHT: BAY CITY ROLLERS --
Number Five

Rounding out the Top Five for the week of January 10, 1976 is the only pure pop song on the list. "Saturday Night" was the Bay City Rollers' first hit in North America, although they had enjoyed considerable success in Britain. The Scottish quintet weren't songwriters. Up until 1974, they relied on cover songs like the Gentrys' "Keep On Dancin'" to attract attention. It wasn't until they teamed up with songwriters for hire Bill Martin and Phil Coulter that they began recording new songs and scoring major hits. Martin and Coulter had their finger on the pulse of the teen market, pumping out tunes like "Remember (Sha La La)," "Shang-A-Lang" and "Summerlove Sensation." Their greatest teen pop creation, "Saturday Night," wasn't originally slated to be released as a single, but after several attempts at hitting the charts in North America failed, they took a chance with it. Making their American television debut on *Saturday Night Live With Howard Cosell*, the tartan-clad Scots played the catchy tune and won the hearts of adolescent girls everywhere. Several weeks later in January 1976, "Saturday Night" hit the top of the charts, staying at Number One for one week.

More, More, More

Andrea True Connection

There is an old show-business axiom that says all singers want to act, and all actors want to sing. This has been proven time after time, sometimes with disastrous results (remember William Shatner's *A Transformed Man?*). Others have been more successful. John Travolta capitalized on his early fame as a television sweat hog to record many albums, scoring several hits. Tired of dominating the pop charts, Whitney Houston took a stab at big-screen fame in 1992's *The Bodyguard* and later, *The Bishop's Wife*. But rarely has there been a more unlikely actress turned pop star than Andrea True. The Nashville-born True traded in her porn-queen status for a run at the hit parade. "More, More, More," the disco ode to excess, was a Number Four hit in 1976.

Success came easily for Gregg Diamond. A talented drummer, by his early twenties he had already amassed an impressive résumé, banging the traps for such acts as Sonny & Cher, James Brown and Joey Dee & the Starlighters. Having already made his mark as a sideman, Diamond decided to give up that life, concentrating instead on a career as a songwriter. For months he struggled, running out of money and almost losing his apartment. Rather than resort to playing drums again, he kept writing, working for weeks on one song.

Banging away at a rented piano, he slowly created a tune that he said "reeked of sex." Without lyrics or a title, he corralled some friends and made a demo. In the coming weeks, Diamond played the instrumental for several friends. Then the break he was waiting for came. Someone who had heard the tape told ex-porn star Andrea True about this great demo he was convinced could be a hit. She was infamous for her performances in the X-rated *Every Inch A Lady*, *Deep Throat II* and *The Seduction of Lynn Carter*. Retired from skin flicks, she was living in Jamaica with her wealthy gynecologist boyfriend, hoping to break into the music biz. True called Diamond, offering him a plane ticket to the West Indies, room and board and studio time in exchange for a crack at the tune. At the very least, Diamond thought, this could be a free vacation.

Catching the next flight to Kingston, the drummer and the porn star met for the first time the very next day. She made good on all her promises, including a week's studio time at Federal Records. Diamond spent several days rerecording the instrumental demo, playing most of the instruments himself. On the third day of recording, the doctor paid a visit to the studio. He was growing impatient with the slow process and asked if Diamond really had a song for his girlfriend to sing. Diamond was stuck. He had the melody but no lyrics. "Just give me forty-eight hours, and you'll have your song."

Pressured, he left the studio to pace up and down the beach. The first three words came out of the blue — "More, more, more." Excited, he went to a bar, downing several rum punches. Tipsy from the alcohol, he started writing the tune's verses in a cab ride back to the house. He sang the uncompleted lyrics to the cabbie. Legend has it that the driver was so impressed with the words, he didn't charge Diamond for the ride.

Later that night, he presented his handwritten notes to True. Then he made an awful discovery: True couldn't sing a note, couldn't hold a tune in a bucket. The pair stayed up all night, with a desperate Diamond acting as vocal coach, teaching her the song. The next day, exhausted, Diamond finished the lyrics and headed for the studio.

Getting True to relax in the studio was Diamond's first job. This was her first time in a professional studio, her big shot at pop stardom, and she was nervous. Diamond wanted her to sound sexy, to really sell the song. But her tension showed through in the vocals. Drawing on his experience as a session musician, he tried to help her loosen up. Dimming the lights in the studio, he instructed True to pretend she was on a porno movie set. By the time he got the take he wanted, True had taken his advice to heart, removing her shoes and panties and loosening her blouse, exposing her breasts. With her vocals in the can, True returned to her boyfriend's house, leaving Diamond to finish up loose ends.

He spent the next two days tinkering with the tape, electronically enhancing True's voice, bringing it up to pitch and double-tracking it to add more depth. Satisfied with the result, he returned to New York with the tape under his arm. He shopped it to an executive at Buddah Records who suggested they take it to a disco, slap it on the turntable and see how the crowd responded. As soon as the music started, the dance floor filled up, and Diamond was offered a deal.

"More, More, More" by the Andrea True Connection reached Number Four on the charts in April 1976. A follow-up album, also produced by Diamond, only contained one single — "NY, You Got Me Dancing" — which stalled at Number Twenty-Seven in March 1977. In the age of disposable disco celebrities, Andrea True was a has-been barely one year after her first hit.

Gregg Diamond went on to work with Whitney Houston and Luther Vandross.

Who Are You

The Who

It was late March 1977, and Pete Townsend was having a bad day. A drawn-out dispute with his for-mer managers had sapped the guitarist and rein-forced his feeling that The Who had sold out — that they were driven by money rather than by music. Punk rock had gripped Britain, and the new

Pete Townsend and The Who in full flight in a still from *The Kids Are All Right*, a 1979 rock-umentary. Left to right: John Entwistle (bass), Roger Daltry (vocals), Keith Moon (drums) and Pete Townsend (guitar/vocals).

New World Pictures

Dave Marsh called *Never Mind the Bollocks, Here's the Sex Pistols* "the best example of deliberate vulgarity rock has ever produced." It's surprising, then, to learn that "Pretty Vacant," the LP's second single, was inspired by an Abba song. Pistols' songwriter and bassist Glen Matlock, a closet Abba fan, lifted the guitar riff from Abba's "SOS" as the basis for a nihilistic anthem that was banned from radio in the UK. "(Guitarist) Steve (Jones) toughened it up," said John Lydon in his book *Rotten: No Irish -- No Blacks -- No Dogs*, "because the original guitar line was very sissy."

brood of brazen bands left Pete feeling like a dinosaur, a relic of an older generation. He was thirty-two years old.

Feeling the need to blow off some steam, Townsend met business partner Chris Stamp at a club called the Speakeasy in London's Soho district. The upcoming events would later be used as the basis of the last great Who single of the 1970s.

Described as seedy and salacious, the Speakeasy was a hangout for many of the new bands of the day. That night, Townsend protégés John Otway and Wild Willy Barrett were performing as the guitarist settled at a table. Several quick double whiskeys later, Townsend was on a roll. Becoming physically abusive, he broke glasses and ranted to anyone who would listen. Midway through his drunken rampage, he spotted two punks at the bar. When told that they were members of the Sex Pistols, he wobbled over and confronted them.

After some hostile back and forth, he grabbed one of the punks by the shirt and lifted him off the ground. "Listen Johnny…" he said, thinking he was talking to Pistols' singer Johnny Rotten. It wasn't Rotten but guitarist Steve Jones and drummer Paul Cook who tried to placate Townsend by telling him they were big Who fans. Townsend was flabbergasted. He had considered the Sex Pistols to be the future of rock and roll — a band to take over from where The Who had left off before they, too, prostituted themselves for commercial success. Townsend's own feelings of self-loathing were so strong that he couldn't even accept the praise from Jones and Cook. Repulsed and cursing, Townsend told them he was disappointed with them and left the club.

The events of the night had left Townsend completely drained. A few feet from the club, he collapsed in a heap, passing out cold in a shop doorway. He slept for a time before a London policeman came by and recognized the rock star. Knudging him in the midsection, the cop roused him and made him an offer. "Wake up, Pete. As a special treat, if you can get up and walk away, you can sleep in your own bed tonight." Rather than spend a night in the drunk tank, Townsend pulled himself together, found a subway station and made his way home.

> A song called "No Future" was originally planned as the first single from *Never Mind the Bollocks, Here's the Sex Pistols*. At the last minute, manager Malcolm McLaren switched the title to the more provocative "God Save the Queen" to inflame the press during Queen Elizabeth's Silver Jubilee.

The next day, he woke up and wrote "Who Are You," a diary-style account of the previous night. The song opens with Pete waking up in the Soho doorway and goes on to trace the surreal events of the evening. The single was well received, with *Rolling Stone* critic John Swenson calling it "...a pounding statement of identity lost and found." Sales pushed it to Number Fourteen on the *Billboard* charts.

For The Who and their fans, the 45's success was dulled by the death of drummer Keith Moon from an overdose of Heminevrin on September 7, 1978, just weeks after the song entered the charts. Ironically, on the LP cover of *Who Are You*, Moon is seated in a chair inscribed "Not to be taken away."

My Sharona

The Knack

In 1979, The Knack resuscitated one of the sacrosanct rock-and-roll traditions of the sixties. Following in the footsteps of "Mony Mony," "Bony Maronie" and "Hang On Sloopy," "My Sharona" took an uncommon female-sounding name, turning it into a platinum-selling single.

When Doug Feiger met the teenage Sharona Alperin, he was an unknown musician with a Beatles' fixation. Despite his band's Southern Californian roots, he modeled their look and sound after the groups of his youth — the Mersey Beat combos with their matching suits and short hook-laden pop songs. Even his band's name was nicked from a British cult movie — 1965's *The Knack and How to Get It*, directed by Richard Lester.

The Mersey Beat posturing paid off. The Knack were hotter than a bandit's pistol, finding themselves in the center of a record-company bidding war, with Capitol (the Beatles' US record label) winning a contract with the young band. The resulting debut album, *Get the Knack*, took off like a rocket, earning a gold record only thirteen days after its release. But it was "My Sharona" that earned them a place in the pop-culture pantheon.

With its edgy, power-chord hook and howled lyrics, "My Sharona" was an ode to teenage sexual frustration. "I had met this girl, Sharona, and fell deeply in love with her," Feiger told *Goldmine*'s Jeff Tamarkin. "She was inspirational and moved me on a very basic level."

Using a riff that guitarist Berton Averre had been playing around with for some time, Feiger molded lyrics that expressed his feelings for Sharona, bending the words to fit around the hiccuping rhythm. The tune came together in an afternoon and was recorded very quickly, virtually live in the studio, with very few overdubs. Producer Mike Chapman says the first time he heard The Knack rehearse the tune, "I knew it was a Number One two bars into the song."

In the Name of Love: Billy Joel composed the elegant ballad "Just the Way You Are" as a birthday present for his then-wife/manager Elizabeth. Joel dropped the song from his repertoire when he married Christie Brinkley. David Bowie's wife Angela was the object of affection in the Jagger/Richards's tune "Angie," a Number One for the Rolling Stones in 1973.

Even as "My Sharona" was climbing the charts, the inevitable backlash began. Critics attacked the risqué lyrics of "My Sharona" and its follow-up "Good Girls Don't," with one writer commenting, if this is how they felt about girls when they were unknowns, "I shudder to think how they are reacting to groupies." One San Francisco artist started the Knuke The Knack movement, while a popular T-shirt of the time gave the well-known *Jaws* tag line a rock-and-roll spin. Embossed over a likeness of The Knack was the slogan, "Just when you thought it was safe to listen to the radio."

Today, Feiger's muse Sharona Alperin has a flourishing residential real estate business in Los Angeles. "When they hear my name, people tell me where they first heard the song and what it means to them," she told writer Judd Justice in 1996. "People say things like, 'You're part of the history of

> Weird Al Yankovic was inspired to write "My Bologna," his 1983 take-off on The Knack's "My Sharona," by the cafeteria food at Cal Poly San Luis Obispo. In 1984, he followed up the success of "My Bologna" with another food tune, "Eat It."

pop culture.' Frankly, I'm not interested in my history. It was fun traveling first class around the world with The Knack, but it was all over before I was twenty-one. Now, when some people hear my name, they say, 'Oh, the real estate agent.' That's my turn-on."

With only limited success after "My Sharona," The Knack fizzled in 1982. A brief reunion in 1991 produced the lackluster *Serious Fun*, after which the band faded completely from view. The Knack may have crashed and burned, but their biggest hit stills garners plenty of play on radio and was featured on the best-selling sound track for the 1994 Generation X romantic comedy *Reality Bites*. Quentin Tarantino was refused permission to use "My Sharona" in *Pulp Fiction* because of the band's apprehension with the film's violent content.

I Don't Like Mondays

Boomtown Rats

A glimpse at a newsroom ticker-tape machine gave rock journalist turned Boomtown Rats singer Bob Geldof the idea for a song based on a disturbing true-life story of an American girl's shooting spree. Geldof read the printout as a reporter asked why she had opened fire. "I don't like Mondays," the high-school sniper replied. Geldof took this line from the newswire as the starting point for a new-wave song that became a classic.

The Boomtown Rats were one of the first acts to emerge from the new-wave scene of 1977, scoring Top Twenty UK hits from their first two albums. Despite their R & B leanings, the band was lumped in with the punk scene and were briefly banned in their home country of Ireland. It wasn't until their third album, *The Fine Art of Surfacing* (1979), that they earned their biggest hit — the superb "I Don't Like Mondays."

In January 1979, Geldof and Rats' piano man Johnny Fingers undertook a grueling radio-only promo tour, visiting thirty-two American cities in thirty-three days. Geldof was in Atlanta, Georgia doing an interview at a college radio station. He was pumping the Rats' latest single "Rat Trap," a Top Ten hit in England but one that had failed to generate

A television game show inspired Peter Gabriel to write an alternative rock-radio staple. The European game show pitted contestants from different parts of the world in a competition for big prizes. "Games Without Frontiers" was Gabriel's reaction to the show. *Rolling Stone* called the tune a "jaunty examination of the similarities between childhood play and adult warfare."

much interest in North America. During a break in the interview, the newsroom's telex machine alarm went off. What Geldof read coming off the wire overwhelmed him.

Brenda Spencer, a young Californian girl, had woken up, loaded a gun her father had allegedly given her for Christmas, leaned out her bedroom window and began taking potshots at the school yard across the street from her house. She only stopped long enough to take a call from a local reporter. "Why are you doing this?" he asked. "Something to do," she replied. "I don't like Mondays, and this livens up the day."

This was a live report. As the singer sat there in the radio booth answering questions, Spencer had returned to her window and fired off several more rounds. The final toll: the school janitor and principal shot dead and eight school kids wounded.

After the interview, Geldof returned to his hotel room and gathered all his journalistic gifts to turn a news story into a song. Deciding not to mention Spencer by name for fear of turning her into a heroine, he kept the details ambiguous. Geldof crafted the lyrics to tell a story about psychosis, not Brenda Spencer's life story. As he sat alone in his hotel room running over the events of the day, he wrote "I Don't Like Mondays" on an acoustic guitar with a soft syncopated rhythm.

"I tried to picture the girl," recalled Geldof in *Is That It?*, a memoir published in 1986. "I tried to visualize the scene: the police captains, the bullhorns, the playground, the parents. The girl must be some sort of automaton. And I wrote, 'The silicon chip inside her head gets switched to overload.' And, of course, why was she doing it? 'Tell me why?' Maybe she's right. Maybe there is absolutely no reason. But it seems the Californian ethos didn't allow for reasons and logic for doing anything. They just did it."

Coincidently, the song made its debut in front of a live audience four months later on a Monday night in San Diego, California — Brenda Spencer's hometown. "I Don't Like Mondays" was an enormous hit in Europe. It topped the *New Musical Express* charts for a solid month in August 1979 and was voted Single of the Year at the British Pop and Rock Awards. It didn't fare as well in the US, only reaching Number Sixty, partly because Columbia Records, fearful of a lawsuit from Spencer's parents, withdrew the record one week after its release.

The song, however, did have one major fan in the United States. From her jail cell, Brenda Spencer remarked that although she didn't like the Boomtown Rats, she approved of the song because it made her feel famous.

Bob Geldof was once described as "a Jagger for the New Depression." "The Rats are the band I sing with," said Geldof in 1978. "It's a job. I don't consider myself to be a big deal. But rock and roll, along with TV and the movies, is a great twentieth-century art form."

Fred Chartrand/Canapress Photo Service

EIGHTIES

Crazy Little Thing Called Love

Queen

Queen's best-known song is "Bohemian Rhapsody," a marvel of studio technology that took seven twelve-hour days to record. It was Number One in Britain in 1975 for a record-breaking nine weeks. In America, it only managed Number Nine. The band would have to wait five years to score their first US chart topper. "Crazy Little Thing Called Love" was Number One for four weeks starting February 23, 1980.

The late Freddie Mercury (real name, Fred Bulsara) was a man of eclectic tastes. Once asked in an interview who his two main musical influences were, he shot back with Jimi Hendrix and Liza Minnelli. Given those mentors, it's not surprising that Queen's music ranged from the glam-rock riffing of *Sheer Heart Attack* to the operatic excesses of *A Night at the Opera* to the jock rock of "We Are the Champions." A musical sponge, Mercury soaked up ideas, spitting them out in a series of irresistibly catchy and kitschy singles. "Killer Queen," "Bohemian Rhapsody," "You're My Best Friend," "Somebody to Love," "We Are the Champions" and "Bicycle Race" all made it to the *Billboard* Top Thirty. In 1980, Queen were at the top of their game, riding high with two back-to-back Number Ones from an album appropriately called *The Game*.

Bertie Higgins's 1982 hit "Key Largo" was inspired by a 1948 Humphrey Bogart/Lauren Bacall film. A gangster story set in Key West, Florida, *Key Largo* was directed by John Houston. Higgins and his girlfriend watched the movie on television late one night. Several weeks later, she ended the relationship. He penned the tune to win her back. It worked. They got married soon after the song came out.

Mercury was on tour with Queen when he got the notion for "Crazy Little Thing Called Love," an ersatz rockabilly tune. Lolling in the bathtub in his suite at the Munich Hilton, he came up with a melody line that didn't sound like anything else the band had ever recorded. Leaping from the tub, he reached for his guitar and worked out the chords to the song. He quickly scrawled some lyrics and made a crude demo on a portable tape recorder. The next day, he introduced the song to the band who were eager to test their rockabilly chops.

Rather than record at their private studio in Montreaux with their customary producer Roy Thomas Baker, the band decided on the more-exciting atmosphere of Munich to cut their next record. Employing German producer Mack, they set out to cut "Crazy Little Thing Called Love." Unlike the labored multitracked productions of their past records, "Crazy Little Thing Called Love" was committed to tape after only three run throughs by the band. The session was kept loose and relaxed, and for the first time in the recording studio, Mercury felt comfortable enough to play rhythm guitar on a track. The resulting tune, says Mercury, sounds very much like the bathroom version. "It's not typical of my work," he told Fred Bronson, author of *The Billboard Book of Number One Hits*, "but that's because nothing is typical of my work."

Released as a single in Britain, "Crazy Little Thing Called Love" rose to the Number Two spot, but that success wasn't enough to convince Elektra Records to ship it to the United States. It had been two years since Queen had scored a Top

Ten hit in the US, and the label feared that this lightweight ditty wouldn't charm the American fans who were used to a harder, more operatic approach from the band. They changed their minds when American disc jockeys began playing imported copies of the song to great reaction. "Crazy Little Thing Called Love" hit the charts in December 1979, rising to the top spot just nine weeks later and sitting there for four weeks.

That success was soon followed by the discofied "Another One Bites the Dust," the second single from *The Game*. Written by bassist John Deacon, the dance song was a favorite of Michael Jackson who urged the band to release it as a single. Like its predecessor, "Another One Bites the Dust" also conquered the hit parade, lounging at Number One for three weeks.

In terms of Queen's success on the American pop charts, 1980 represented their grandest moment. They placed three more singles ("Under Pressure" with David Bowie, "Body Language" and "Radio Ga-Ga") in the lower regions of the Top Thirty in the next four years before the hits dried up in 1984. Their best work behind them, the band's prolific career was tragically cut short on November 24, 1991 when Freddie Mercury succumbed to AIDS.

In 1985, Bronson asked Mercury about his feelings toward "Crazy Little Thing Called Love." "I love it now as I did then," he replied, "but it's easy to love the thing that brings you money."

> "Uptown Girl," Billy Joel's 1983 single, was written for supermodel Christie Brinkley. They met after the accidental death of Brinkley's boyfriend Oliver Chandon, heir to the Chandon Champagne estate. Joel wooed her with the song, and the two were soon married.

Whip It/ Satisfaction/ Jocko Homo

Devo

Herky-jerky. The thinking man's Kiss. Unorthodox. Comical. Catchy. All these terms described Devo, the five self-described "spud boys" from Akron, Ohio, who burst on the new-wave scene in 1978. Driven by a desire to strip away modern music of its excesses, they created a robotic, postmodern sound that de-evolved rock and roll to its barest roots. "The music that was coming out then was concert rock and disco," said Devo cofounder Mark Mothersbaugh. "Concert rock was just stupid, bloated and overblown. It was the epitome of what America was about. (We are conspicuous consumers and proud of it.) Then there was disco music which was kind of like a beautiful woman with no brain.

"The music we were writing at that time was like the Flintstones meet the Jetsons. It was really much more influenced by Captain Beefheart, M.C. Escher and Muddy Waters. We really respected Andy Warhol and the pop-art movement and the concept that an artist — that an idea and a concept — was bigger than the specific media you worked in."

This sensibility led to a dozen musically radical records that remain as humorous as they are adventurous. Starting with their biggest hit, here are the stories behind three of Devo's best-known songs.

WHIP IT

Devo fooled everyone with the release of "Whip It" in 1980. On the surface, the single appears to glamorize sado-masochism and masturbation, two subjects near and dear to the heart of every red-blooded North American — just ask Jerry Springer. This misconception propelled the danceable tune to the Top Twenty. The provocative double entendre of the line "Whip it good!" drew the ire of church groups, with one preacher railing against them for "abandoning God's principles governing sex." Actually, the song was written with a higher purpose in mind.

"We thought of 'Whip It' as people pulling together and whipping a problem," said Mothersbaugh. It may be the highest charting self-help song ever, having reached Number Fourteen in November 1980.

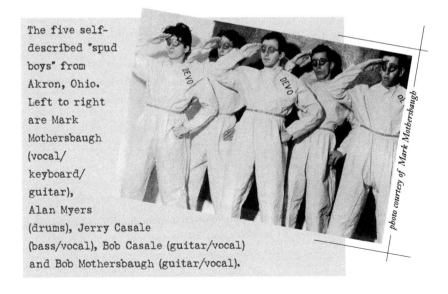

The five self-described "spud boys" from Akron, Ohio. Left to right are Mark Mothersbaugh (vocal/keyboard/guitar), Alan Myers (drums), Jerry Casale (bass/vocal), Bob Casale (guitar/vocal) and Bob Mothersbaugh (guitar/vocal).

photo courtesy of Mark Mothersbaugh

SATISFACTION

Devo's debut, 1978's long player *Q: Are We Not Men? A: We Are Devo*, led the listener down a path less traveled, smashing into a postmodern wall. A robotic cover of the Rolling Stones' chestnut "Satisfaction" deconstructs the song to the point of unrecognizability, stripping the sixties' classic of its humanist veneer and rendering it to its barest form. "It was a song that was important to us because when we would come out and play in the early days in Ohio, we just got people pissed off," said Mothersbaugh. "They would want to get in fist fights with us. People were trying to figure out what the fuck we were. What we were doing with our music. It was the cover songs that actually helped give people a handle as to what we were about and what our music was about. They could say, 'Oh, here's a sixties' classic that has been ingested, processed and regurgitated a decade later."

Mothersbaugh explained the tune's genesis. "It was probably around 1975 or 1976, and we were living in Akron, Ohio. A friend of mine owned a garage behind a car wash. We used to have to drive through the car wash every day to go to rehearsal. The place

photo courtesy of Mark Mothersbaugh

This rare illustration from a 1920s' religious tract titled "Jocko-Homo Heavenbound" partially inspired Devo leader Mark Mothersbaugh to write one of his most famous songs.

was cold. It wasn't heated. It wasn't set up for humans to actually spend any time there other than to dump shit — it was a storage unit or something.

"We were all standing around in full winter clothes — probably snow pants and mittens. [Guitarist] Bob Cassale started playing the riff that was actually the germination of the song. That little Persian goose-step riff. We were just kind of cracking up. Just the fact that we were freezing to death, and you could see your breath in front of you, had a lot to do with the way the song sounded and came out. I remember when we were playing it without lyrics on it, it felt like a slinky going down steps before it had form. So we kind of liked that. [Bassist] Jerry [Cassale] started singing "Paint It Black" to it. It didn't really work, but it made us laugh. Then I started singing "Satisfaction," and it made everybody laugh. The pieces fit together nicely and neatly."

Devo's "Satisfaction" was too odd to break the Top Forty in North America but fared well in Britain where musical eccentrics are embraced with open arms. The *New Musical Express* raved about it, calling it one of the "most original singles of the year."

JOCKO HOMO

Four decades after its release, a horror movie starring Charles Laughton inspired a classic new-wave song. *The Island of Lost Souls* is the source of the line "Are we not men?," made famous by Devo in 1978's "Jocko Homo." "Fucking amazing movie," said Mothersbaugh.

The idea for the song had occurred to Mothersbaugh several years before after watching the late, late show on television. "I had a little hand-held tape recorder that I would use to tape off my little black-and-white eleven-inch TV," he said. "We didn't have video recorders in 1972, so in my apartment, I would tape the sound tracks to movies I liked. *Island of Lost Souls* was one that just kind of hit at the right time.

"Charles Laughton is the mad scientist who is trying to evolve these subhumans, these pathetic animals into a superior life form. Instead, he is creating these hideous creatures — as they describe themselves, 'Not human. Not man. Not animal. Things.' They say it in this wailing pathetic voice. He controls them with a whip. He'd stand on top of the rock at their meeting place and snap it, and go, 'What is the law?' They'd all go, 'Not to walk on all fours. Are we not men? Not to spill blood. Are we not men?'"

The 1933 movie climaxes in a beautifully shot scene as the subhuman creations run through the jungle, casting eerie shadows against the House of Pain. "[They] don't want to go to the House of Pain," continued Mothersbaugh, "which is [Laughton's] laboratory where he is doing these experiments that are not working out the way he was hoping they would. When the shadows went by, I just remember going 'Holy shit' because it reminded me of the factories in downtown Akron just a couple of blocks from where I lived. The old factories that were built during the industrial revolution. I just remember thinking, 'I know all these people.' I watched all the shadows go by. 'I live here. I live on the Island of Lost Souls. I work at the House of Pain.' That was obviously the chorus and the rallying theme behind the song. But the lyrics were inspired by a pamphlet called Jocko-Homo Heavenbound. Some reverend in Ohio wrote it."

"Jocko Homo" was not released as a single but nevertheless, remains one of Devo's best-known tunes.

More influential than their record sales would indicate, the band was an electronic avant-garde force whose influence spreads into the nineties. Devo fans include Nirvana (they covered "Turnaround," a 1978 Devo tune on 1992's *Incesticide*), Nine Inch Nails and even heavy metallists Metallica. "I think what we represented was a different flavor," said Mothersbaugh on Devo's legacy. "We expanded horizons in a conceptual way."

Take Off

Bob and Doug McKenzie

G'day, eh? Years before rock-video hucksters Beavis and Butthead hit the airwaves, another television duo pierced the screen, making the leap from TV to the Top Twenty. Bob and Doug McKenzie, two eh-holes from the Great White North, became one-hit wonders in 1982 with the novelty tune "Take Off."

The beer-swilling, tuque-wearing hosers Bob and Doug McKenzie were the creation of Rick Moranis and Dave Thomas, members of the SCTV comedy troop. The characters came about as the result of the Canadian Broadcasting Corporation's request to SCTV's producers for two minutes on each show of Cancon — distinctive Canadian programming. Moranis and Thomas balked at the thought, jokingly suggesting that maybe two parka-clad hosers sitting in front of a map of Canada might meet the CBC's standards for Canadian content. "Great idea," said the producer. "Do you think we could get a Mountie in there somewhere?"

Soon after, Rick and Dave (as Bob and Doug McKenzie) were in front of the camera, stubby beer bottles in hand, the smell of back bacon filling the studio. The first day, they improvised fifteen two-minute Great White North spots, six of which were deemed suitable for air. The spots were cheap to produce (they had the production values of a cable access show), but above all, they were funny, introducing the typical Canadian phrases "hosehead" and "take off, eh?" to SCTV's North American audience.

The duo had no idea how popular Bob and Doug were becoming until they received a call from the Saskatchewan Roughriders football club, asking them to perform with the team's cheerleaders. Deplaning in Saskatchewan was a scene they will never forget. Hundreds of Bob and Doug fans showed up in plaid shirts and tuques to cheer on the comedians. After that successful appearance, the fan mail began pouring in, with requests for Bob and Doug posters and autographed pictures. As fast as you could say, "Coo roo coo coo, coo coo coo coo," the hosers — starting out as a Cancon filler for the show — became national icons and pop-culture phenomena.

photo courtesy of Anthem Records

Anthem Records, an independent Toronto company, approached Thomas and Moranis with the idea of doing a comedy album to cash in on the wave of McKenziemania. In the studio, sitting in front of a re-creation of the set from the television show, the two comedians drank

The original hosers Bob and Doug McKenzie, played by Rick Moranis and Dave Thomas, took tuques, flannel shirts and stubby beer bottles to the Top Twenty in 1982.

beer and improvised four hours worth of material. The rough tape was edited down to album length, and while it was funny, something was missing. Moranis, who had been a Toronto DJ before turning to acting, felt the record would never get Top Forty airplay without a hit single. They needed a song.

Toronto song writers Carey Crawford and Jonathan Goldsmith were hired to write the music. Listening to a demo of the tape, Crawford, Goldsmith, Moranis and Thomas brainstormed lyrical ideas, coming up with "Take Off." Rush lead singer Geddy Lee, who had attended elementary school with Moranis, added his hoser-rock credentials to the project.

> Remember the 1982 novelty hit "Pac-Man Fever" by (Jerry) Buckner & (Gary) Garcia? Listen carefully to the Pac-Man gobbling sound effect. It was recorded directly from a video machine at a delicatessen -- in the background you can hear a customer ordering lunch.

Produced for just a few thousand dollars, Bob and Doug McKenzie's *Great White North* album eventually sold 350,000 copies in Canada and 650,000 units in the US where it was distributed by PolyGram. Released at the height of hoser-mania, "Take Off" hit Number One in Canada and reached Number Nine on the *Billboard* charts in March 1982. Moranis and Thomas followed the record's success with a book and a full-length movie — 1983's *Strange Brew*.

Bob and Doug's popularity approached Beatlesque proportions. Moranis and Thomas were mobbed on the streets, and a hoser parade organized in Toronto by the record company drew hundreds of cars, stopping traffic from one end of the city to the other. "Oh, my God. This is embarrassing," Thomas thought at the time, with typical Canadian reserve.

The success of the hosers ultimately overwhelmed the show that introduced them to the world, opening up opportunities for Moranis and Thomas outside the confines of SCTV. Both left the show. Moranis parleyed the *Great White*

The 1981 Joe Dolce hit "Shaddap Your Face" was a huge worldwide hit, spawning dozens of cover versions. The novelty tune has been recorded in Japanese, Chinese, Greek and Hungarian. Even Brit rockers EMF (remember "Unbelievable" in 1991?) waxed a thrash rendering of the song.

North's success into a string of appearances in money-making movies (*Ghostbusters; Honey, I Shrunk the Kids;* and *Little Shop of Horrors*), while Thomas has remained a constant presence on television, hosting his own syndicated series and starring on *Grace Under Fire*.

Burning Down the House

Talking Heads

Talking Heads are regarded as one of the most vital bands to emerge from New York's new-wave scene. Noted for their musical innovation and button-down shirts, they proved to their new-wave peers that it *was* hip to be square. Talking Heads scored their biggest hit with "Burning Down the House," a funk jam from the 1983 long player *Speaking in Tongues*.

Scottish-born David Byrne met drummer Chris Franz and bassist Tina Weymouth at the Rhode Island School of Design in 1970. Befitting their art-school background, Franz and Byrne performed in a band called the Artistics. After graduation, the trio moved to Manhattan, renting a cramped loft on Chrystie Street that doubled as a rehearsal hall for their new and as yet untitled band.

They had a list of possible band names taped to the wall of their loft. Visitors were invited to add their suggestions to the roll. Naming the band was a time-consuming process since the art-school grads were searching for a moniker that didn't denote any specific kind of music. Serious contenders were emblazoned on drummer Chris Franz's kick drum. The Vogue Dots? Rejected. Too new wave. The Tunnel Tones? Nope. The World of Love? All spurned.

Marvin Gaye's 1985 comeback single "Sexual Healing" was inspired by a conversation with biographer David Ritz. On a visit to Gaye's apartment, he discovered a cache of pornographic books and magazines. Disgusted, he suggested Gaye needed some "sexual healing." The singer was inspired by the phrase, quickly jotting down a set of lyrics. He added his words to an old reggae track that had been kicking around his home studio for months, creating the song that would put his career back on track and earn two Grammy awards. Ritz was given a cowriter's credit on the tune.

It took a visit from Wayne Zieve, a fellow RISD grad, to name the group. Leafing through *TV Guide*, he came across the term "talking head" — TV jargon for a head-and-shoulders shot of a news commentator. "...a talking-heads shot was to be distinguished from its opposite cousin, action footage, by the fact that it was 'all content, no action,'" said Weymouth in Adam Dolgins's book *Rock Names*. The band had finally found a name to match their musical philosophy. Franz rushed out and bought a red shirt, adding the band's new name in silver letters. Wearing the shirt on Bleeker Street one day, a man approached him. "Is that the name of a band? That is a terrible name." The incident made the band laugh, so Talking Heads it was.

Once named, they began playing in public. Their first gigs were at CBGB on the Bowery. *The Penguin Guide to New York* described the bar as "the heart of the city's punk-rock movement" in the late 1970s, adding "it's the archetypal dive — dark, worn, graffitied and odorous of beer." Club owner Hilly Kristal agreed. "It has been pretty accurately described as long and dungeon-like," he said.

Kristal remembers the first Talking Heads gig when they opened for the Ramones. "There were three of them then," he says, as Jerry Harrison didn't join the band until 1976. "I think they were probably the most disciplined group. They really worked. They practiced constantly until they got a feeling of where they wanted to go musically. They got acceptance very quickly."

So quickly, in fact, that they became one of the first bands of the CBGB crew to sign a deal with a major record label. They released ten albums for Sire Records over the next eleven years, placing three songs on the *Billboard* Top Forty, including "Burning Down the House."

The song started as a funk jam in the group's rehearsal space. Chris Franz, who had recently attended a Parliament-Funkadelic concert at Madison Square Garden, was hyped on the hard-kicking funk sound of the group. To paraphrase one of P-Funk's best-known tunes, they "tore the roof off that sucker."

Still pumped from the concert, Franz led the Heads in a hard-driving, yet upbeat, jam. Talking Heads had recently come off a world tour where they had been joined by R & B and funk side players like Bernie Worrell on keyboard and

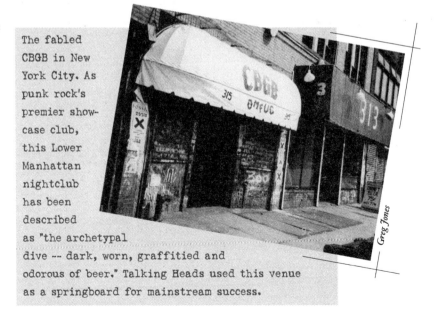

The fabled CBGB in New York City. As punk rock's premier showcase club, this Lower Manhattan nightclub has been described as "the archetypal dive -- dark, worn, graffitied and odorous of beer." Talking Heads used this venue as a springboard for mainstream success.

Greg Jones

Busta Jones on bass. That experience honed the group's funk chops, and Franz knew how hard the band could play. Pushing them to really let loose, he yelled "Burn down the house," a P-Funk crowd chant. Singer Byrne liked the sound of the chant, changing the line to "Burning down the house," for the finished version of the song. Layering an urgent bass-guitar line against quickly paced drumbeats, Talking Heads produced a prime slice of eighties' blue-eyed funk.

The energetic song broke into the Top Ten, partially due to an innovative video that garnered heavy rotation on MTV. Expanding on the song's enigmatic themes of anxiety and self-denial, Bryne crafted a visually unique video for his band's biggest hit. Shot in Union City, New Jersey, the clip featured surreal images of Byrne's face alternated with flames projected against the side of a house, intercut with performance footage.

"I guess it was a good title," Franz told *Rolling Stone*, "because I heard it on classic-rock radio twice today.... Hey, it was a classic title.... What we really wanted to do was rock the house."

Maniac

Michael Sembello

Michael Sembello was a Grammy award-winning session musician before he penned a tune about a mass murderer that hit the top of the charts. "Maniac," a cut from the multiplatinum *Flashdance* sound track, topped the *Billboard* charts for two weeks in 1983.

After a seven-year stint as Stevie Wonder's guitarist, Michael Sembello was looking to expand his horizons. Working as a sideman was a shadowy existence. Life on the edge of the spotlight, while lucrative, wasn't enough. He wanted to write and perform his own music — to take center stage. In 1982, he had written "Mirror Mirror" for the Pointer Sisters. To his surprise, they turned it down, calling it a "hokey nursery rhyme." He believed in the tune, using his connections to get it released. Diana Ross heard it and turned it into a Top Ten hit, convincing Sembello he had what it took to write and perform hit songs.

One night in late 1982, Sembello and his writing partner Dennis Matosky took a break from the studio to watch a movie. Horror aficionados both, they decided on *The Texas Chain Saw Massacre*, the ultimate slasher flick. It's a grisly account of a circle of friends in the Texas desert terrorized by a family who manufacture and eat luncheon meats made of human flesh. Critics hated this movie. Panned for excessive violence, they noted the "rib-tickling dialogue" and "bloody special effects that are disgusting rather than frightening." According to Harry and Michael Medved, authors of *The Golden Turkey Awards: The Worst Achievements in Hollywood History*, the low-budget film is most notable as one of the worst films ever made. Others, however, consider the film to be a classic of the genre.

Nonetheless, it inspired the two songwriters to head back to the studio to create a song based on the theme of the movie. Once in the studio, Sembello crafted a song about a homicidal maniac who takes pleasure in dismembering people. Playing with unusual time signatures, Sembello thought the tune might fit on the sound track for an upcoming slasher flick. Committing the song to tape, it was filed away on a shelf in the studio.

Several weeks later, producer Phil Ramone approached Sembello to submit some material for a movie sound track he was working on. The film was *Flashdance*, the unlikely story of Alex (played by Jennifer Beals), ironworker by day and exotic dancer by night, with aspirations of one day joining the Pittsburgh Ballet. Sembello agreed to take on the project and worked up some musical ideas in his home studio.

Asking his wife (Cruz Baca, a former backup singer for Sergio Mendez) for help, she grabbed a tape from the shelf, dubbed the new material and couriered it to Ramone at Paramount. By the end of the week, Paramount called, raving about one of the songs on the demo tape. It was a perfect fit for one of the dance sequences in the film, and they were prepared to make an offer. As the songs on the demo were untitled, Sembello asked the executive to give him some details on the song. "It's the one at the end of the tape about the maniac," was the reply.

Sembello was dumbfounded. He hadn't intended to send

"Maniac" to Paramount. Sembello soon figured out that Baca had used the old "Maniac" tape to dub the new material without realizing it was at the end of the cassette. It was a happy accident, and the tune (with certain lyrical changes) was used in one of *Flashdance*'s elaborately choreographed dance scenes.

Flashdance became a national sensation, earning millions of dollars at the box office. From a pop-culture perspective, the film had more than just a monetary impact. Spawning the off-the-shoulder oversize T-shirt look, *Flashdance* changed the way many women dressed (at least in 1984). And if imitation is the sincerest form of flattery, it also inspired at least two porno movies: *Fleshdance* and *Flashpants*. More importantly, for Sembello, the song earned him an Oscar nomination for Best Song and a Grammy nomination for Best New Song of the Year. He walked away empty-handed in those categories, although he did share a Grammy with other artists on the *Flashdance* sound track for the Best Album of Original Score for a Motion Picture.

Baca laughs when she notes that her husband isn't much of a dancer, but, ironically, it was a dance song that propelled him to the top of the charts and gave him the taste of fame he craved.

Billie Jean

Michael Jackson

An emotionally disturbed fan inspired Michael Jackson to write the song that went to Number One, earned a Grammy for Song of the Year and broke the color bar on MTV.

"Billie Jean" was the single that launched 1983's *Thriller* into platinum orbit.

The letters started arriving in 1981. Jackson received hundreds of fan letters a week — some intimate, others winsome — but these were different. A teenage woman wrote dozens of notes to Jackson, enclosing pictures of a baby she claimed he had sired. In the dispatches, she wrote of her love for the singer and how happy they could be raising their love child if only he would respond to her. At first, Jackson ignored the letters, but as they began to pile up, he realized how beset this mystery woman was. In one letter, she noted some physical resemblance between the singer and the child and angrily wondered how the former child star could ignore his only heir.

As the months passed, the language in the letters became more urgent, more disturbed, and Jackson became concerned for his safety. Ever since John Lennon's fatal run-in with Mark David Chapman, obsessed fans were treated as a menace by musicians.

Her last message to Jackson came packaged neatly in a box. Inside was a photo of the woman, a weapon and a note begging Jackson to use the weapon to kill himself at a certain date and time. She would do the same, right after she killed her baby. In the next life, maybe they could all be together, she wrote.

Jackson's concern turned to outright fear with the arrival of that final parcel. He had nightmares about the woman showing up at his home, trying to fulfill her bizarre suicide pact. He framed her picture, placing it on a coffee table so he could study her face and never forget it. Copies of the photo were turned over to his security people in case the woman showed up at the front gates of his home.

Although Jackson never met this crazed fan (she was sent to an insane asylum), he did use the experience as the basis for "Billie Jean." In the lyrics, Jackson didn't refer to the girl or the incident specifically for fear of inspiring more harassing mail from troubled fans. Instead, he turned the story into a generalized tale about false allegations, hearsay and paternity-suit paranoia.

The lyrical images conjured up a very real picture for Jackson. So intense was his feeling for "Billie Jean" that he was able to record the tune's remarkable vocal in just one take. "His voice quivers and shakes; at times, he's singing so hard he can barely spit out the long conversational lines," wrote Dave Marsh in *The Heart of Rock & Soul: The 1001 Greatest Singles Ever Made*.

Ironically, the song that turned Michael Jackson into a megastar almost wasn't included on *Thriller*. Producer Quincy Jones didn't think the song was strong enough for an album cut, let alone a single. In *Michael Jackson: The Madness and the Magic*, J. Randy Taraborrelli writes that the singer "was extremely angry about this and still has not forgiven Quincy for questioning his judgment."

Jackson and Jones also differed over the tune's title.

Quincy felt people might assume Jackson was singing about tennis pro Billie Jean King and wanted the title changed to "Not My Lover." Once again, Jackson disagreed, but not before consulting sister LaToya who, in a moment of psychic clarity, advised him to stick with the original title.

Pumped from his victory over Quincy Jones, Jackson took on an even bigger challenge: MTV. In its formative years, the successful twenty-four-hour music station had a strict "it's gotta be rock and roll" policy, meaning that very few videos by artists of color were ever aired. In MTV's first year and a half of production, less than 3 percent (twenty-five of 750) of all videos shown featured black performers. The music policy was so restrictive that video director Bob Giraldi called MTV "a bunch of racist bastards, pure and simple." When "Billie Jean" was first submitted to the network, it was rejected until CBS allegedly threatened to pull all their videos. Bowing to corporate pressure, MTV began running "Billie Jean" in heavy rotation on March 2, 1983. Michael Jackson had broken MTV's color bar, clearing the way for other African-American acts.

Buoyed by frequent play on MTV and a stunning appearance on the NBC special *Motown 25 – Yesterday, Today and Forever* in March 1983, Jackson set a new standard for himself, taking "Billie Jean" to the top of the *Billboard* charts for seven weeks — his biggest hit to date.

She Blinded Me With Science

Thomas Dolby

Thomas Dolby thought audiences might be finding his music too demanding. A technocrat who had been fiddling with computers and homemade synthesizers since the age of eighteen, he set out to dumb down his compositions and in the process, scored his lone Top Forty hit. "She Blinded Me With Science" reached Number Five on the *Billboard* Hot One Hundred in May 1983.

Thomas Morgan Dolby Robertson was born in Cairo, Egypt to archaeologist parents. As a child, he tagged along with his parents, traveling the world. The only constant in his life was the piano lessons he took at each new boarding school. He loved music but had other interests as well. Always fascinated with electronics, he started fiddling with ham radios as a child, graduating to computers and elaborate tape machines as he got older. In university, his eclectic interests included meteorology and projectionism. Bored with structured education, he dropped out of school without earning a degree to embark on a career in the music business.

Using a homemade PA system, he worked as sound engineer with many British new-wave bands including the Fall and the UK Subs. Inspired by Kraftwerk and Brian Eno, he

Boy George flippantly dismissed one songwriter who claimed Culture Club had ripped him off. "Handy Man" composer Jimmy Jones cried foul over the group's "Karma Cameleon," a 1983 Number One. "I might have heard it once," George told *Rolling Stone*, "but it certainly wasn't something I sat down and said, 'Yeah, I want to copy this.' We gave him ten pence and an apple."

built a high-tech recording studio in his home, learning the craft of record production. His reputation as an electronic genius soon spread, and he found himself producing records for the Thompson Twins, the Camera Club and Lene Lovich (for whom he wrote "New Toy," a hit in Europe). With those successes behind him, Dolby set out on a solo career in 1981 with the release of "Urges" on the Armageddon label. He found time to produce records for Joan Armatrading, M and Foreigner while releasing a stream of electro-pop discs.

In the media, he cultivated a mad-scientist image, surrounded by a bank of computers with blinking lights. Playing up on that perception, he penned "She Blinded Me With Science" as a novelty song in hopes of broadening his audience.

"I think it's the most meaningless song I've ever written," he told *Creem*'s Michael Goldberg. "It's about a sort of fuddy-duddy old scientist who gets obsessed with his lab assistant. When I made that song, it was with the thought in my head that people were finding my music too demanding, and that maybe I should let loose and make a record that was basically nonsense like everything else on the charts. And it's just a sad reflection on the state of things that it was successful."

The ascendancy of the song owes a great deal to the accompanying self-directed video. Visually rich, the video shows Dolby visiting a home for deranged scientists. There he is given shock treatment and receives counseling from famed British scientist Magnus Pike who also supplied the shouted refrain "Science" in the song. Dolby's father puts in an appearance as, no surprise, an archaeologist. The video was in heavy rotation on MTV as the song slowly climbed the charts, peaking at Number Five on the Hot One Hundred on May 14, 1983.

It was his last visit to the rarefied strata of the Top Five, although he has continued to record, produce records and score films.

Sweet Dreams (Are Made of This)

Eurythmics

At the time of its release, "Sweet Dreams (Are Made of This)" was considered to be a high-tech master-piece. Cool. Semiotic. Icy. European electro-pop that rode an impossibly catchy riff to the top of the American charts. But the high-gloss electronic veneer masked the tune's decidedly low-rent beginnings.

Musician Dave Stewart first met Annie Lennox in a health-food restaurant in the Hampstead area of London. Lennox, a classically trained flautist, took his order for a plate of cabbage but denied his second request that she marry him — immediately. Nuptial bliss may not have been on the menu that night, but a romantic and professional relationship did come out of that first meeting. They soon moved in together, forming the Tourists (with Peet Coombes) in 1977. An energetic new-wave act, the Tourists registered a British Top Five hit with a remake of Dusty Springfield's "I Only Want to Be With You."

The song's sentiments aside, the Tourists had split by 1980, and the romance was on the rocks. Lennox reports that the day her relationship with Stewart ended, Eurythmics began. The unusual name is defined by the

American Heritage Dictionary as "...the choreographic art of interpreting musical composition by a rhythmic, freestyle graceful movement of the body in response to the rhythm of the music." By defining the name, they announced a new direction, steering away from the new-wave pop of the Tourists into murkier, more complicated rhythmic music. A critically acclaimed album, *In the Garden* was released in 1981. The pressure of constant road work to promote the album with little commercial reward left Stewart with reoccurring health problems, while Lennox suffered a nervous breakdown.

After a short hiatus, the duo regrouped, assembling a makeshift eight-track warehouse studio in the Chalk Farm section of London. One night, after several weeks of work, the pressure became too much. A terrible fight broke out between the ex-lovers. Stewart, always a techno-hipster, retreated to the comfort of the recording console, while Lennox withdrew to the far end of the cavernous warehouse.

Noodling around on the synthesizer, Stewart came up with a throbbing rhythm layered over a chunky synth bass riff. Lennox, sensing that Stewart was on to something, set aside her animosity and joined in, improvising the now-famous synthesizer riff. It sounded so good that Lennox began singing, adding a stream-of-consciousness lyric over the catchy melody. "Sweet dreams are made of this," she sang, "who am I to disagree." Thirty minutes later, the song was finished. It was the fastest tune they had ever written. Lennox

Women of the Eighties: "The Beautiful Ones," an album track from *Purple Rain*'s sound track, was rumored to be Prince's favorite cut on the record. It should have been -- he wrote it for his girlfriend Susannah Melvoin, sister of his guitarist Wendy. Toto's 1982 chart topper "Rosanna" was written for actress Rosanna Arquette who was then dating guitarist Steve Lukather.

commented, after the fact, "it is not often that complete ideas come out like that."

Getting the tune on tape was more complicated. Below the jerry-built studio was a timber factory, and the pair had to wait until the workers downstairs had turned off their ban saws before they could record the vocals. Stewart later joked that if the sound of the factory could be heard on the record, it was because he had forgotten to close the windows.

The song's hook may have been supplied by synthesizers, but old-fashioned glass milk jugs added texture to the chorus of the song. Stewart filled several milk jugs with different levels of water, pitched to specific notes. Banging them with a mallet provided an industrial-sounding counterpoint to Lennox's vocal.

The warehouse tapes were meant to be used as a demo, a rough blueprint for a more-detailed production in a proper studio. But the tapes so impressed RCA that they elected to release them with only a minimum of rerecording. The entire recording budget of the *Sweet Dreams (Are Made of This)* long player added up to roughly $700, a small fraction of what is spent on most major label releases. "Sweet Dreams (Are Made of This)" sat on the *Billboard* charts for seventeen weeks, spending one week in the top spot in September 1983.

Proving that great songs are open to more than one interpretation, "Sweet Dreams" was given an alternative treatment by Marilyn Manson in 1995. His was a bleak rendering that exposed the vulnerable underbelly of sexual tension only implied in the original.

Jump

Van Halen

Inspirations for songs occasionally appear out of thin air; sometimes they appear over the airwaves. A live news broadcast gave David Lee Roth the idea for "Jump," the Number One single that established Van Halen as the tallest of Top Forty's heavy-metal poppies.

David Lee Roth was under pressure to write songs for Van Halen's upcoming album. Titled *1984*, Warner Brothers planned a publicity blitz based on a January 1, 1984 release date. Moving away from their tried-and-true formula of including cover songs on every album, Van Halen resolved to flex their songwriting muscles and produce an album of originals. But their deadline was looming.

Roth came up with a novel way of writing lyrics. Cruising through the Hollywood Hills in a 1951 Mercury Lowrider with Larry the roadie as chauffeur, Roth would recline in the back seat and wait for inspiration to hit. One afternoon after lunch, the duo was driving around listening to a synthesizer track on cassette. Guitarist Eddie Van Halen had written the track two years previously only to have it spurned by the band. "We don't need this shit," was reportedly the reaction of one band member. At the goading of producer Ted

Dire Straits guitarist Mark Knopfler wrote their only Number One hit after shopping for home appliances. In the television department, he overheard two guys talking, making fun of a video they were watching on *MTV*. One guy commented to the other that musicians don't work very hard for their money. His friend shot back sarcastically, "Yeah, maybe they get a blister on their little finger." Knopfler was amused by the exchange, writing it down in the store. It became the basis for "Money for Nothing."

Templeton and Warner Brothers, the heavy-metal band was persuaded to resurrect the lilting synthesizer riff.

Sprawled in the tufted leather backseat of the vintage car, Roth let his mind drift to a television newscast he'd seen the night before. Live coverage showed a man perched on the ledge of a skyscraper, threatening to jump. Imagining himself in the crowd outside the skyscraper, Roth wondered what their reaction would be. "There's always somebody who yells, 'Go ahead and jump!'" he thought. Playing on this idea, he changed the circumstances somewhat. In his scenario, Roth is a man interested in a woman at his local bar, but he is plagued by self-doubt. "Might as well jump," he says, convincing himself to approach the woman. Using Larry as a sounding board, Roth leaned over the front seat, asking the roadie what he thought of the lyrics. "He's probably the most responsible for how it came out," Roth told *Musician*.

With its brash mix of synthesizers and screaming guitars, many critics cited "Jump" as a latter-day Who single, like "Won't Get Fooled Again," only more tuneful. Dave Marsh, dean of American rock critics, called "Jump" "heavy metal *in excelsis*" and rated it Number Twenty-Eight out of the greatest 1001 rock-and-roll singles of all time.

"Jump" became Van Halen's fastest-selling single ever. Released in January 1984, it was fueled by a video which reportedly cost only $600 to produce. In heavy rotation on MTV, "Jump" debuted in the middle of *Billboard*'s Hot One

Hundred. Six weeks later, it had climbed to Number One, a position it held for five weeks.

With visions of a solo career dancing in his head, David Lee Roth left Van Halen in 1985. Little has been heard from him since.

Blasphemous Rumours

Depeche Mode

Tunesmith Martin Gore courted controversy in 1984 by publicly questioning his commitment to Christianity. "Blasphemous Rumours," a single from Depeche Mode's long player *Some Great Reward*, wowed them in the clubs but saw little chart action in North America because of its contentious content.

As the seventies became the eighties, many young English musicians rejected the guitars and drums of their punk peers, opting instead for synthesizers and drum machines. The resulting wave of electro-pop bands swept Europe. The music was mellifluous and danceable (if somewhat robotic and chilly), played by self-described "new romantics" with rococo-coiffed hair and futuristically cut clothes. At the forefront of the techno bands were four lads from Basildon, Essex, England who took their name from a French fashion magazine — Depeche Mode (translation: "fast fashion").

After a series of sold-out shows at the Bridge House Tavern in London's Canning Town, the band signed a deal with Mute Records, beginning a relationship that would take both parties to the top of the charts. They were instant critical darlings. One early write-up in the *New Musical Express* called their music, "danceable, electric, earnest and endearing, with more poise than pose and proud to appeal to all." In 1981, shortly after inking the deal with Mute, songwriter Vince Clarke left Depeche Mode to form Yazoo with Alison Moyet. Synth player Martin Gore took over the creative reigns, becoming the group's main songwriter and composing twenty-six hit singles in the next decade.

Gore expanded on the band's early sound. The poppy electro-beat sound of Clarke's "I Just Can't Get Enough" was displaced by a darker, more intricately layered texture. Gore wrote about profound topics, frequently blending strong sexual overtones into the mix. In "Master and Servant," for instance, Gore makes allusions to the submissive-dominatrix relationship. "Blasphemous Rumours" pushed the boundaries even further. This time, Gore took on the church.

In the early eighties, two bands had hits with songs inspired by Vladimir Nobokov's novel *Lolita* -- the story of an older man who falls head over heels for a young girl. Sting wrote "Don't Stand So Close to Me" for the Police in 1981, perhaps remembering his experiences as a teacher at the Northern Counties Teacher Training College in Newcastle. Three years later, Wang Chung had a Top Twenty hit with "Dance Hall Days," a clever takeoff on the name of the book's central character Delores Hayes.

The song stems from two separate incidents. Gore read a tabloid account of a boy who tried, unsuccessfully, to take his life. His reason? The sixteen-year-old lad declared himself "bored with life." Gore was shaken by the story. How could a teenager, with his whole life ahead of him, try to take his own life? Next, Gore heard a story of a troubled eighteen-year-old who had recently reaffirmed his faith in God in an attempt to turn his life around. Forty-eight hours later, he was tragically killed in a car crash.

Both events affected Gore deeply. His faith in the church was rocked. If there was a God, how could he allow such terrible things to happen? For the first time in his life, he felt cut adrift from the church. Seeking the comfort of his friends, he told them of his feeling that Christianity had failed him. Describing the incidents that led him to this epiphany, someone quipped, "God must have a sick sense of humor." The line stuck with Gore, becoming the lyrical hook of the "Blasphemous Rumours'" chorus.

The iconoclastic "Blasphemous Rumours" didn't reach the Top Forty in the United States, but it hit the Top Ten in Europe where Depeche Mode were superstars or, as *Rolling Stone* dubbed them, "the kings of arena techno-pop."

Wake Me Up Before You Go-Go

Wham!

Yorgos Kyriako Panayiotou was inspired to write a hit song after seeing a note his friend Andrew left his mother. Under the name George Michael, Yorgos penned "Wake Me Up Before You Go-Go," a Number One hit in 1984 for Wham!.

As teenagers, Andrew Ridgeley and George Michael were tight friends. Meeting at school in Bushey, England, the two often cut class to discuss their love of music and aspirations of pop stardom. After graduation, they took the first tentative steps toward realizing their dream. Forming the Executive, a ska band, the duo tried to write hit tunes. That band was short lived but did produce several demos of original music. Under the new name Wham!, the tapes fell into the hands of Mark Dean, label head of Innervision Records. Impressed, Dean signed the teenagers on the strength of "Wham! Rap," an autobiographical tale about being on the dole and rising above the shame of unemployment.

"Wham! Rap" underwhelmed the record-buying public in its initial release. The follow-up single, however, bolted the dynamic duo (who still lived at home with their parents) to the top of the British charts. "Young Guns (Go For It)" was just the first of a string of hits (including a rerelease of

"Wham!Rap") for Innervision that turned Wham! into one of the biggest acts in the United Kingdom. They were so hot, Michael once remarked, that "[Wham!] would be on the front page whenever Princess Di wasn't having her hair done."

Unfortunately, what the two young singers didn't know about the music business could fill the London Library. They signed a bad deal, and after finding huge success, they had to go to court to nullify their relationship with Dean and Innervision. Michael and Ridgeley, both now barely twenty years old, weren't without a deal for long. Epic Records anted up, scooping the popular pair, preparing to break them into the United States.

They needed a surefire hit to launch the debut record on Epic. "Careless Whispers," a leftover from the Executive days, was a good song but not upbeat enough. Did they have anything else? Michael thought back to their school days, to one night in particular when he stopped by at Ridgeley's house to pick him up for an evening of nightclubbing. While he waited for his friend to get ready, he noticed a scrap of paper in his friend's bedroom. It was a note Ridgeley left taped to his door for his mother to wake him up for school. It read, cryptically, "Wake me up up before you go go." Apparently, when he wrote the note, the young Ridgeley had just come back from several hours of dancing at a local disco. Tired and drowsy, he mistakenly scribbled "up" twice, so as a joke, he completed the note with "before you go go."

Michael thought the line would make a great title for a song. It had a sense of nonsense that appealed to his sense of humor and brought back images of the Motown music the pair loved. One of their favorites was Smokey Robinson's "Going to A-Go-Go," a 1966 classic that took the French slang for discotheque (a go-go) to the Top Twenty.

Michael incorporated the line into what British writer Paul Du Noyer called "a big bouncy bastard" of a song that broke the band into the United States. Entering the chart at Number Eighty in early September 1984, "Wake Me Up Before You Go-Go" hit the apex ten weeks later, staying at Number One for three weeks.

Panic

Smiths

At the time of its release, "Panic," the Smiths' 1986 single, was thought to be a denunciation of disco. The band's bard Morrissey had made some disapproving remarks to the press on certain aspects of black music, which seemed to explain the song's sentiment. Actually, the contentious "hang the DJ" chorus of the song was a little more specific and had nothing to do with disco music.

In the mid-eighties, the Smiths inspired many column inches in the press. In British pop circles, the band appeared to be the lone boat against the current. While most bands played up the carnality of their music, Morrissey promoted celibacy. Other groups hit the charts with good-time dance songs. The Smiths wrote a requiem for the child victims of the sixties' moors murderers Ian Brady and Myra Hindley. Acts like Wham! took advantage of their boyish good looks. Morrissey wore national health spectacles. Poised as a modern-day Oscar Wilde, the singer, with his eloquent miserabilism, was always quotable and great fodder for the front pages.

After a successful early run at the charts and considerable acclaim in the media, the Smiths hit a mid-eighties' dry spell on the singles' charts. Five consecutive singles failed to break into the Top Twenty despite a sweep of the 1985 *New Musical Express* reader's poll. (They won Top Group, Johnny Marr took honors as Best Instrumentalist and Morrissey and Marr shared an award as Best Songwriter.) The long-winded titles of the tunes — "There Is a Light That Never Goes Out" or "Please Please Please, Let Me Get What I Want" — might have had something to do with the dearth of hits, but whatever the reason, the Smiths needed a place on the charts.

Never one to bite his tongue, Morrissey penned a tune pointing the finger at those he felt were impeding his band's success — Britain's DJs. He was upset that lightweight acts like Wham! were commanding the airwaves instead of the Smiths. The main target of Morrissey's ire was most likely BBC Radio1 disc jockey Steven Wright, a very vocal critic of the Smiths. Morrissey was fiercely protective of his band and didn't appreciate Wright's anti-Smiths diatribes. Ignoble as it may look, the singer sought revenge on Wright in the song.

Another incident provided the tune's sing-along chorus. In April 1986, Morrissey was listening to the radio, anxiously awaiting news on the nuclear accident at Chernobyl. A grim-voiced announcer broke into the programming, describing the catastrophic events in Ukraine. Immediately following the newscast, the DJ spun the fluffy, high-gloss "I'm Your Man" by Wham!. "That DJ should be killed," thought Morrissey, enraged by the announcer's insensitivity to the great tragedy.

With anger building inside him, he sat down and wrote "Panic" with a lyric encouraging the death of all DJs. In a shimmering display of their songwriting chemistry, guitarist Johnny Marr provided an assertive musical attack for Morrissey's lyrical wrath. Recorded too late to be included on the Smiths' next long player *The Queen Is Dead*, "Panic," with its crowd-pleasing "hang the DJ" chant, was offered only as a single. The rarity of the record doubtlessly had something to do with its success, becoming a collector's item immediately on release. Ironically, radio jumped on the song,

When Mick Jones was writing the Clash's classic *London Calling* album, the über punk was sharing a London council flat with his grandmother. Tunes written in the flat include "Lost in the Supermarket," "Clampdown" and "The Guns of Brixton."

pushing it to the brink of the Top Ten in 1986 and breaking the Smiths' run of bad chart luck.

The song remains a jewel in the Smiths' crown. In 1992, Labatt sponsored a vote to determine Britain's Top Five Hundred all-time favorite tracks. Polling readers of diverse magazines, from *The Daily Mirror* to the *New Musical Express*, a list was compiled and published in book form. The Smiths placed seven songs on the honor roll, with "Panic" clocking in at Number 135.

Public Enemy
Number One

Public
Enemy

When Carlton Ridenhour was an arts student at Long Island's Adelphi University in the early eighties, he discovered graphic design wasn't his only forte. Frustrated by the bad sound quality on most early rap records, he decided to become a rapper even though he didn't have any musical background. "[I] can't even play Lotto," he told *Rolling Stone* in 1989. Using the stage name Chuck D., he formed Public Enemy, one of the biggest-selling and most controversial rap groups of the 1980s.

Ridenhour met Hank Shocklee at university where Shocklee was supporting himself by running weekend rap parties and managing DJs. Schocklee was impressed with Ridenhour's promotional ideas, bringing him on board to publicize his concerts. Ridenhour excelled at his part-time job. Due to his aggressive marketing tactics, the weekend parties were always packed. He enjoyed the promotions business and was becoming more involved with the music, immersing himself in hip-hop culture.

A driven man with definite ideas about how things should be done, Ridenhour was offended by the shoddy quality of the rap records of the day. Rap was still in its infancy, and more often than not, production values on the records were low-fi. Muted voices and echo chambers obscured the lyrics, while ungainly mixing de-emphasized the beat. One night, riding around in a car with some friends, listening to the latest hip-hop tapes, Ridenhour griped loudly to his friends. "Shit, I can't hear a motherfucking word he's saying." That night, he vowed he would do a better job.

Around the same time, a trained guitarist named Bill Stephney had taken over the campus radio station. Stephney had recently jumped on the hip-hop bandwagon, realizing that the DJ's turntable work was creative — a valid musical form. He quickly instituted a three-hour rap show on Adelphi's radio station. Shocklee and Ridenhour were invited as guests and subsequently offered their own show. It was a move that would help transport rap from the underground to the *Billboard* charts.

The pair initially saw the show as a marketing opportunity, a cheap way to advertise their upcoming rap parties. But there was another advantage. Determined not to play the same record twice on the show, they had to come up with creative ways to fill up 180 minutes of airtime. As there was a severe shortage of rap records, to flesh out the show, they programmed their own beats, rapping over them. With no musical instruments at their disposal, they used a turntable to crib beats from existing records as a background for their raps. Using the technology offered by the radio station, Ridenhour strove to offer the high production value he found so lacking on most rap records. The show, and their raps, became very popular.

During this time, Ridenhour wrote a groundbreaking rap as an answer to a challenge issued by a friend. Flavor Flav (rapper William Drayton) taunted Ridenhour, saying that he was an amateur rapper. The radio host replied to the charges with a blistering rap called "Public Enemy Number One," a boastful rant layered over a noisy, aggressive beat. "Known as the poetic lyrical son," he rapped, "I'm public enemy number one."

The tune proved that Ridenhour was a credible rapper. The small campus station was overrun with requests for "Public Enemy Number One." This brought the rapper to the attention of Rick Rubin, founder of Def Jam Records, who had just inked a distribution deal with CBS. Rubin offered a deal to Ridenhour and Shocklee who promptly turned him down, feeling they would be treated like "indentured servants" if they signed to a major label.

Soon after, Rubin recruited Bill Stephney into the Def Jam family. Stephney convinced the doubtful duo that Rubin and company were alright and would treat them fairly. Naming themselves after their signature tune, Public Enemy signed with the record label in 1987.

Increasing the lineup to include a surreal and visually intimidating crew of rappers and a DJ — Professor Griff (Richard Griffin) 'Minister of Information'; Flavor Flav, DJ Terminator X (Norman Rogers); and a four-piece plastic Uzi-packing backup group, the S1Ws (Security of the First World) — Ridenhour drew on his arts background to design a look for the band, one previously unseen in rap circles. Chuck D.'s ball cap, drawn down tight to his nose, countered Flavor Flav's outlandish "coal lamper" appearance. The unsmiling S1Ws' combat fatigues gave them a stern militaristic aura. The effect was striking — and just a bit menacing. Writing in *Rolling Stone*, Lewis Cole called this configuration "a political rap group as seen through the eyes of a Marvel Comics illustrator."

Public Enemy's first Def Jam offering, 1987's *Yo! Bum Rush the Show*, took its title from the story of a B-boy gate-crashing a nightclub. The band set itself a cut above the rest, using Chuck D.'s thundering vocal delivery to great effect, butted against a lean, hard sound supplied by DJ Terminator X. With the release of the first album, Public Enemy saw themselves bum rushing the music industry. After moving 300,000 units of *Yo! Bum Rush the Show* (and triple that for subsequent releases), the band named after a song became the most influential rap act in the industry, imitated by many, but equaled by none.

Love Rescue Me

U2

U2 were in the United States to record an album that would pay homage to their heroes — the seminal figures of American music that had helped mold their multiplatinum sound. One night, a curious dream, the result of too much partying, led Bono Vox (real name, Paul Hewson) to write the lyrics to one of U2's most sincere songs, "Love Rescue Me," from 1988's *Rattle and Hum*.

After scoring a Paul Bunyon-size hit with *The Joshua Tree* (1987), Irish rockers U2 were poised on the ladder between mammoth achievement and international stardom. The *Rattle and Hum* project was conceived as a multimedia assault — a "live" record, videos and concert motion picture — designed to penetrate any outlying parts of the world that weren't yet U2 fans. It worked. Despite taking a sound trouncing from reviewers, *Rattle and Hum* went on to sell fourteen million copies, establishing Bono, Edge (David Evans), Adam Clayton and Larry Mullen as the biggest band in the world.

In the winter of 1987, U2 set out to write what would become *Rattle and Hum*. Seeking a change of venue in which to write new songs — Dublin being a cold, wet place in the winter — U2 chose Los Angeles, a city overflowing with all that is healthy *and* decayed in the blueprint of the American dream they planned to chronicle. The band's guitarist Edge rented a house in Beverly Hills for his wife and kids, with Bono as a temporary houseguest. (The residence would later gain ignominy as the site of the murder of José and Kitty Menendez at the hands of their sons Lyle and Erik.)

After a night of fraternizing and drinking, Bono slept fitfully in the guest house, dreaming of one of his idols, Bob Dylan. A lifelong Dylan devotee, Bono had met the fabled folkie several times, once performing with him in 1984. The Dylan tune "Maggie's Farm" had long been a staple in U2's live set. In his dream, Bono saw Dylan onstage, singing a song about a man whose life was falling apart while those around him lavished him with praise and turned to him for redemption. In the end, all the man craved was the love and salvation that was demanded of him. It is conjecture whether the lyrics in the dream were actually a metaphor for Dylan's life and career — an ephemeral treatise

C. Procaylo/Canapress Photo Service

Bono, lead singer of Irish supergroup U2 sports a muscle shirt in 1997. "Love Rescue Me" was originally planned as a duet between U2 and Bob Dylan before Dylan stepped down, citing conflicts with his new band the Traveling Wilbury's.

on the folk singer's unwanted place in history as the mouth-piece of a generation.

Bono woke, jotting down the lyrics from the dream through sleepy eyes. Some time later, Bono met Dylan and brought the hastily written lyrics. "Is this one of yours?" Bono asked, showing Dylan the song. Dylan assured the younger singer it wasn't but said he found the rough-hewn lyrics engrossing. At the meeting's end, the two agreed to flesh out the lyrics, turning Bono's dream into a song.

The songwriters collaborated on the lyrics, with U2 providing the music. Dylan actually recorded a country ballad version of "Love Rescue Me" which was to be included on *Rattle and Hum*, but he later asked that the song not be used to avoid a conflict of interest with his band the Traveling Wilburys. U2 rerecorded the tune, with Bono using Dylan's unique phrasing as a guide, but with the addition of the Memphis Horns which lent the song a country-soul flavor.

While "Love Rescue Me" did not chart, *Rattle and Hum* was Number One on the album charts for six weeks.

One

Metallica

Metal kings Metallica riffed their way into the Top Forty with an antiwar song inspired by a novel by a blacklisted writer. "One," the story of a mutilated, bedridden soldier, peaked at Number Thirty-Five on the *Billboard* charts in March 1989.

Metallica's fourth album, *...And Justice for All*, delivered on drummer Lars Ulrich's promise that the band would make a record "with no sacrifices, no compromises, no corners cut." A thrash masterpiece of epic proportions, the sixty-five-minute record bristles with emotional power, and with most songs clocking in at over six minutes, it challenges the listener to keep pace with the bristling speed guitar. Taking the album's name from a Norman Jewison film that explores the corruption and hypocrisy in the court system, the band expands on that theme, producing an album of unyielding lyrical content. "Eye of the Beholder" is a diatribe against censorship, inspired by the *Frankenchrist* obscenity case that bankrupted Jello Biafra's Alternative Tentacles record label. Another cut, "The Shortest Straw," is a heavy-handed look at the McCarthy era Communist witch-hunt.

...And Justice for All's most fully realized track is "One,"

a dramatic antiwar parable of a maimed soldier, arms and legs amputated, waiting to die. Two books led to the creation of this song. The band's manager recommended they read Victor Navasky's *Naming Names*, an account of Senator Joseph McCarthy's infamous blacklisting of suspected Communists. In that book, they came across the name Dalton Trumbo, a writer who had scripted several Hollywood classics including *Kitty Foyle*, *Spartacus* and *Thirty Seconds Over Tokyo*. As one of the Hollywood Ten, he was briefly jailed for refusing to answer McCarthy's questions at the House of Representatives Un-American Activities Committee hearings. Blacklisted in Hollywood, Trumbo assumed the name Robert Rich, winning an Academy Award in 1956 for Best Motion Picture Story for *The Brave One*. In 1960, Trumbo reemerged, writing the screenplay to *Exodus* under his given name.

The band was fascinated with Trumbo and the ostracism he suffered at the hands of anti-Communist zealots. They may have seen him as a kindred spirit because as a thrash metal band, they often felt on the outside of the mainstream music industry. Checking out his work, they found a dog-eared copy of Trumbo's 1939 novel *Johnny Got His Gun*, the story of Joe Bonham who goes off to war only to come home severely disabled. Written two years before the United States entered World War II, the novel's message was popular in the left-wing antiwar movement. By 1941, the tide had changed. The US was embroiled in the war, and the book, viewed as dangerous propaganda, was pulled from distribution. *Johnny Got His Gun* resurfaced in the late sixties, selling thousands of copies to young men about to be shipped off to Vietnam.

Using the book as a starting point, the band crafted a song about a man who, as Ulrich put it, comes back from war as a "living brain type of thing." Drawn in horrific detail, a graphic video — the band's first — accentuated the sorrowful inhumanity of the protagonist's plight. Shot in black and white, the clip intercuts shots of the band with footage from Trumbo's own 1971 film adaptation of *Johnny Got His Gun* (starring Timothy Bottoms). Metallica's management had to track down one of the two existing prints of the motion picture from an Italian distribution company. The print was in terrible shape, but director Michael Salomon was cleverly able to cut and paste enough of the film stock to create an effective video. Relying heavily on sound bites from the film, Salomon dubbed Bottoms's dialogue into the song to tell the tale of Joe Bonham. Unlike most rock videos, "One" was an entirely realized mini film, telling a complete story from start to finish. Debuting on MTV's Headbanger's Ball in January 1989, the video quickly rose to Number One on the station's Top Fifteen countdown.

"One" won Metallica a Grammy nomination in 1989 in the newly minted Best Metal Performance, Vocal or Instrumental. The previous year, they suffered an embarrassing defeat to irrelevant sixties' rockers Jethro Tull in the Hard Rock/Heavy Metal category. But according to the *LA Times*, they still managed to shake "the Shrine Auditorium chandelier with a performance unlike anything ever seen or heard on a Grammy show." They reigned victorious in 1989, having brought metal music to the Top Forty (Number Thirty-Five) and taking home the Grammy. Commenting on Metallica's performance at the Grammy's, Ulrich seemed gladdened that his band had finally broken into the mainstream. He told the *Washington Post*, "We didn't come out and perform satanic rituals on stage or rape girls, and from our point of view, ['One'] was a good song."

NINETIES

Smells Like Teen Spirit

Nirvana

When Nirvana was in the studio recording "Smells Like Teen Spirit," the band didn't think the song was anything remarkable. Producer Butch Vig, however, knew straightaway it would be a monster hit. He later told a reporter, "It was just blowing me away. I was jumping around the room." A savage guitar-pop tune, "Teen Spirit," with its classic us-versus-them theme, came along at a time when the alienated youth of America were looking for a new bellwether. The single's release turned Nirvana leader Kurt Cobain into a pop star and cultural icon — a true grunge godhead.

Much has been written about this song, but it is Cobain's lyrics that drew the most notice. "Smells Like Teen Spirit" was greeted as the roar of rebellion, a rallying cry to angry disaffected kids. Actually, the phrase's origins are humbler than initially thought. Long before Nirvana signed to Geffen Records, Cobain was living in Olympia, Washington, a suburb of Seattle. One night, he and his friend Kathleen Hannah (of the Riot Grrrl group Bikini Kill) decided to go out and literally paint the town. Armed with spray cans, they vandalized several buildings with their favorite tag lines — the inflammatory "God Is Gay" or the nonsensical

"Amputate Acrobats." Finishing off, they defaced a pickup truck with the fluorescent slur "Queer" before returning to Cobain's home on North Pear Street. While Cobain watched, Hannah wrote the slogan "Kurt Smells Like Teen Spirit" in large sloppy letters on his apartment wall. Cobain was flattered, thinking the graffiti was a tribute — an evocative statement of his youthful rebellious spirit. Actually, it was a joke. The "Teen Spirit" Hannah actually had in mind was an antiperspirant for young women. It wasn't until the song was riding high on the charts that Cobain learned an underarm deodorant had provided the inspiration for the tune.

The song's most famous line, "Here we are now, entertain us," was dissected by music writers as a cynical line about youths' diminished expectations in the aftermath of the Reagan/Bush golden years. In fact, it was a favorite Cobain party trick. To break the ice at social gatherings, he would often say to the hosts, "You invited us here, now entertain us."

Musically, rock critics often cite the debt "Teen Spirit" owed the 1976 Boston hit "More Than a Feeling." The chord changes are analogous, a debt Cobain gladly

Mark J. Terrill/Canapress Photo Service

A rare smile from Nirvana leader Kurt Cobain. The late guitarist was moved to write Nirvana's biggest hit "Smells Like Teen Spirit" after a spray-painting spree in Olympia, Washington.

acknowledged. "'Teen Spirit' was such a clichéd riff," he told *Rolling Stone* writer David Fricke in an interview published in January 1994. "It was close to a Boston riff or 'Louie Louie.'" Structurally, the tune, with its soft and quiet then loud and hard dynamic, was a blatant rip-off of Cobain's heroes The Pixies.

The immense success of "Smells Like Teen Spirit" and the subsequent platinum status of the album *Nevermind* was an anathema for Cobain. In interviews, he said he was embarrassed by the record's glossy radio-ready production, telling Michael Azzerrad, in the biography *Come As You Are*, that *Nevermind* was "closer to a Motley Crüe record than a punk-rock record." Playing the role of antistar to the hilt during Nirvana's 1993 fall tour, Cobain often omitted "Smells Like Teen Spirit," the band's biggest hit, from set lists.

Jeremy

Pearl Jam

Rising from the ashes of Green River and Mother Love Bone, two seminal grunge bands, Pearl Jam made a splash in 1991 with the release of the multiplatinum *Ten*. The album (kept out of the top spot on the charts by Billy Ray Cyrus) turned them into superstars and made a troubled kid from Richardson, Texas a household name. "Jeremy" hit the Top Five on alternative rock charts all over North America in 1991.

Eddie Vedder was working as a hotel security guard in San Diego when he received a tape from a new Seattle band looking for a vocalist. He had performed with several bands, but things never seemed to work out. He quit Bad Radio because the members didn't take the music seriously enough. Sometimes his shyness got the best of him. Once, he even wore goggles with the lenses blacked out so he wouldn't have to look at the audience. However, life as a security guard didn't appeal to him much, so he decided to give music another crack.

The tape was sent by Stone Gossard and Jeff Ament, former guitarist and bassist, respectively, with Green River and Mother Love Bone. They were auditioning vocalists after Andrew Wood, their last singer, died of a heroin overdose. The cassette contained three instrumental guitar tracks which Gossard hoped Vedder could put lyrics to. After listening to the tape, Vedder fashioned a mini rock opera, a trio of songs that he insists are not autobiographical in any way. In the first movement, "Alive," a mother is drawn sexually to her son because he reminds her of her dead husband. The story continues in "Once" where the son is so traumatized by the experience that he becomes a serial killer. "Footsteps" closes the trilogy when the son is captured and executed. Vedder recorded the vocals in his home studio and mailed them to Seattle.

Gossard and Ament were blown away by Vedder's tape. The combination of intense vocals with strong lyrics was just what they were after. Vedder was invited to join the band to rehearse and write more songs. Upon arrival in Seattle, Vedder was given more tapes and the writing began in earnest.

The product of a troubled childhood, Vedder identified with alienated youth and found fodder for his songs in the stories of angry teens. A newspaper story from Richardson, Texas provided the inspiration for a song that would become the centerpiece of Pearl Jam's debut *Ten*.

Matthew McCarthy/Canapress Photo Service

Eddie Vedder plays it up for the crowd at a 1996 concert. The album *Ten* turned Pearl Jam into superstars, and made a troubled kid from Richardson, Texas a household name.

On January 8, 1991, Vedder read the story of Jeremy Wade Delle, a Richardson High School sophomore. Rebuffed by a teacher for missing a class, Delle was sent to the principal's office to get an admittance slip. He returned instead with a .357 Magnum. "Miss, I got what I really went for," the shy teenager said before placing the barrel of the gun in his mouth and pulling the trigger in front of a class of thirty.

Sixteen-year-old Brian Jackson was standing outside the classroom when he heard the bang. The sound, he said, was "like someone had just slammed a book on a desk." "I thought they were doing a play or something," he continued. "But then I heard a scream, and a blond girl came running out of the classroom, and she was crying." Wondering what had happened, he went in and saw Jeremy dead on the floor. "The teacher was standing against the wall, crying and shaking," he reported. "Some people were standing around her, holding her as if to keep her from falling."

Like Vedder, Delle was from a broken family and was described by classmates as a loner. Vedder identified with Jeremy, having spent many hours wondering whether life was worth living. But the story made him angry as well. Vedder often said he would be dead by now if it had not been for music, and he thought about all the good experiences he would have missed. Maybe if Jeremy had something to fall back on as Vedder had, this tragedy could have been avoided.

With Delle's story churning in his head, Vedder composed a song about a daddy who didn't give affection and a boy who finally spoke in class. When it came time to record "Jeremy," Vedder sang as though his life depended on it — and maybe it did. "If it wasn't for music," Vedder said at the MTV Video Awards in 1992, "I would have shot myself in front of that classroom."

"Jeremy" was Pearl Jam's first Top Ten single.

Rhythm of My Heart

Rod Stewart

Rod Stewart is a great interpreter of other people's songs. With the right material, Stewart's voice can really soar. In 1991, he found a tune that matched his style perfectly. Written by Canadian Marc Jordan, "Rhythm of My Heart" hit the Top Five.

The story of "Rhythm of My Heart" starts years before the song was actually written, when Jordan was a young boy. "My dad was a classically trained light opera singer," said Jordan, "but he sang everything. He sang jazz, big-band stuff, musical theater and folk songs. All sorts of things.

"He loved Irish, Scottish and Maritime folk songs. He loved that music and collected it. I heard it growing up as a child — all these wonderful Maritime folk songs that were really very much like the Irish and Scottish folk songs of the settlers. That music was in me when I grew up, and I think it had a big part in the fact that I could write 'Rhythm of My Heart' because it is really based on one of those Celtic melodies I heard as a child. Not a specific melody, just an amalgam of all the songs that I heard and the rhythms and melodies. The song came very quickly. It wasn't hard to write because it all made sense."

At the time he wrote the song, Jordan was living in Los Angeles, having moved south from his native Toronto. "I started out as a recording artist," he said. "I got my first deal in Los Angeles while I was living in Toronto. I did a couple of records for Warner Brothers with the Steely Dan people. I moved to Los Angeles after I lost my recording contract, and I needed money to keep myself alive. It was the writing that kept me going."

The year was 1983 and Jordan was barely making ends meet as a performer, although he had a publishing deal at Warner Chapell Music, penning tunes for Diana Ross, Kansas and Kim Carnes. Once "Rhythm of My Heart" was written, Jordan needed to make a demo of the song — a necessary step in selling the tune. "We did a demo of it in the Lawrence Welk Publishing Offices Studio in Hollywood," he said. "I phoned the [musician's] union and got a bagpipe player who showed up in a kilt, and he blew his brains out. It was four in the morning when we finally got a [bagpipe] part we could use. That song was finished early in the morning — about six or seven o'clock. The engineer actually left, it was such a late session."

Peg Mosik

Singer-songwriter Marc Jordan drew on his father's record collection as inspiration for the Celtic-flavored "Rhythm of My Heart." "He loved Irish, Scottish and Maritime folk songs," said Jordan.

The demo was mixed and submitted to Warner Chapell who sent it to Rob Dickens, then head of Warner Publishing. Dickens loved the song but was unable to place it with a major recording artist at the time. However, the tune was picked up by a Dutch Elvis impersonator who released it as a single in 1984.

Years later, Dickens was put in charge of revitalizing Rod Stewart's career. "He was the guy who found 'Downtown Train' for Rod and a few of the hits he had in the early nineties," continued Jordan. "He remembered ['Rhythm of My Heart'] for about six or seven years, and when he was looking for a Rod Stewart single, he pulled it out and played it for Rod. Rod said, 'I can do it,' and boom."

Stewart loved the Celtic feel of the tune, stamping what *Q Magazine* called his patented raspy "tartan-scarf-wearing treatment" on Jordan's lyric. The up-tempo ballad seemed radio ready, but at the last minute, there was a snag. "It's an interesting thing; ['Rhythm of My Heart'] is an antiwar song about a man who goes away to war, or to some kind of struggle, and wonders if love has been a casualty of the war," Jordan elaborated. "Then he comes home, and he realizes, no, when men go away to war, they may be altered, but things remain intact. The strange thing was that about a week before the single was to come out in London, the BBC said, 'We won't play this unless you remove any reference to war.' [England was] in the Gulf War at the time.

"It was a huge dilemma for me. [Producer] Trevor Horn

You can go anywhere in the mail. In May 1997, in a case of life imitating art, a twenty-six-year-old man mailed himself in a large wooden crate to a friend who lived one hundred miles away. Scott Harner made his unusual travel plans after hearing the story of Walso and his long-distance love Marcia in "The Gift," a Velvet Underground song. How much does it cost to mail yourself? Postage due was $180 for the four-hundred-pound package.

was calling. Everybody was calling, wanting me to change the lyrics. I actually took a shot at it. I couldn't really make it happen, and then the war ended in three days. It was a short war! I dodged a bullet there."

Released in early 1991, the single tore up the charts, revitalizing Stewart's career. It was his biggest hit since 1989's "Downtown Train" — reaching Number Five in the United States and topping the charts in many other countries. "You just watch it," said Jordan, "almost like a horse race. You try to guess where it is going to go. I thought it would only go to the mid-thirties, but it kept going and going and going. What I also found out was that it was a hit in almost every country in the world. I didn't actually realize what a huge international star Rod was."

Tears in Heaven

Eric Clapton

In the days immediately following his son's death, Eric Clapton turned to his guitar for solace. Sequestered in his home in England, he tried to find a way to wash away the hurt of this latest tragedy. Years before, he had written "Layla" under similar emotional distress. In those painful, lonely hours, he composed "Tears in Heaven," a requiem for his son.

March 19, 1991 was an exciting day for four-and-a-half-year-old Conor. His dad, Eric Clapton, took him to the Ringling Circus in New York City. There, wide-eyed in amazement, he saw acrobats and trapeze artists live for the first time. After the show, Clapton dropped Conor at the apartment of his mother, Lori Del Santos, in the swanky Galleria Building on East 57th Street, before returning to his hotel uptown. It had been a great day for father and son. Clapton had just come off several years of intense work and had been unable to spend time with the young boy. He feared he would become an absentee father, just as his father had been. It was his plan to take the next year off to try to get to know his son.

The next day, a housekeeper opened a window to air out

Songwriters always have their ears attuned for catchy phrases -- even in times of confusion. In a scene reminiscent of *Kids Say the Darndest Things*, Neil Finn, tunesmith for the now-defunct Crowded House, wrote "Pineapple Head" (an album track from *Together Alone*). "It started with my son Liam who had a fever. He was delirious, and I was standing by with a cloth to cool him down, and he just started talking about all these things," Finn said in *Mojo*, reported by David Hepworth in 1994. "'Pineapple Head! Pineapple Head!' Then he said 'detective is flat' and 'getaway car.'" So, instead of staying there and doing what a father should do, I ran downstairs and committed it to a song. Until my wife Sharon came in and

a bedroom. The little boy, still dressed in his pajamas, climbed out on the ledge of the window while his mother was out running errands. Possibly trying to emulate the tightrope walkers he had seen the previous night, he lost his balance and fell 750 feet to the roof of an adjacent building.

Eric Clapton arrived at the scene minutes after the accident. The paramedics, police and ambulance were already there, trying to save Conor's life but to no avail. He was pronounced dead on the scene and was buried eight days later. George Harrison and Phil Collins attended the funeral, while Keith Richards, John Mayall and Prince Charles sent sympathy notes.

The tragedy was compounded by newspaper reports that tried to lay the blame on Eric Clapton. The condominium had not been equipped with protective window guards, a mandatory feature in all New York State apartments housing children under the age of twelve. One newspaper claimed Clapton would be brought up on charges relating to the absence of window guards, although one city hall official told the press, "It is highly unlikely we would want to capitalize on a tragedy such as this."

Clapton withdrew from public life in the months following Conor's death. Trying to put his life back together, he attended AA meetings and went into therapy. He kept a typically English stiff upper lip but wondered if he was suffering enough. "[I had] to go into analysis to sort that bit out," he said later. "...from the way I was raised and being English...we pretend we're okay, and we take care of business," he told *Rolling Stone*'s James Henke. "But inside, it's a different story." The greatest healing tool, however, turned out to be his oldest friend — his guitar. In the early summer of 1991, Clapton accepted a commission to write a score for *Rush*, a film adaptation of Kim Wozencraft's novel about a narcotics agent who becomes addicted to drugs. The guitarist recorded fifteen of the tunes he had written during his self-imposed exile, including "Tears in Heaven."

Released in early 1992, the popularity of "Tears in Heaven" eclipsed the film, generating thousands of newspaper

looked at me in horror and said, 'What are you doing down here?'" Finn also credits Liam with writing the line "here comes Mrs. Hairy Legs" in the Crowded House hit "Chocolate Cake."

Canapress Photo Service

Eric Clapton coaxes notes from his guitar at a 1995 concert. In times of turmoil, Clapton often turned to his guitar for solace. In the days immediately following Conor Clapton's tragic death, the elder Clapton dealt with his pain the best way he knew how -- by writing a requiem for his son.

column inches from critics eager to discuss Clapton's tender, understated tune. Undertaker Richard Putt reported in the press that "Tears in Heaven" was the most-requested song at funerals that year. Critical response was mostly positive, although one former colleague questioned Clapton's motives for releasing the tune so soon after Conor's death. Writing and recording it was logical, the friend said, but "releasing it as a single was self-indulgent beyond belief."

Clapton answered this harsh criticism with typical grace and eloquence. "My audience would be very surprised if I didn't make some reference to [Conor's death]. I didn't want to insult them by not including them in my grief." In another interview, he praised the opportunity that *Rush* provided him to express his feelings through "Tears in Heaven" and have it "come out while there was still an audience for it."

Potentially the song's toughest critic, Lori Del Santos was moved by "Tears in Heaven." "The sound of Eric's voice, the music — it made me weep," she told CBS News of the tune which she heard for the first time in a shopping mall. "I know [Eric] is saying those words in "Tears in Heaven" because he is worried that they didn't spend enough time together…. Eric is frightened that if he met Conor in heaven, our son might not recognize him."

The sentiment of the song endeared Clapton not only to the public, but to the music industry as well. In 1992, he received an MTV Award for "Tears in Heaven" and was honored as an outstanding recording artist by the Royal Variety Club. That year at the Grammy's, host Gary Shandling quipped, "If you're up against Eric Clapton in any categories, I'd go home now."

"I don't think I deserve this," he told the audience. "There were better songs." Later, after his sixth trip to the stage, he made a heartrending speech. "I feel incredibly guilty. I don't know why I feel so guilty about taking so many of these. I don't know what to say. I'm very moved and very shaky and very emotional. I want to thank a lot of people, but the one person I want to thank is my son for the love he gave me and the song he gave me. I have received a great honor, but I've lost the one thing I truly loved."

Clapton had nine nominations, and he left the Shrine Auditorium that February night clutching six statues, including an award for "Tears in Heaven."

Under the Bridge

Red Hot Chili Peppers

A song written as an exorcism of inner demons, lamenting the death of a dear friend, was never meant to be released. Anthony Kiedis had penned the song as an entry in a song diary. He certainly didn't think "Under the Bridge" would hit Number One.

Fairfax High in Los Angeles could rightly lay claim to the title "the rock-and-roll school." Phil Spector, Herb Alpert, Jerry Leiber and Guns and Roses' guitarist Slash all learned about readin', writin' and 'rithmetic here. Nirvana shot their famous "Smells Like Teen Spirit" video in the Fairfax gymnasium. As the seventies became the eighties, a trio of teenage boys would meet here, finding celebrity as the Red Hot Chili Peppers. Hillel Slovak and Michael "Flea" Balzary had a band called Anthym, a jive-funk outfit whose music presaged the punk-funk sound of the Chili Peppers. After graduation, Kiedis hooked up with his high-school friends as the band's emcee.

"Their parents call them crazy, and the girls call them all the time," he would squawk from the stage. "But I call them like I see them, and I call them…Anthym!"

Anthym split before committing anything to tape, with Flea departing to slap the bass for punk legends Fear and Slovak teaming up with What Is This? The three remained friends, with Slovak and Kiedis becoming particularly close.

Initially bonding over their love of music, they soon discovered a mutual magnetism to the dark side of life in Los Angeles. Entire days were erased from their memories as they mixed dangerous quantities of LSD, cocaine and heroin. The pair would stray to perilous parts of LA to score, frequently buying from gang members under a bridge in a particularly seedy part of the city.

In 1983, the three funkateers started a new band — Tony Flow and the Miraculously Majestic Masters of Mayhem. After one gig, the group agreed that the cumbersome name had to go. Redubbed the Red Hot Chili Peppers, they tore up every room they played in, often performing in the nude. Soon they were offered a speculative recording deal with EMI America.

Unfortunately, as Slovak and Flea were signed to other record deals, they had to be replaced on the band's 1984 eponymously titled debut. The guys continued to play live and regrouped to record 1985's acclaimed *Freaky Styley* long player.

Meanwhile, drug use was rampant in the band. Slovak indulged to an alarming degree. On tour, he courted drug dealers in every city, scoring at each stop. In 1988, his heavy use took its toll. He walked out on the band during their European tour, unable to play. The good times came to an abrupt end on Sunday June 26, 1988. The guitarist overdosed, slipping into a coma before dying alone in his apartment.

Kiedis was desolate. Not only had he lost his best friend, but, as he was still using, he had to reexamine his life. He decided to get clean. Isolation from the lure of Los Angeles was the only way to kick his habit. After Slovak's memorial service, Kiedis packed a bag and headed to Mexico. For one month he lived in a modest fishing village, living in a hut on the beach, drying out.

While Kiedis was away, drummer Jack Irons decided to leave the band, blaming the music industry for what had happened to Slovak. When Kiedis returned, he found his band in bedlam. "The death of Hillel changed our entire attitude," he said later of that time. "Losing your best friend at the age of twenty-six is a mind- and soul-blower. But there was definitely an inspiration which came from Hillel dying which helped sharpen the focus of the band. Flea and I were left with each other, and we decided, 'Here's something we started a long time ago that we haven't finished.'"

Recruiting new members guitarist John Frusciante (whose audition for the band included showing his erect penis) and Chad Smith (drums), the reborn Red Hots recorded *Mother's Milk*. Its heart-stopping single "Knock Me Down" was dedicated to their dead colleague.

Kiedis was still healing. Feeling the loss of his friend profoundly, he longed to reestablish contact with his family and old friends. He wanted his predrug life back. Feeling isolated, he sometimes felt as if Los Angeles, his home for the last fifteen years, was his only constant companion.

Driving in his car one afternoon with these thoughts swirling through his head, he began to sob. His mind wandered to his old friend Alain Johannes who often flippantly remarked about guardian angels. He saw them everywhere — in the Hollywood Hills, at his home, in crowds. They looked out for him, he said, "more than any human being in the world." Kiedis thought he must have a guardian angel. Otherwise, he would be dead too, just like Hillel.

Alone in his car, he sang, "Sometimes I feel like I don't have a partner..." Arriving home, he couldn't shake his strange mood. He realized that no matter how low he sunk, he was still in better shape than he was as a drug addict. Needing a release for these feelings, he sat down and put pen to paper. Expanding on the theme established in his car, he wrote a soul-searching song about the bridge where he used to buy drugs and the things that went on beneath that bridge. Once finished, he thought the lyrics were too sentimental, too sad for the Red Hots, and he didn't even bother to show them to the band.

Enter Rick Rubin, a hot New York producer with an eclectic list of credits on his résumé — from rappers Public Enemy to thrash-metal rockers Danzig. He was the perfect choice to helm the Red Hot Chili Peppers' next album, *BloodSugarSexMagik*. Leafing through Kiedis's notebook, "Under the Bridge" caught his eye.

Kiedis hadn't even considered including the song. It was almost folkie sounding, and he figured Rubin would hate it. The producer insisted on hearing it, urging the singer to sing it on the spot. Kiedis gave him an a cappella version. Rubin loved it and convinced Kiedis to present it to the band. The band agreed it should be on the record.

Recording commenced in Lauren Canyon in an abandoned hacienda once owned by Rudolph Valentino. Built in 1917, it was also rumored that the Beatles once dropped acid there on a visit to the United States. The band recorded live off the floor, producing the best material of their career. "Give It Away," a frenzied speed rap, would later win a 1992 Grammy as Best Hard-Rock Song. Even more popular was "Under the Bridge," a song which even the band admitted didn't have much of a hook but revealed a level of songwriting maturity missing from their other records. It was the band's first ballad. Its stripped down production — little more than sparse guitar and Kiedis's vocal — recalled Jimi Hendrix's gentle "Little Wing." *Rolling Stone* scribe David Fricke praised "Under the Bridge," saying it is "light on radio-friendly pomp and direct in its confessional detail." He went on to describe the tune as "a nervy slice of melodrama that is streets away from mosh-ville" and the locker-room chuckles the band was known for.

As for the actual location of the bridge, Keidis is not saying. "It's downtown," he told David Fricke. "But it's unimportant. I don't want people looking for it."

"Under the Bridge" was released in February 1992, following up the hot single "Give It Away."

Cop Killer

Body Count with Ice-T

A speed-metal band that started out as a hobby for rapper Ice-T brewed up a storm of controversy that made headlines. Generating the type of rage usually reserved for terrorists or other enemies of state, Ice-T's band Body Count was publicly denounced by some heavyweight individuals. Even George Bush threw in his two cents, calling the record "sick." "It makes me feel good," Ice-T told *Rolling Stone*, referring to the strife surrounding his record, "like I haven't been just standing on a street corner yelling with nobody listening all this time." At the vortex of the storm was "Cop Killer," a track from Body Count's 1992 debut.

Ice-T (born Tracy Marrow) took his stage name from Iceberg Slim, a black exploitation writer. The release of a series of hard-core hip-hop records earned him notoriety for his violent, realistic renderings of ghetto life. It's a life he understands. While rapping made him a millionaire with a mansion in Beverly Hills, he grew up on the mean streets of South Central Los Angeles. Shot twice, once during the commission of an armed robbery, his *Original Gangster* (the title of his 1991 release) swagger is authentic.

Body Count was born of the rapper's longtime love of

thrash-metal music. In the summer of 1992, Ice-T joined the Lollapalooza tour, bashing out a hard-driving set list that included "Cop Killer." Audiences loved the band, so the next logical step was to make a record. Given the multiplatinum success of Ice-T's rap recordings, a national distribution deal was quickly solidified with Time Warner Inc. The resulting record unleashed a barrage of speedy riffs, with Ice-T's inflammatory lyrics about killing a policeman. With no hip-hop beats in sight, Body Count's debut appealed to a whole new audience that wouldn't normally be caught dead listening to rap.

Ice-T admits to having some problems with the police, but he swears "Cop Killer" isn't a rallying call to gun them down in the streets. It's a song about getting even, an eye for an eye; for every kid gunned down by police, so shall a cop die. Ice-T explains he wrote the song from the perspective of a psychopath driven to the edge of reason — an individual he can understand but whose behavior he doesn't condone. "It's a record about a character," he told Alan Light in *Rolling Stone.* "I know the character, I've woken up feeling like this character. When I saw the [LA] riots on TV, I wanted to get out there, but I've never clicked over." Still, he wondered why all this attention was paid to a protest record that speaks about killing the police while nobody raises an eyebrow when kids are harmed by the cops.

Time Warner sensed there might be a problem with the inflammatory nature of the song and talked Ice-T out of calling the album *Cop Killer.* They convinced him that such a title would hurt sales as stores might refuse to stock the record. A compromise was reached. The album was officially titled *Body Count,* but the cover featured "Cop Killer" tattooed on a man's chest, gang style.

Body Count hit the stores in March 1992, debuting at Number Thirty-Two on the *Billboard* Top Fifty album chart. The real problems started when a policeman in Houston,

Film director Quentin Tarantino wasn't known as a songwriter, but according to his résumé, he has cowritten at least one tune. The song "Scooby Snacks" by Fun Loving Criminals borrows so heavily on samples from Tarantino-directed films *Reservoir Dogs* and *Pulp Fiction* that he sued and had his name added to the song's credits.

Texas heard the song and alerted his collegues at the Fraternal Organization of Cops. Deciding that this song was going to get their fellow police officers mowed down in the line of duty, they launched a campaign against the piece, Ice-T and Time Warner. Other detractors surfaced almost immediately. Oliver North called for charges of sedition to be brought against Time Warner. No fewer than sixty members of the United States Congress signed a letter calling "Cop Killer" "vile" and "despicable." The corporate office of Time Warner received bomb threats while employees of their subsidiary companies Sire and Warner Records were fending off death threats. In Texas, a group of cops under the banner CLEATS called for a national boycott of all Time Warner products. Chicago police jumped on the boycott wagon, sending thousands of copies of the following protest letter to TW executives:

> We, as members of the Chicago Police Department and members of their families, are appalled and offended that you and your country are willing to promote the Ice-T song called "Cop Killer."
>
> We are urging you to remove this song from the record stores and the media. Until such time, we intend to boycott any and all products, movies and amusement parks, such as your Six Flags, that are owned and operated by Time Warner.
>
> With all the turmoil in the world today, this song promotes more civil unrest.
>
> If you continue to promote this song, rest assured

that you will be held liable and accountable for officers that are killed as a result of subjects using this song as a plea in their defense.

In the midst of this external pressure, Time Warner, which had always promoted the artistic freedom of its performers, was suddenly being attacked from within. Arch-conservative Charlton Heston showed up at a shareholder's meeting disputing Ice-T's constitutional right to compose and perform songs such as "Cop Killer." Other TW insiders agreed, fearing that a national boycott would damage their company's reputation. Opera singer and TW chairperson Beverly Sills bowed to the external pressure and with Ice-T's blessing, stopped production on Body Count's album. The record had already gone gold, and Ice-T reasoned that "all the new people who are buying the record are snooping assholes. That's not why we want to sell records." The death threats ceased and the record became an instant collector's item.

Did "Cop Killer" contribute to violence against police? No. In 1992, cop killings were down 20 percent.

Informer

Snow

Maybe it's in the genes. The grandson of fabled Toronto outlaw Paddy McCarren, Darren O'Brien (aka Snow) had been in trouble with the law several times — twenty-three times to be specific. Breaking and entering, assault causing bodily harm, aggravated assault, the list goes on. In fact, when "Informer," his catchy, Jamaican dance-hall-influenced hit, was starting its long climb to the top of the charts, the Irish Catholic rapper was doing time.

O'Brien grew up in the mean streets of Toronto's Allenbury public-housing project. Multicultural in the extreme, O'Brien's old "hood" saw families from all over the globe living side by side. "White, black, it don't matter," O'Brien told *Rolling Stone*. "We were all brought up together." This cross-pollination was at the root of the rapper's musical education. In his early teens, he used to dress up like Kiss, miming to their records. It wasn't until a neighbor played him tapes from a Jamaican DJ called Barry Gee that O'Brien (or Snow, as his Rasta friends nicknamed him) found a different musical path — rap.

A stint in Ontario's East Detention Center for two counts of aggravated assault in 1989 (he was consequently acquitted and freed) gave Snow the determination to pursue a career in music. Upon release from jail, he made his way to New York in search of a record deal. For once, luck seemed to be on his side. He was discovered and signed to a record label. Snow produced both the album and video for "Informer" before heading back to Canada to face charges on an old assault rap.

The nine-month sentence he received in that court action seemed to stymie his burgeoning career. Behind bars, he didn't know that "Informer" had been released and was being played on *MuchMusic*, the Great White North's *MTV* equivalent. None of his fellow inmates believed him when he told them of his New York adventure. "Yeah, right," they would say sarcastically. His reputation was tarnished on the inside, but his legacy of criminal action kept him safe from his disbelieving peers.

Everything changed one night early in 1992. A fellow con who had been released phoned Snow in jail with some exciting news. "I just saw your video on *MuchMusic*," he said. "No, you couldn't have seen it. It's not out yet," was Snow's skeptical reply.

He told one or two people, not wanting the word to get around just in case it wasn't him or worse yet, in case his friend had mistaken lightweight rapper Marky Mark for him. On Friday and Saturday nights, the inmates were allowed to watch movies and then half an hour of *MuchMusic* before lights out. Snow knew that *MuchMusic* worked on a four-hour rotation, so he would have a chance to watch later that night. "Damn, I hope it's me," he thought. "Not Marky Mark."

After the movie, he paced up and down the adjoining hallway by the TV room. He was nervous. All of his jailhouse friends were inside, watching and waiting. Just minutes before lights out, he heard a familiar sound. "Bana bana bana…" — the new stylee opening of his song. Running into the TV room, he stood by the television, rapping along with the video in perfect patois. The inmates cheered as he sang and his stock rose in jail. "I was alright because it wasn't Marky Mark," he told a reporter years later.

His newfound fame spread through the facility, all the way up to the warden. One day, after Snow had been released on a day pass, the warden requested a meeting. "I saw you on 'Electric Circus,'" said the warden, referring to a *MuchMusic* dance show. "My son was watching too. He thinks your music is garbage. And, I saw a bar in the back of the set. You're not permitted to drink. I have to give you thirty days and no more passes."

Snow was crushed. How could he promote his record if he was denied passes? "No way," he said, denying that he had been drinking at *MuchMusic*. He was desperate. This was his chance at a better life.

"I'm just kidding," the warden said, revealing his cruel joke. "My son actually loves your stuff." From that point on, everything changed. In keeping with his newfound star status, he was accorded better treatment in jail. "They started saying, 'Okay. This kid has something going for his life,'" said Snow. "They started treating me a little different."

Snow was released after serving nine months — just in time to see "Informer," the rap about a police snitch become hotter than jerk chicken, hitting the top of the charts. Even as the tune sat at Number One for seven weeks, he was on parole, sworn to stay sober and attend anger management classes. The success of the song turned the twenty-three-year-old rapper's life upside down. He went to jail in a paddy wagon and left in a limousine. On the inside, he was a punk with a long record. Now he was a star with a hit record.

Creep

Radiohead

The members of the Oxford, England-based Radiohead hated the song "Creep." They wouldn't even perform it live, assigning it to the status of a warm-up number for sound checks and studio sessions. Guitarist Jon Greenwood particularly abhorred the tune and always sought new ways to undermine its effectiveness whenever the band played it. Even songwriter Thom Yorke (a dead ringer for comedian Martin Short) thought his own lyrics were "crap." So the Brits were surprised when an accidentally recorded take of "Creep" became their breakout single in the United States.

Thom Yorke was cagey about the origins of "Creep" — a song so swollen with sexual frustration and unhealthy thoughts, it seemed ready to burst at the drop of a guitar riff. Was it a true-to-life story of carnal obsession and self-loathing? Yorke was tight-lipped. "I wrote it in college," is all he would say.

In early Radiohead rehearsals, "Creep" was presented to the band and immediately rejected. Its whispered introduction — words of love to a woman, the beauty of whose skin makes the singer cry — was deemed too wimpy. The tune's middle section, with the menacing proclamation "But

I'm a CREEP!," was too psychotic, too strange even for this group of British punk popsters. The band wrote and fine-tuned other tracks for their Capitol/EMI CD debut *Pablo Honey*.

Signed on the strength of aggressive guitar pop songs like "Vegetable" and "Prove Yourself," Radiohead's sound has been described as "The Who by way of the early Jam," with substantial melodies and hummable choruses. The play list for the album did not include "Creep."

During one recording session, the band played "Creep" as the warm-up for another number. Guitarist Greenwood was upset. He loathed the song and wanted the band to drop it permanently from their repertoire. Unable to convince the lads to forget about it, he took matters into his own hands. Playing the musical saboteur, he waited until the band was about to play the chorus, then cranked his amplifiers up to ten. To ensure it was loud enough, he quickly strummed the guitar several times. On the chorus, all hell broke loose. Greenwood unleashed a wall of sound — all feedback fury and distortion — that he hoped would ruin the tune, making it unbearable to listen to.

What Greenwood didn't know was that the studio engineer had switched on the recording console, committing the guitar assault to tape. During the tune's playback, everyone agreed something was different. Greenwood's renegade playing brought the song to life. The song rocked. "Hey, what the fuck was that?" Yorke excitedly said to Greenwood. "Keep that! Do that!"

The guitarist's plan had backfired. "Creep" abruptly went from the slush pile to the Top Forty. "If that guitar hadn't exploded where it exploded," said Yorke in 1997, "there's no way it would have got on alternative radio. And we wouldn't be anywhere." Included on *Pablo Honey*, "Creep" hit the charts with a vengeance in Britain and drew considerable critical response in North America. "'Creep'...has to be the most audacious pop move since the Police scored a Number One single with a song more or less about stalking ['Every Breath You Take'] in 1983," wrote Glenn Kenny in the September 16, 1993 issue of *Rolling Stone*.

Trent Reznor, the evil genius behind Nine Inch Nails, wrote the electronic sound track for the popular computer game *Quake*.

The unexpected single established the band worldwide, becoming their first chart entry. Even though "Creep" struck a chord with many listeners, the band was taken aback at its popularity. Yorke called it a "freak" success, while Greenwood still seemed keen to disassociate himself from the song. "It's not like our song anymore," he told *Rolling Stone*. "When we play it, it feels like we're doing a cover."

Spoonman

Soundgarden

Like many of Seattle's Sub Pop Records alumni, Soundgarden were noted for their raw heavy-metal sound. Longtime fans were surprised with the release of "Spoonman," a largely acoustic track featuring the spoons as a lead instrument.

Soundgarden entered Seattle's famous Bad Animals Studios with enough material for two full-length albums. Following up the critical and commercial success of 1991's *Badmotorfinger* wouldn't be easy, and the band was determined to be prepared. The band honed their chops on the road while songwriter Chris Cornell practiced his craft, writing lyrics for Alice Cooper and Flotsam and Jetsam.

Working with producer Michael Beinhorn, the heavy metalists trimmed down their tunes to fifteen, picking a diverse group of songs geared to expand the band's sound. The selection process was a democratic one. The four band members would vote for each song, and only those unanimously agreed upon were deemed good enough to be included on the record. Guitarist Kim Thayil told a reporter, "There were some songs that maybe one of us liked, but that wasn't enough to justify the band doing them."

Some of the choices were painful for the individual

members. Bassist Ben Shepherd loved a song called "Cold Bitch," fighting for its inclusion. He was vetoed by the others, and while the song has turned up as a B-side on several singles, he is philosophical about the tune. "It feels like an alienated child from the family or the one that was left behind."

During the recording of the as-yet-untitled album, Cornell took a night off to watch a video called *Superclown*. He misread the title as *Superunknown*, and thought it was a cool term. Although it is a nonsense name for a record, the rest of the band liked it and adopted it as the album's working title.

The completed tracks were a disparate lot — aggressive, intelligent and experimental. Cornell called the album unfocused, "...but in a good way." He likened the record to a movie sound track where each tune offered a different feel, adding up to one atmospheric whole. "Let Me Down" was a blues-based rocker, while "My Wave" recalled California's surf-punk sound. The tracks that followed mixed it up even farther, blending psychedelic ballads with the title tune's almost Motown feel. Many reviewers noted the band's growth, pointing out that "Spoonman," *Superunknown*'s first single, appeared to pay homage to The Who. The band admitted the debt to the British supergroup, allowing that the tune's percussion was reminiscent of "Magic Bus," a 1968 hit.

The quirky percussion on "Spoonman" was supplied by one of Soundgarden's Seattle heroes. Street musician Artis the Spoonman, who began playing the spoons in 1974, was a familiar face in Pike Place Market. When Soundgarden was first starting out, they would often head down to the market to listen to the mohawked busker play his spoons. Years after their first meeting, Cornell immortalized Artis in *Superunknown*'s strongest track. Since busking was his only source of income, Artis was hired to play on the record and appear in the video, becoming a local legend.

Offspring repaid a fan's loyalty by hiring him to sing on one of their most popular records. A forklift operator from Orange County, California, Jason Whittaker was given one line in the band's hit "Come Out and Play." He intones the tune's most famous line "You gotta keep 'em separated."

Released in the spring of 1994, *Superunknown* wasted no time in declaring its arrival. Debuting at the top slot on the *Billboard* charts, the album ultimately outsold the hot acts of the day including Candlebox and fellow Pacific Northwesterners Nirvana. Reviews were kind, with one critic throwing a backhanded compliment in the band's direction: "Soundgarden have come through with the great Led Zeppelin album they have been threatening to put out since 1988."

"Spoonman" was the record's lead release, spawning a video (the first of seven culled from the album) and no less than six different single versions including one on clear vinyl, a cassette single and a seven-inch picture disc.

What's the Frequency, Kenneth?

R.E.M.

A peculiar incident involving a convicted killer and a stodgy television talking head inspired Michael Stipe to pen "What's the Frequency, Kenneth?" — the first single release from *Monster*, R.E.M.'s hardest rocking album to date.

The release of two back-to-back acoustic albums had turned R.E.M. into international superstars. *Out of Time* (March 1991) and *Automatic for the People* (October 1992) were quiet, deeply personal records that reflected the band's somber mood. Although their star was rising in the world market, for R.E.M., it was the best of times and the worst of times. During the recording of those records, guitarist Peter Buck, drinking heavily, sunk into a deep depression following the dissolution of his marriage. Buck's melancholy mood pervaded every note on that dark duo of records.

When it came time to record their next record and mount their first tour in five years, the band opted for an upbeat strategy. Drummer Bill Berry demanded the change, threatening to hang up his drumsticks if they made another acoustic album, thereby jeopardizing a musical partnership that had been established over a decade before.

Writing commenced in September 1993, and the band

The members of R.E.M. must have loved to eat out in restaurants. They have immortalized two Southern eateries on two separate albums. The *Dead Letter Office* 1987 instrumental cut "Walter's Theme" was a tribute to Walter's Bar-B-Que, one of their favorite dining spots. The phrase *Automatic for the People*, used as the title for their multi-platinum 1992 long player, was borrowed from Weaver D's Delicious Fine Foods restaurant in Clarke County, Georgia. At the soul-food restaurant, when a customer placed an order, the waiters responded with the chirpy catchphrase "Automatic," as if to say, "No problem."

pumped out a series of straight-ahead rockers that saw the acoustic instruments of the past albums gathering dust in the closet. After writing forty-odd songs for consideration, by mutual consent, the quartet pared down the number to twelve tunes that fit their idea of what a roaring rock-and-roll record should be. Naming the completed tracks *Monster* (a sly homage to a Steppenwolf album of the same name), the band unleashed their hard-edged sound to the public exactly one year after the writing began. *Monster* debuted at Number One on the *Billboard* Two Hundred in September 1994.

The album kicks off with a three-minute and fifty-nine-second electric guitar blast, signaling R.E.M.'s return to a stripped-down sound. The inspiration for "What's the Frequency, Kenneth?" was ripped from the headlines of the day. A newspaper account of a strange encounter between CBS news anchor Dan Rather and a street person moved Michael Stipe to compose the song. Walking to the CBS television studio in New York one day, Rather was accosted by William Tager, a disturbed ex-convict who had served time for manslaughter. During the verbal assault, Tager repeatedly yelled, "What's the frequency, Kenneth?," a nonsense phrase that Stipe later identified as streetspeak. Rather was shaken but unhurt by the encounter.

Stipe built on that event, crafting a tune that thumbs

its nose at the media. He later told *Musician Magazine*'s Vic Garbarini, "[It's] about people playing into the bullshit about the media drawing lines among young people in this country — that group is about cynicism, and this group are idealists. And yes, it's also commenting on how we go about trying to research and analyze things we don't understand, like people younger than ourselves, rather than using our intuition and figuring it out from that end." Whatever Stipe's enigmatic lyrics are about, he commented, "'Kenneth' is such a joy to sing, I don't care what the words are about."

The phrase "losing my religion," the basis of R.E.M.'s 1991 Top Five hit, was an antiquated saying from the American South. It means "at wit's end," or "at the end of your rope."

"Kenneth's" tempo slows near the end. During the song's live recording, bassist Mike Mills slowed down the pace. The rest of the band instinctively followed his lead, not realizing he was having an appendicitis attack and would have to be rushed to the hospital. After Mills's recovery, the band never found time to rerecord the song, so it was released as is.

"What's the Frequency, Kenneth?" had the unexpected side effect of allowing Dan Rather to show his lighter side. In a comedy bit on David Letterman's *Late Show*, Rather was seen rigidly conducting R.E.M. in a run through of the song. The publicity generated by that performance, and R.E.M.'s own gritty video that won major airplay on *MTV*, helped push "What's the Frequency, Kenneth?" to the midpoint of the Top Forty.

The Macarena

Los Del Rio

In 1996, everybody did The Macarena. Hillary Rodham Clinton did the Spanish dance at the Democratic Convention. Chita Rivera shook her booty Latin style along with a crowd of fifty thousand fans at Yankee Stadium. Even Bob Dole got into the act. Falling off a stage in Chico, California, Dole covered by saying he was doing that "new Democratic dance, The Macarena." All this attention came as a shock to the song's creators Antonio Romero Monge and Rafael Ruiz, better known as Los Del Rio. Colleagues for thirty-two years, the duo has released a record a year for as long as they have been together. "The Macarena" became their biggest hit and the first Spanish song to top the US *Billboard* chart.

As curious as it may seem now, "The Macarena" almost didn't get released when it was recorded in 1993. Despite a career spanning more than three decades, Antonio Romero Monge and Rafael Ruiz had never scored a chart-busting hit. As Los Del Rio, the two men were cult darlings in Don Hermanas, a small city in Spain. Monge wrote the infectious number in homage to Diana Patricia Cubillan, a sensuous Flamenco dancer whose erotic moves entranced him after seeing her perform in a Venezuelan nightclub. Depending on which report you believe, Monge either named the song after a saint whose statue is carried through the streets of Seville every year or a neighborhood in that Spanish city.

Initially, Los Del Rio's record company didn't want to release the tune. The record label's quandary was with the line "Dale a tu cuerpo alegria, Macarena" ("Give your body some joy, Macarena") — pretty racy stuff for Spanish radio. The company yielded, releasing "The Macarena" with little or no promotion in April 1993. Despite the lack of publicity, the tune became a minor summer hit in Spain.

The story could have ended there. With no international promotion, "The Macarena" fell off the charts in Spain and seemed destined to become a footnote in Los Del Rio's prolific career. Then came a series of unrelated events that propelled them into the glare of the international spotlight. In 1994, their record company was snapped up by music-industry colossus BMG, and after Los Del Rio performed for the Pope, a BMG excutive commissioned a video for "The Macarena." The clip's director made a decision that would ultimately make the tune the Number One dance song of the nineties. He hired Mia Frye, an American dance instructor based in Paris, to choreograph easy-to-remember dance moves for the tune. "My main focus," she said, "was to remove anything that was too fast. It was important not to include moves that were dependent on

Duran Duran took their name from a character in the campy sci-fi film *Barbarella*. It was no surprise, then, that they released a tune called "Electric Barbarella" on 1997's *Medazzaland* CD. Leader Simon LeBon denied the song was inspired by the film. In an interview with *Toronto Sun*'s Jane Stevenson, he said "[Keyboardist] Nick [Rhodes] worked the lyric for that one, and he wanted a four-syllable name, and somebody had already used "Macarena." "Barbarella" just seemed like the right one."

THE MACARENA

Just in case you missed
it, here's how you dance
The Macarena:

Right and left arms
    straight out front,
    palms down.
Right and left arms
    straight out front,
    palms up.
Right hand grasps inside
    of left arm at elbow.
Left hand grasps inside
    of right arm at elbow.
Right hand behind right
    back of neck.
Left hand behind left
    back of neck.
Right hand on left front
    pants pocket.
Left hand on right pants
    pocket.
Right hand on right
    front pants pocket.
Left hand on left front
    pants pocket.
Move rump to the left.
Move rump to the right.
Move rump to the left.
Clap hands and jump
    ninety degrees to the
    right.

the beat. I wanted to be sure that even a child with no sense of rhythm could dance The Macarena." She came up with a series of nonchallenging line-dancing moves that were easy to memorize and perform.

The song about the sassy temptress Macarena made the rounds in European nightclubs, earning little radio play but packing dance floors all over the continent. In late 1995, the Bayside Boys, a Miami remixing team, reworked a club mix of the tune, adding an English monologue about a woman who rejects her soldier boyfriend Vitorino to hang out with his two best friends. Samples from *The Graduate*, with Anne Bancroft cooing, "I'm not trying to seduce you," were thrown in to add extra steam.

A hit in the clubs, the Bayside Boys' "The Macarena" wasn't an immediate radio favorite. After eighteen weeks on the charts, it peaked at Number Forty-Five before falling off the hit parade in December 1995. Then, as the weather got hotter, so did the song. "The Macarena's" club success continued to spread, and suddenly the song was on the charts again. Thirty-three weeks after the Bayside Boys originally entered the charts, "The Macarena" went all the way to Number One, making it the slowest rising pop single in history.

By then, it seemed the public couldn't get enough of "The Macarena."

Soon there were three versions of the tune on the pop charts — the Bayside Boys', the original Los Del Rio rendering and a copycat take on the ditty by Los Del Mar.

The tune had hips gyrating everywhere — not just in trendy nightclubs. In Malta, they did the dance at the Nationalist Party rallies. Beer drinkers at Oktoberfest in Munich wagged their lederhosen to "The Macarena." Kids and grandmothers alike were waving their arms to the catchy song, propelled by the bouncy rhythm, not the steamy story. "The Macarena" is a rare Number One hit that transcended generations, vocations and ethnicity. It's huge appeal crossed all lines, sucking everyone in, even the rhythmically challenged.

By the end of the year, the very clubs that had propelled "The Macarena" into public consciousness had grown tired of repeated requests for the dance tune. One club posted a copy of the CD upside down on the staff bulletin board, warning their DJs not to play it. Another club retired the song in what they called a "crispy celebration," burning a copy of the disc on the sidewalk outside their establishment. The craze was over.

Ironic

Alanis Morissette

A song from Alanis Morissette's multiplatinum *Jagged Little Pill* CD hit heavily on the charts but left English teachers scratching their heads. "Ironic" was her fifth Top Five single in 1996. "The most ironic thing about that song," said one DJ, "is that it is mostly not about irony at all. It's about bummers."

Ottawa-born Alanis Morissette has been singing since she was old enough to walk. In 1977, at the age of three, she memorized the entire score of *Grease*, and using a nail-polish bottle as a microphone, she often sang it in a loud, clear voice for her family. The three Morissette kids were obsessed with show business. Chad, Wade (her twin brother, born June 1, 1974, older by twelve minutes) and Alanis practiced dance routines they learned from watching videos and often acted out scenes from movies and television. Soon the boys moved on to more practical pursuits — Chad veering toward a career in business, while Wade became interested in sports. Alanis, though, was single-minded. She wanted to feel the heat of the spotlight.

In school, she participated in musicals such as *Annie*, and by 1984, she was writing her own songs, composing both lyrics and music. At age ten, she sent a tape of her songs to singers Lindsay and Jacqui Morgan, close friends of the family. One song, "Fate Stay With Me," knocked out the couple. They helped Alanis rewrite the tune, adding structure to her crude melody, teaching her how to write a song. A few months later, having taken the Morgans' advice to heart, Alanis was writing polished songs.

The year 1991 saw the realization of her dream — a full-length CD titled *Alanis*. She cowrote each of the ten dance tracks, scoring a Top Five Canadian hit with "Too Hot." Canadian success continued with the 1992 release of *Now Is the Time*, moving 100,000 units and earning a gold record. Alanis's brand of dance pop earned her the label of "the Paula Abdul of Canada."

Although successful in Canada, the first two records were not released in the United States. With an eye toward an American release, she left Ottawa for Toronto to work with different songwriters and expand her sound. It was not a happy time. The next two years saw a series of disastrous relationships and unfulfilled creative needs. In 1994, she began commuting to Los Angeles, meeting with a series of songwriters in hopes of finding someone with the creative spark needed to kick her songwriting skills up a notch. She found her man in the form of Mississippi-born Glen Ballard, a seasoned record-industry veteran who had been associated with records by Michael Jackson and Wilson-Phillips — discs that had sold a reported 100 million copies.

MCA set up a meeting between the two in February 1994, and they immediately connected. "Musically and cerebrally, Glen and I were so on the same wavelength, it all came together," she told *Mojo*. One night, while working on a song that never got finished, they had an idea for another. In twenty minutes, they had written "Perfect." Later that night, they recorded it, and that original demo appeared on *Jagged Little Pill*. Later, Alanis would call that night one of the most "overwhelming spiritual moments" she's ever had.

"Perfect" established a methodology for their collaboration. Sitting together — Alanis on the floor, Ballard settled in a chair — they would strum acoustic guitars, working on snippets of lyrical and melodic ideas. When inspiration came, Alanis would enter a zone, almost as though the music was being channeled through her from some spiritual source. Songs were written and recorded the same night — sometimes taking only a couple of hours from the germination of an idea to a finished demo. The work was so stream of consciousness that Alanis would occasionally replay a tape recorded the night before and have no recollection of the tune or how they wrote it. Using this method, the pair penned twenty songs, including "Ironic," with twelve making the final cut for *Jagged Little Pill.*

The first sign of the album's eventual popularity came early. LA radio station KROQ sneak previewed "You Oughta Know" on May 16, 1995, weeks before *Jagged Little Pill*'s official release date. Public reaction was swift as the KROQ phone lines lit up. Listeners loved the song. The Alanis juggernaut had begun.

Subsequent *Jagged Little Pill* singles were snapped up by a record-buying public hungry for any song from the twenty-one-year-old Canadian. "Hand in My Pocket," "You Learn" and "Head

Camapress Photo Service

Contrary to her mellow, meditative style of writing, in live performance, Alanis Morissette is a whirling dervish as pictured in this 1996 photo from a London Hyde Park concert.

Over Feet" all topped the charts. But it was "Ironic" that picked up kudos from the public while earning scorn from the academic community. A debate played out in the newspapers questioned whether the song actually contained any real irony. A headline in the *Washington Post* blared "Now THIS Is Ironic; It's Like a Hit Song that Got the Words Wrong." Reporter Richard Leiby called the song an example of "irony abuse," writing, "Just wrap quotes around a word, capitalize it or add an exclamation mark, and you've got Instant Irony!"

Saying the opposite of what you really mean is rhetorical irony. *Webster's* cites the example of saying "It's a lovely day" when it is raining. Classic irony is more complicated. Leiby cites satirist Jonathan Swift's *A Modest Proposal* as an example: "As a solution to the Irish famine, an economist proposes that the babies of the Irish poor be sold as food to the rich landlords — to raise money to prevent starvation." Alanis is trying for situational irony, defined as "a combination of circumstances or a result that is the opposite of what is or might be expected or considered appropriate." Does she hit the mark? Carol Myers-Scotton of the University of South Carolina doesn't think so. She gave the song a poor mark, citing the "rain on your wedding day" line as bad luck, not irony. Catholic University professor Glen Johnson agrees, saying the tune lacks the "doubleness" required for proper irony. "There should be two levels," he told Leiby, "some meaning other than the surface meaning."

Academics may have given the record a failing mark, but record buyers were unfazed, pushing the song to the top of the charts.

Sheryl Crow's 1993 album *Tuesday Night Music Club* was named after a group of friends who worked together in informal sessions at Bill Bottrell's Pasadena, California studio. Members included Crow, David Baerwald, Kevin Gilbert and the band Wire Train. The musicians would gather and work on songs. By the end of each Tuesday "we'd have recorded either a piece of shit or a great work," Crow said.

Anybody Seen My Baby?

Rolling Stones

Mick Jagger and Keith Richards have been writing songs together for over thirty years. Prolific in the extreme, their alliance has yielded hundreds of songs and moved millions of pieces of vinyl. In 1997, on the eve of the release of *Bridges to Babylon*, the Rolling Stones' twenty-third studio album, a quandary arose. The proposed first single sounded suspiciously like another song. Something had to be done. "We don't steal songs," quipped Keith. "We've got enough."

When Mick Jagger was writing "Anybody Seen My Baby?," he was working toward an R & B groove. Rhythm and blues was Jagger's first love. In middle school, he and Richards had become fast friends because of their mutual admiration of the American beat music of Chuck Berry, Muddy Waters and Bo Diddley. A few years later, the Rolling Stones came together as a band to play the music they loved. "When we started, we were just playing blues and rhythm and blues because that's what we liked," Jagger once told a reporter. "We were playing it well, and nobody else was doing it. We were blues purists who liked ever-so commercial things but never did them onstage because we were...so wary of being blues purists, you know what I mean?"

Years later, the Rolling Stones could hardly be described as blues purists. Three decades in, the Stones have appropriated virtually every American music genre — rock and roll, jazz, soul, disco and country. Adept at many styles, Jagger was working toward an updated, less-raw R & B sound for "Anybody Seen My Baby?" — a Gamble and Huff soul feel for the nineties. Starting with a slow, chunky bass line, he built the tune around a melodic chorus of lost love.

An interview given during his early songwriting days explains Jagger's composing modus operandi, thoughts that may explain his state of mind when writing the lyrics for "Anybody Seen My Baby?" "I was very emotional as a teenager, but then most adolescents are, like overdramatizing situations, and that's why there's always been a very big market for adolescent love songs," revealed Jagger. "You know, those songs that are based on the frustrations of an adolescent. Anyone who understands that, consciously or unconsciously, and writes fantasies based on that premise, gets hits. A song like "Young Love," which was very popular

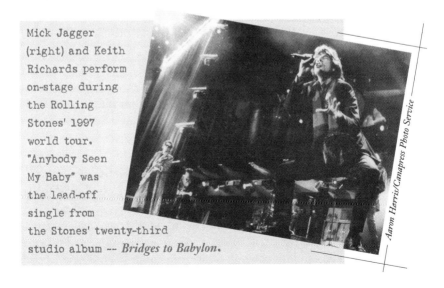

Mick Jagger (right) and Keith Richards perform on-stage during the Rolling Stones' 1997 world tour. "Anybody Seen My Baby" was the lead-off single from the Stones' twenty-third studio album -- *Bridges to Babylon*.

Aaron Harris/Canapress Photo Service

Oasis songwriter Noel Gallagher openly admitted that he borrowed liberally from other people's songs in his works. "No composer is ever a virgin," he said. "You never start from scratch." This attitude got him in a little bit of trouble from the members of Monty Python. The comedians sued Oasis for plagiarism. In contention was the album track "Whatever" that seemed to borrow a little too heavily from the 1973 Python tune "How Sweet to Be an Idiot."

when I was around fourteen, was a heart-tugging song when you were that age."

"Anybody Seen My Baby?" is the Stones' strongest new song in years. "It's kind of lightish," Jagger told *Access Magazine* in November 1997. "It's not heavy heavy, but it's definitely R & B." Propelled by Jagger's powerful vocal, he sells the melancholy chorus, establishing the hook of the song. It was the chorus, however, that caused some contention in the Rolling Stones' camp.

Guitarist Keith Richards says while they were recording the track in the studio, there was a familiar ring to the tune, "but nobody put their finger on it until we'd finished it." Richards's daughter was the keen-eared listener who caught the problem.

"I was in England a few weeks ago, and I was playing it in the front room, and my daughter arrived with her friend in the kitchen," Richards told *Toronto Sun* reporter Jane Stevenson. "And they don't know what's playing, and it's wafting through the house, and they started to sing "Constant Craving" over the top, and it was, 'Oh — time to make a phone call.'"

A call was placed to the Stones' lawyer. He advised offering a cowriting credit to k.d. lang and Ben Mink, the Canadian composers of the 1992 hit "Constant Craving," lest the Stones be tarred with the ugly brush of plagiarism. A nondeliberate plagiarism lawsuit was not unprecedented. Songwriters have been on guard since the publishers representing songwriter Ronnie Mack successfully sued George Harrison for copyright infringement in 1971. They claimed his Number One "My Sweet Lord" bore an unreasonable resemblance to the 1963 hit "He's So Fine." United States District Court Judge Richard Owen ruled in favor of the publishers, although he conceded that Harrison did not deliberately plagiarize the song. That case dragged through court for five years. The Rolling Stones wanted to avoid a similar situation and found a compromise with the Canadian composers.

Lang and Mink were satisfied with the arrangement although Jagger was less so. He admitted to respecting lang although he didn't own any of her records. "I don't think it really sounds like it myself," he told Stevenson. "It's just a lot of nervous lawyers."

"Anybody Seen My Baby?" reached the Top Ten on the *Billboard* charts in the fall of 1997.

I'll Be Missing You

Sean "Puff Daddy" Combs with Faith Evans

The year 1997 may be remembered for posthumous tribute songs ruling the charts. Elton John's warmed-over "Candle in the Wind" raised millions for charity in memory of Diana, Princess of Wales, while another song eulogizing a slain rapper was part of a very different campaign, ensuring his memory would not die. "I'll Be Missing You" kept Notorious B.I.G./ Biggie Small's flame alive on the charts.

"You're nobody until somebody kills you," are the closing lines on Notorious B.I.G.'s posthumously released CD *Life After Death*. The disc's cover shows the rapper posing next to a hearse, his name emblazoned on the vanity license plate. Violent death is a common theme in hip-hop culture, but these references are particularly telling given the events of Sunday March 9, 1997.

A night of party hopping with his friend/producer/ mentor Sean "Puff Daddy" Combs brought Notorious B.I.G. (whose real name was Christopher Wallace) to the Soul Train Awards, hosted by *Vibe* in Hollywood. Biggie was a star on the rise, with a hit album under his belt — 1994's *Ready to Die* — and another soon to be released. Hype spun all around the former drug dealer from Brooklyn's Fort Greene. Newspapers ran running ads urging people to "Think

B.I.G.," keeping Biggie's three hundred pounds of rapping wrath front and center. After a few drinks and a bit of glad-handing, he headed out to his Chevy Suburban for the drive home. As party goers and two of Biggie's best friends watched, a dark sedan pulled up alongside his vehicle. Several shots were fired, and seconds later, Biggie was dead, slumped over the dash of the Chevy. He was just twenty-four years old. Police report it was the one hundredth drive-by shooting in Los Angeles that year.

In the following weeks, LAPD searched for a motive in the shooting. One theory held that Biggie was murdered as the result of a personal financial quarrel involving a Compton Southside Crip gang member who had briefly worked for the rapper. Police also investigated the possibility that Biggie was killed as a result of an East-West feud between New York's Bad Boy Records and Los Angeles' Death Row Records. At the time of this writing, Biggie's murder case remains unsolved.

It is an unwritten rule in the music business that nothing sells records like an unexpected death. Otis Redding, Buddy Holly, Jim Croce, Tupac Shakur and Kurt Cobain all had posthumous records snapped up by bereaved fans in a outburst of public mourning. Biggie's sophomore effort, the double CD *Life After Death* released one week after his demise, debuted at Number One, hanging around the Top Ten for a full fifteen weeks.

The success of the disc was in part due to the market-ing efforts of the record's producer Sean "Puff Daddy" Combs. Combs, best known as the brains behind multiplat-inum discs by Boyz II Men, R. Kelley, Mariah Carey and Lil' Kim, spearheaded a "Remember" campaign to keep Biggie's name in the headlines. Among the events he organized were a New Orlean's-style funeral cortege in the streets of Brooklyn in March 1997 and an unprecedented thirty-seconds of silence on two hundred radio stations across the United

States. The jewel in the crown of Puffy's "Remember" campaign was a musical tribute, a triple-platinum single called "I'll Be Missing You."

The tear-jerking single featuring Biggie's widow Faith Evans was recorded to raise money for Biggie's two children — all profits from the song to be put in trust for the kids. As the leadoff track on Combs's solo debut *No Way Out*, "I'll Be Missing You" was also seen by some critics as a fail-safe way to kick off his singing career. Writing in *Spin Magazine*, Sia Michel cynically called the release "marketable mourning," suggesting that Combs was cashing in on the death of his friend. Combs answered his critics in the documentary *Born Again*: "I'm a Biggie fanatic," he said. "I have his name tattooed on my body. Remembering Biggie is never going to stop."

Heartfelt tribute or clever marketing ploy? Either way, "I'll Be Missing You" is a strikingly effective single. Combs cribbed the melody from the 1983 Police hit "Every Breath You Take," changing the sampled song's minor-chord melancholy into what *Rolling Stone*'s David Fricke called "a radiant hymn of brotherly love and community's loss." The use of a recycled melody lent "I'll Be Missing You" a built-in sense of familiarity, but according to Combs, that didn't guarantee it would be a hit. "It's not easy to use a hit record and make it become a hit that sells two million copies," Combs told Anthony Bozza in *Rolling Stone*. "Try it, be my guest, go sample…. I mean, I may do it, but it's an art form."

"I'll Be Missing You" shot to the top of the charts, earning another platinum record for the twenty-seven-year-old rap mogul. Statistically, 1997 will go down in Combs's personal history as a very successful year. His solo record and offshoot productions dominated the rap, pop and R & B charts, but at the end of the year, his thoughts turned to his departed friend. "I would do anything," he told Bozza, "I would turn the hits into negative hits if I could just be with Biggie again."

Tubthumping

Chumbawamba

A casual listen to Chumbawamba's breakthrough hit suggests that it's just another addition to the long-held tradition of drinking songs in English pop music. The band had a different idea when they wrote the tune. Devout anarchists, Chumbawamba would like nothing more than for their music to be the rallying cry for those feeling government oppression. In 1997, "Tubthumping" went to Number One in most major North American markets.

Chumbawamba are not an overnight sensation. The five men and three women from Leeds, England have been struggling since 1982 when they banded together, taking their name from a dream one of the band members had. In the dream, he saw two public washrooms — one labeled "Chumba," the other labeled "Wamba." Neither word made sense to him, and he didn't know which loo to use. The dream resonated with the band, and they adopted the nonsense word as their moniker.

Politically charged songs have rarely done well on the charts, particularly when they seemed to take the piss out of conventional thought. A case in point was their 1986 debut on their independent label Agit-Prop. After watching *Live*

Oasis fans have long wondered about the mysterious Elsa mentioned in the lyrics of "Supersonic." She was not a groupie although she did hang around the studio while the boys were recording. Elsa was a stray dog befriended by the band that had, to put it delicately, a gastrointestinal problem. One night, she compounded her problem by gobbling a whole box of Alka Seltzer. Noel Gallagher was so amused by the flatulent dog that he paid her his highest compliment by exalting her in song.

Aid, the anarchists were disgusted by the sentiment of the concert. In their estimation, the benefit exploited the underprivileged and only served to boost the egos of the performers. Their response was an album called *Pictures of Starving Children Sell Records*. Not surprisingly, in the era of Sir Bob Geldof and the feel-good mania surrounding *Live Aid*, the album failed to chart.

More controversial records followed on their next indie label One Little Indian. A collection of tunes called *Jesus H. Christ* deliberately plagiarized Top Forty songs and was deemed unsuitable for release. *Anarchy* almost made it to the record stores, but it was banned because of a graphic depiction of a baby being born on its cover.

Other records actually saw the light of day. *English Rebel Songs* was an album of a cappella folk music, while their next release, *Slap*, was a tribute to techno. In total, Chumbawamba recorded eight records for One Little Indian before entering the studio to work on the as-yet-untitled *Tubthumper*.

The sessions began, as all the others had, with a collection of tunes worked up by the band during their live shows. A few weeks into recording, One Little Indian expressed concern over the content of the album. They suggested scrapping the whole project, telling the band to take some time off to write new material. The band rankled at this, opting instead to dissolve their association with the label. With the record in the can but no label to release it, all looked lost. But several tense months later, VH1 programmer Lee Chestnut heard the single "Tubthumping" on a compilation disc. He loved the catchy tune and after doing some homework, found out that Chumbawamba was a free agent. He alerted Republic Records' honcho Monte Freeman who requested a copy of the record from the band's English management. After only one listen, he was prepared to deal.

An offer from major label Republic/Universal in America seemed like an unlikely choice for a band of fiercely independent British anarchists. But as vocalist Dunstan Bruce explained to *Los Angeles Times* scribe Jerry Crowe, "Anarchy isn't about being in your own little exclusive club…. We want as many people as possible to hear what we've got to say because we think what we've got to say is of much more value than what, say, the Spice Girls or Oasis have to say." The deal was signed, and the album was given worldwide release. Their message would soon reach an audience far larger than they ever would have imagined.

Naming the album *Tubthumper* — according to their Web site, British slang for "an orator, ranter, a soapbox preacher" — they released the first single, "Tubthumping," in October 1997. A mix of dance beats and catchy call-and-response vocals, the band describes "Tubthumping" as much more than an ode to the pleasures of drinking. "It's a song for those people who don't really have a voice," said Bruce, whose working-class vocal provides the song's insanely appealing hook. "It's a song for all those people who only get a chance to express their opinion when they stand up in a pub drunk and start mouthing off about something, or when they're singing on the way home from the pub."

Band member Danbert "the Cat" Nobacon expanded on those sentiments in an interview with Paul Freeman. "The idea for 'Tubthumping' is in the lines 'I get knocked down; I get back up again.' It's about someone who works in a crap job. He goes off to the pub and still has the life inside him to rise above it. That's a universal theme."

"We were writing about things in our community and our lives," he continued. "But it does cross over. Despite the details, people in Venezuela or Canada, in a lot of cases, can see something in their lives that is parallel."

When "Tubthumping" became an international hit, Chumbawamba had to face critics who charged that they had sold out, that they weren't real anarchists, that they had become part of the capitalist machine. Nobacon denied that major success had dulled their subversive edge. "We accept the contradiction of being anarchists and working for a major corporation," he said. "But life is full of contradictions. If we'd stayed doing pamphlets, then we'd still be reaching only two hundred people. Just because we're suddenly popular, why should we lose our credibility?"

Selected Bibliography

Bronson, Fred. *The Billboard Book of Number One Hits: The Inside Story Behind the Top of the Charts.* New York: Billboard Publications, Inc., 1985.

Cain, Robert. *Whole Lotta Shakin' Goin' On.* New York: The Dial Press, 1981.

Christgau, Robert. *Christgau's Record Guide.* New Haven and New York: Ticknor & Fields, 1981.

Cooper, Alice, as told to Gaines, Steven. *Me, Alice.* New York: G.P. Putnam's Sons, 1976.

Dawson, Jim and Propes, Steve. *What Was the First Rock 'N' Roll Record?.* Boston and London: Faber and Faber, 1992.

DeCurtis, Anthony with Henke, James with George-Warren, Holly. *The Rolling Stone Album Guide.* New York: Random House, 1992.

Demorest, Steve. *Alice Cooper: Shock Rock's Glitter King*. New York: Popular Library, 1974.

Edwards, Henry and Zanetta, Tony. *Stardust: The David Bowie Story*. New York: Bantam Books, 1986.

Fein, Art. *The L.A. Musical History Tour*. Boston and London: Faber and Faber, 1990.

Gritter, Headley. *Rock 'N' Roll Asylum*. New York: Putnam Publishing Group, 1984.

Hibbert, Tom. *Rockspeak! The Dictionary of Rock Terms*. London/New York/Sydney: Omnibus Press, 1983.

Kent, Nick. *The Dark Stuff*. England: Penguin Books, 1994.

Kiersh, Edward. *Where Are You Now Bo Diddley?*. Garden City, New York: Dolphin Books, 1986.

Larkin, Colin. *The Guinness Encyclopedia of Popular Music*. Enfield, Middlesex: Guiness Publishing Ltd., 1993.

Lydon, John with Zimmerman, Keith and Kent. *Rotten: No Irish — No Blacks — No Dogs*. New York: Picador USA, 1994.

Marsh, Dave. *The Heart of Rock & Soul*. New York: Plume Books, 1989.

Marsh, Dave with Swenson, John. *The Rolling Stone Record Guide*. United States: Randon House, 1979.

Morrell, Brad. *Nirvana and the Sound of Seattle*. New York: Omnibus Press, 1993.

Nolan, A.M. *Rock 'N' Roll Road Trip*. New York: Pharos Books, 1992.

Norman, Phillip. *Elton: The Definitive Biography*. London: Arrow Books, 1991.

Palmer, Robert. *Jerry Lee Lewis Rocks*. New York: Delilah Books, 1981.

Smith, Joe with Fink, Mitchell. *Off the Record: An Oral History of Popular Music*. New York: Warner Books, 1988.

Stein, Cathi. *Elton John*. Great Britain: Futura Publications Limited, 1975.

Taraborrelli, Randy J. *Michael Jackson: The Magic and the Madness*. New York: Ballantine Books, 1991.

Thompson, Dave. *Never Fade Away: The Kurt Cobain Story*. New York: St. Martin's Paperbacks, 1994.

Tosches, Nick. *Hellfire: The Jerry Lee Lewis Story*. New York: Delacorte Press, 1982.

Walker, Dave. *American Rock 'N' Roll Tour*. Emeryville: Thunder's Mouth Press, 1992.

Whitburn, Joel. *The Billboard Book of Top 40 Hits: 5th Edition*. New York: Billboard Books, 1992.

Index

A

"Abraham, Martin and John" 65
Ace 139-141
"Across the Universe" 135, 137
A Hard Days Night 67
"A Hard Days Night" 71
"Ain't That A Shame" 9, 33
*A Kick In the Head Is Worth Eight
    In the Pants* 150
"Albert Flasher" 115
"A White Sports Coat (and A Pink
    Carnation)" 120
"American Pie" 119-122
American Woman 132
. . . *And Justice For All* 220
Andrea True Connection 158-160
Anka, Paul 19
"Anybody Seen My Baby?" 268-271
Approaching Day 125
"At the Hop" 39, 46
Atkins, Chet 36, 37
Axton, Mae 34, 35

B

"Baby" 30
Bachman-Turner Overdrive
    132-134
"Bad, Bad Leroy Brown" 125-128
Barry, Jeff 72, 74
Bartholomew, Dave 7
Baxter, Les 36
Bay City Rollers 153, 156, 157
Bayside Boys, The 262, 263
Beach Boys, The 124
Beatles, The 66-69, 88
Bee Gees, The 150-152
Berry, Chuck 27-29
"Billie Jean" 192-194

Blackboard Jungle, The 25, 26, 27
Blackwell, Robert "Bumps" 30-33
"Blasphemous Rumours" 204-206
Blood, Sweat and Tears 86
"Blowtop Blues" 31
"Blue Bayou" 75
"Blueberry Hill" 9
"Blue Suede Shoes" 38-41
Body Count 244-247
Bogart, Neil 106, 107
"Bohemian Rhapsody" 173
Bono 217-219
"Book Of Love" 51-53, 120
Boomtown Rats, The 167-169
"Boppin' the Blues" 41
Bowie, David 1, 2, 135-138, 165
Boy George 196
"Bo Diddley" 20-22
"Break It To Them Gently" 115
Brenston, Jackie 10-12
Bridge Over Troubled Waters 123
Bridges To Babylon 268, 269
Brinsley Swartz 139
Brownsville Station 129-131
B.T.O. 132-134
"Burning Down the House"
    185-188

C

"Campbells Are Coming, The" 97
Campbell, Glenn 50
"Can't Buy Me Love" 66-67
"Careless Whispers" 208
Carnes, Kim 232
Carrack, Paul 139-141
CBGB's 186, 187
Champs, The 48-50
Chandler, Chas 101

Chess, Leonard 21
Chess Records 12, 21
Chuck D 213-216
Chudd, Lew 7
Chumbawamba 275-278
Clapton, Eric 101, 68-69, 139, 235-239
"Clampdown" 212
Clark, Dick 39
Clash, The 212
Cobain, Kurt 225-227
Combs, Sean "Puff Daddy" 272-274
"Come Out and Play" 256
"Convoy" 153-154
"Cop Killer" 244-247
Cooper, Alice 145-149, 254
Cornell, Chris 254-256
Cramer, Floyd 36
"Crazy Little Thing Called Love" 173-175
"Crazy, Man Crazy" 23
Creedence Clearwater Revival 17, 110
Creem 1, 196
"Creep" 251-253
"Crimson and Clover" 111
Croce, Jim 125-128
Crofts, Dash 50
Cropper, Steve 110
Crowded House 236-237
Crow, Sheryl
"Crying" 75
"Crystal Blue Persuasion" 111
Cummings, Burton 115
Cyrus, Billy Ray 228

D
"Dance Hall Days" 205
Dark Side of the Moon 127
Depeche Mode 204-206
Devo 176-180
Def Jam 214
Diamond, Gregg 158-160

Diddley, Bo 20-22
Dinning, Jean 22
Dinning, Mark 21
Dion 15, 65
Dixon, Willie 21
Dolby, Thomas 195-197
Dolce, Joe 184
"Don't Stand So Close To Me" 205
Don't Mess Around With Jim 126
Domino, Fats 7-9
"Do the Bop" 39
"Downtown Train" 233, 234
"Do You Think I'm Sexy?" 151
Durden, Tommy 34, 36

E
Elliott, Cass 88
EMF 184
English Rebel Songs 276
Eurythmics, The 198-200
"Every Breath You Take" 253
"Eye In the Sky" 140
Ezrin, Bob 146, 147, 148, 149

F
"Fame" 135-138
"Fat Man, the" 7-9
"Fire" 101-104
Fine Art of Surfacing, The 167
Finn, Neil 236-237
Flack, Roberta 122
Flashdance 190, 191
Flores, Danny 48-50
Fogarty, John 110
Foley, Ellen 147
Four Seasons, The 70-71
Freeman, Max C. 23-26
Freed, Alan 29
"From Me To You" 68
"Funky Broadway" 87

G
Garfunkle, Art 123

Gaudio, Bob 70-71
Gaye, Marvin 186
Get the Knack 164
Girl Can't Help It, The 9
"Goin' Home" 9
Gore, Martin 204-206
Gouster, The 135
"Great Balls of Fire" 42-47
"Green Tambourine" 105-107
Greenwich, Ellie 74
Greenwood, Jon 251-253
Gross, Henry 124
Guess Who, The 115, 132, 145

H

"Hang On Sloopy" 81-84, 164
Hambone Kids, the 21
"Hand In My Pocket" 266
Hannah, Kathleen 225, 226
Harder They Come, The 124
Harrison, George 67, 236, 270
Haley, Bill 23-26
"Hang On Sloopy" 81-84
Hawkins, Screamin' Jay 17-19
"Head Over Feet" 266-267
"Heartbreak Hotel" 34-37
Hendrix, Jimi 1, 101-104, 109,
    173, 243
"He's My Star" 30
"He's So Fine" 65, 270
Heston, Charlton 247
"Hey Joe" 102
Hit Parader 1
"Hold On, I'm Comin'" 93-95
Holly, Buddy 20, 119, 120, 273
"Honey Don't" 40
"Hound Dog" 13-16
"How Can You Mend A Broken
    Heart?" 152
"How Long" 139-141
Howlin' Wolf 21
"Hully Gully, The" 79

I

"I Can't Quit Her" 86
Ice-T 244-247
"Ida May" 28
"Ida Red" 28
"I Don't Like Mondays" 167-169
"If I Had A Hammer" 78
I Got A Name 128
"I Got A Name" 128
"I'll Be Missing You" 272-274
"I'll Have To Say I Love You In A
    Song" 128
"I Live In A Split Level Head" 100
"I'm A Man" 22
"I'm In Love With My Little Red
    Tricycle" 100
"I'm Just A Lonely Guy" 21
Imperial Records 7
"I'm Walkin'" 9
"I Put A Spell On You" 17-19
"In Dreams" 75
"Informer" 248-250
In The Garden 199
"Ironic" 264-267
"I Think We're Alone Now" 111
"I've Been Loving You Too Long"
    109
"I've Gotta Make You Love Me" 116
"I Want Candy" 81, 82
"I Want To Hold Your Hand" 66,
    68-69

J

Jackson, Michael 192-194
Jagged Little Pill 264-266
Jagger, Mick 268-271
James, Tommy 111-113
"Jelly Jungle (Of Orange
    Marmalade) 106
"Jeremy" 228-230
Jesus H. Christ 276
"Jive Talkin'" 150-152
"Jocko Homo" 176, 179, 180

Joel, Billy 73, 165
John, Elton 1, 138, 142-144, 272
Johnson, Johnnie 27, 28
Jones, Quincy 193, 194
Joplin, Janis 1, 109, 121
Jordan, Marc 231-234
"Junker's Blues" 8
"Jump" 201-203

K

Kansas (rock group) 232
"Kansas City" 14
"K.C. Lovin'" 14
"Key Largo" 174
Kiedis, Anthony 240-243
"Killing Me Softly (With His
    Song)" 122
King, Billie Jean 142, 143, 194
Kleinbard, Annette 60
The Knack 164-166
Knack And How To Get It, The 164
Koda, Cub 129-131
Kooper, Al 86

L

LaBostrie, Dorothy 30, 31, 32
"Land of 1,000 Dances" 87
"Layla" 235
"Leader of the Pack" 72-74
Leiber, Jerry 13-16, 240
Leka, Paul 105-107, 114, 115, 116
Lemon Pipers, The 105-107
Lennon, John 66, 67, 68, 121,
    135-138, 192
Let It Be 135
Lewis, Jerry Lee 42-47
Lieb, Marshall 59, 60
Life After Death 272, 273
Life and Times 125, 126
"Lion Sleeps Tonight, The" 63-65
"Little Demon" 19
Little Richard 30-33
"Lonely Boy" 19

"Long Time Gone" 65
Lopez, Trini 78
Los Del Rio 260-263
Love It To Death 146, 147
"Love Rescue Me" 217-219
"Love Rollercoaster" 153, 155, 156
Lovin' Spoonful, The 88-92
"Lucy In the Sky With Diamonds"
    144

M

"Macarena, The" 260-263
"MacArthur's Park" 106
Mamas and the Papas, The 88
"Maniac" 189-191
Manilow, Barry 153, 154, 155
Martin, George 67, 69
"Maybellene" 27-29
"Mbube" 63, 64
McCall, C.W. 153, 154
McCartney, Paul 66-69
McCoys, The 81-84
McKenzie, Bob and Doug 181-184
McLean, Don 119-121
Meatloaf 147
Metallica 220-222
Michael, George 207-209
"Money" 127
Monge, Antonio Romero 260
Monotones 51-53, 120
"More, More, More" 158-160
Morissette, Alanis 264-267
Morton, George "Shadow" 72-74
"Mother and Child Reunion"
    123-124
Monster 258
"Mony Mony" 111-113, 164
MTV 144, 188, 192, 194, 197, 202,
    217, 219, 230, 238, 249, 259
MuchMusic 249, 250
"Mustang Sally" 87
Myers, Jimmy 23-26
"My Sharona" 164-166

N

"Na Na Hey Hey Ciao Ciao" 116
Na Na Hey Hey Kiss Him
    Goodbye 114-116
Napoleon XIV 96-100
"Nashville Cats" 90
Nelson, Ricky 50
Nine Inch Nails 253
Nirvana 225-227, 240
Not Fragile 133
Notorious B.I.G. 272, 273, 274
Now Is the Time 265
N.Y. — You Got Me Dancing"
    160

O

Oasis 270, 276
Offspring 256
Ohio Players, The 153, 155, 156
"Oh, Pretty Woman" 75-77
Okeh Records 18, 19
"One" 220-222
"Only the Lonely" 75
"Only Women Bleed" 145-149
"Operator (That's Not the Way It
    Feels)" 126
Orbison, Claudette 75-77
Oribison, Roy 75-77
Otis, Johnny 13, 14

P

"Paint It Black" 90, 179
Panayiotou, Yorgos Kyriako 207
"Panic" 210-212
"Paradise By the Dashboard
    Light" 147
Parker, Colonel Tom 34
Parsons, Alan 140
Patrick, Charles 51-53
Pearl Jam 228-230
Pepsodent 52
Perkins, Carl 38-41
"Philadelphia Freedom" 142-144

Phillips, Sam 11, 39, 40, 43, 44, 46
Pickett, Wilson 86
*Pictures Of Starving Children Sell
    Records* 276
Pink Floyd 127, 140
Pinz, Shelley 105
"Please, Please Me" 66, 69
Police, The 205, 253
"Poor Little Fool" 50
"Poor People of Paris" 36
Pop, Iggy 73
Presley, Elvis 14, 15, 34-37, 40, 42
Prince 199
Public Enemy 213-216
"Public Enemy Number One"
    213-216
"Purple People Eater, The" 54-56
"Purple People Eater Meets the
    Witch Doctor, The" 56
Purple Rain 199
"Puppy Love" 96
Pythian Temple 24

Q

Queen 173-175
Queen Is Dead, The 211

R

Radiohead 251-253
"Rag Doll" 70-71
Rattle and Hum 217, 219
Ray, Johnny 96
Ready To Die 272
Redding, Noel 101, 102, 103
Redding, Otis 108-110
Red Hot Chili Peppers 240-243
Reeves, Glen 35, 36
"Remember (Walking In the
    Sand)" 72, 73
R.E.M. 257- 259
Reznor, Trent 253
"Rhythm Of My Heart" 231-234
"Rice Is Nice" 106

Richards, Keith 268-271
Ridgeley, Andrew 207-209
Rivera, Chita 260
Robbins, Marty 120
Rock and Roll Hall of Fame 9, 28
"Rocket 88" 10-12
Rolling Stones, the 1, 90, 101, 145,
    165, 178, 268-271
Rolling Stone 1, 88, 163, 188, 206,
    213, 215, 227, 237, 243, 244,
    245, 248, 274
Ross, Diana 153, 155, 189, 232
Royal Teens 70
Ruiz, Rafael 260

S
Sam and Dave 93-95
Sam the Sham and the Pharaohs
    78-80
Samudio, Domingo 78
"Satisfaction" 176, 178, 179
"Saturday Night" 153, 156
S.C.T.V. 181, 182, 183
Seals, Jim 50
Searchers, The (movie) 55
Sebastian, John 2-3, 88-92
Sedaka, Neil 63
Sembello, Michael 189-191
Seville, David 56
Sex Pistols, the 20, 162, 163
"Sexual Healing" 186
Sgt. Pepper's Lonely Heart Club
    Band 109
"Shaddap Your Face" 184
"Shame, Shame, Shame" 136
Shangria-Las, The 72-74
"Shannon" 124
"She Blinded Me With Science"
    195-197
"She Loves You" 66, 67, 68
"Shelter Of Your Arms, The" 96
"Short Shorts" 70
Simon and Garfunkle 123

Simon, Paul 123-124
"(Sittin' On) The Dock of
    the Bay" 108-110
Slap 276
Sledge, Percy 85-87
Slovak, Hillel 240,241, 242
"Smells Like Teen Spirit" 225-227,
    240
Smiths, The 210-212
"Smokin' In the Boys' Room"
    129-131
Snow 248-250
"Soul Man" 95
Soundgarden 254-256
"Sour Suite" 115
"Space Oddity" 1
Spector, Phil 57-60, 240
Spencer, Brenda 168, 169
"Spoonman" 254-256
Springsteen, Bruce 121
Steam 114-116
Stewart, Rod 151, 231-234
Stipe, Michael 257-259
Sting 205
Stoller, Mike 13-16
Strangeloves, The 81-83
"Sweet Dreams Are Made Of This"
    198-200
Sub Pop Records 254
Sullivan, Ed 88
Sun Records 38, 39, 40, 90
Sun Studios 10, 11, 42, 43,

T
"Take Off" 181-184
"Takin' Care of Business" 132
Talking Heads 185-188
Taupin, Bernie 143
"Tears In Heaven" 235-239
Teddy Bears, The 57-60
"Tequila" 48-50
Ten 228, 229
Ten Commandments, The (movie) 79

Texas Chainsaw Massacre, The 189-190

"Theme From Mahogany (Do You Know Where You're Going To?)" 153, 155

"They're Coming to Take Me Away, Ha-Haaa!" 96-100

"Thirteen Women" 24, 25

Thornton, "Big Mama" 13-16

"Tie A Yellow Ribbon" 65

"Time" 140

"Time In A Bottle" 127, 128

"To Ev'ry Girl — To Ev'ry Boy" 96

Tokens, The 63-65

"To Know Him Is To Love Him" 57-60

"Too Hot" 265

Tourists, The 198, 199

Townsend, Pete 101, 161-163

Trumbo, Dalton 221, 222

Tubthumper 276, 277

"Tubthumping" 275-278

Tuesday Night Music Club 267

Turner, Ike 10, 12

Turner, Tina 12, 59

"Tutti Frutti" 30-33

"Twist and Shout" 66, 67

U

U2 217-219

"Under the Bridge" 240-243

"Unbelievable" 184

"Uptown Girl" 175

V

Van Halen 201-203

Vedder, Eddie 228-230

Velvet Underground, The 233

Vig, Butch 225

W

"Wake Me Up Before You Go-Go" 207-209

Wall of Sound 60

Wang Chung 205

Waters, Muddy 21, 28, 176, 268

"We Are the Champions" 173

Weavers At Carnegie Hall, The 64

Webb, Jimmy 106

"Wee Wee Hours" 28

"(We're Gonna) Rock Around the Clock" 23-26

Wham! 207-209

"Wham! Rap" 207, 208

"Whatever" 270

"Whatever Gets You Through The Night" 138

"What's the Frequency, Kenneth?" 257-259

"When A Man Loves A Woman" 85-87

"Whip It" 176, 177

Who, The 161-163

"Who Are You" 161-163

"Whole Lotta Shakin'" 42

Wilson, Brian 124, 154

Wilson, Jackie 93

"Witch Doctor" 56

"Wonderin'" 30

"Wooly Bully" 78-80

Wooley, Sheb 54-56

"Workin' At The Car Wash Blues" 128

Y

Yankovic, Weird Al 166

Yanovsky, Zal 88

Yorke, Thom 251-253

"You Ain't Seen Nothin' Yet" 132-134

"You Don't Know Like I Know" 94

"You Got It" 77

"You Know That I Love You" 81

"You Learn" 266